THE
REPUBLICAN
RIVER

THE REPUBLICAN RIVER

A VISITOR'S GUIDE TO DEMOCRACY IN MIDDLE AMERICA

DENIS BOYLES

 CALAMO

THE REPUBLICAN RIVER: A VISITOR'S GUIDE TO DEMOCRACY IN MIDDLE AMERICA. Portions of this book originally appeared under the title Superior Nebraska, published by by Knopf Doubleday Publishing Group, 2006.

978-1-7329009-0-5

This revised edition published 2018 by Calamo Press, New York.
Book design: Kim Hall, The Inhouse Design Studio.
Photographs in this book are from Wikimedia, except where noted.

Currente-Calamo
244 Fifth Avenue, Ste D169
New York, NY 10001

info@currentecalamo.com Brief portions of this book appeared in
The *American Enterprise and National Review Online*.

TABLE OF CONTENTS

AUTHOR'S PREFACE.

P arts of this book first appeared twelve years ago under the title *Superior Nebraska* and published by Doubleday. There were the usual pre-publication conversations. In one of these, I rather emphatically explained that this is a book mostly about the people who live along the banks of the Republican River and that while the Republican did indeed flow through Superior, Nebraska, it wasn't really *only* about that fine town, but mostly about a necklace of towns strung along the big arc of the Republican, like a halo atop Kansas. However, the editor, a lifelong New Yorker, said he had consulted with his Manhattan-based marketing team and that they all had been firm in their conviction that it was impossible to publish a book with the word "Republican" in the title.

So I then tried to explain that the point of the book is to make clear the misconceptions most New Yorkers have about the Midwest, but especially Kansas, especially after the success of Thomas Frank's 2004 best-selling *What's the Matter with Kansas?*, a book which had helped people from places other than Kansas validate their misconceptions about the place. On the other hand, this book, I said, is much more about Kansas than Nebraska, so "Superior Nebraska" may mislead book buyers. After consulting again with his marketing team I was told that, really, there's no difference between Kansas and Nebraska. I protested but he didn't buy it—and neither did many, many thousands of book-buyers who were confused by the title.

So I've revised and updated this book to the summer of 2018, rewritten large parts of it and added new material. It now carries the title it should have carried before. This is a book about the Republican River and the towns that live next to (and sometimes under) it.

INTRODUCTION

RETURN OF THE PART-TIME NATIVE.

You may have heard this one: A guy grows up in Kansas, goes to the big city, becomes a writer, then comes home again, where he sees nothing but acres of pure dumb and tells everybody in Kansas how stupid they are.

Not me, that's for sure. No, the chap in this particular case is a man named Harrison George. The time is the early 1930s and in the Midwest, the dust is still settling on houses, cars and trucks.

George is a member of the politically furious class. He had been an early adapter to the new radicalism of the International Workers of the World, but by the time we meet him, he's a busy Communist party apparatchik shuttling between assignments in California and New York. His line, not surprisingly, is propaganda disguised as journalism. So when he finds himself passing through his old home state, he steps off the Santa Fe long enough to grab a quick lunch at a Harvey House restaurant, and as he eats, he ruminates about the sorry state of the world, Kansas's little patch in particular, making a mental note or two for later use.

George isn't an obscure hack, either. He had made a name for himself in the wider world as one of several Kansas-bred Communist heavyweights. I understand that a "Kansas Communist" may seem like an impossibly dissonant concept, like a "liberal Republican", but anything's possible in Kansas, where libertarian values adhere to the state's image like bugs on a windshield. Even the word "liberal" has a curious ring to it, which is perhaps why the local press never uses the term, preferring "moderate" as the more euphemistic option. But when George was passing through, Kansas Communists were

3

not at all uncommon. For example, as he was lunching in Kansas, the Communist Party of the USA was being run by Earl Browder, a typewriter repairman from Wichita. Browder was part of a red circle that included James Cannon, the famous Trotskyite, who came from Rosedale; and L.E. "Louis" Katterfeld, who, with Kansas City's Gertrude Harmon, was present at the birth of the Communist Labor Party of America (later the CPUSA) in 1919. Katterfeld went to a country school just south of where I'm sitting now in Cloud County before moving a little farther west in the state. For all these people, and for reasons that still resonate, a Kansas association was not just mere biographical note, but an important credential; in a movement largely dominated by the foreign born, a "New York Communist" made perfect sense. It took being a Kansan to provide proof of an American Communist's patriotic *bona fides.* If you could say "even in Kansas" you could prove a certain dull point: ask Bernie Sanders and Alexandria Ocasio-Cortez, who, to demonstrate their magical attraction, staged a rally at a 5,000-seat convention center Wichita. It didn't matter that there were 1,000 empty seats. It was *Kansas* and they were *Socialists.* "We must have gotten off at the wrong stop because people told me Kansas was a Republican state," Sanders told the crowd. "It doesn't look like it." Then he went back outside. A few months later, Trump drew three times as many people to a rally in Topeka, a town that has one-third the population of Wichita.

The association of Kansas with the left has long been the stuff of ironic political commentary. As *Time* noted in a 1938 cover story on Browder, the Party's leader was born in Wichita, "and he never lets...his public forget it." One of Browder's more memorable slogans: "Communism is 20th Century Americanism." Dutifully noted *Time's* anonymous correspondent, "His life is an American biography."

Earl Browder

The same could be said of you, me and hundreds of millions of other Americans, of course, but I suppose what *Time* meant was that Communists were Americans, too—and who could be more American than a guy from Wichita?

Like Browder, Harrison George wore the mantle of Kansas hard-toiler with pride. His story was that he had been born in a dugout—a one- or two-room hole-in-the-ground with a roof—near Oakley, Kansas, in 1888 (although I could find no local records to support this claim). "That little spot of homestead on the Kansas prairie where my pioneer mother bore me is more sacred to me than the Stock Exchange quotations on U.S. Steel Common or American Can Preferred," as he put it in a 1937 poetic pamphlet called *This Fourth of July*. His self-portrayal as a son of the sod was rich in detail: George smoked a corn cob pipe and spoke with a pronounced prairie twang, and while it's quite possible that he was indeed a hardscrabble kind of guy, Whittaker Chambers later reported he was a typical "middle-class American revolutionist."

By the time his train stopped in Kansas, George had not only become active in the Industrial Workers of the World and edited the IWW newspaper, he'd done time for sedition during World War I, been put on trial by the party for trying to lead a Communist *putsch* and married comrade Browder's sister. He'd written a column for the *Daily Worker* called—in solidarity with the Loyalists in the Spanish Civil War—"Red Sparks by Jorge" and gone to China and to the Philippines, working to start Communist movements there. His convincing if peculiar cover: kinky American health nut. To meet the needs of Filippino Communists, George had started a small chain of enema therapy clinics. Over the years, he'd also written a very tall pile of propaganda pamphlets, containing the sort of bombast that still rings familiar today:

> [Capitalists] demand that jobless workers starve by the millions rather than for the rich to pay taxes sufficient to expand the W.P.A. and insure the wives and babies of workers against slow starvation, disease and death!

> They...do *not* love this country. They love their stocks and bonds. Only the workers and the toiling farmers and hard working small business men, and professionals and intellectuals who struggle for progress now love this country.

But the George opus that holds the greatest interest for us at the

moment is the one that had its beginnings in that Harvey House restaurant by the Santa Fe tracks, a 1938 screed for a college review, *Kansas* Magazine[1], entitled—what else?—"What's the Matter with Kansas?"

It is useful, and important, to note that neither Harrison George nor Thomas Frank—whose own *What's the*

William Allen White

---

1 At the time an annual periodical published by Kansas State College Press in Manhattan.

Matter With Kansas? was widely respected by readers from New York to Boston—coined that loaded question. It was appropriated from an old cowboy saying by William Allen White, the legendary editor of the Emporia *Gazette*, whose essay of the same name appeared on his paper's front page on August 15, 1896.

Like the work that would later bear and abuse White's title, the original piece spoke to the politics of the day. However, for White, the title was explicitly ironic, intended to demolish leftwing populists, then as now on the loose in Kansas and elsewhere, spreading a message of improvised socialism. White's adversaries were advocating inflation as a means of reducing agrarian debt—and warring with the Republicans, whom White supported. His point was that Kansans knew exactly what they were doing, politically, and didn't need anybody to tell them otherwise.

But the particular object of White's scorn were those outsiders with contempt for Kansans' bedrock values of hard work and thrift. "Go east and you hear them laugh at Kansas," he wrote, in a passage that might have been composed yesterday, "go west and they sneer at her...Go into any crowd of intelligent people gathered anywhere on the globe, and you will find the Kansas man on the defensive. The newspaper columns and magazines...are now filled with cartoons, jibes and Pefferian[2] speeches..."

It is brilliant people like these, he continued, in mocking respect, who will tell you we need more men like themselves, men who "hate prosperity, and who think because a man believes in national honor, he is a tool of Wall Street...That's the stuff! Give the prosperous man the dickens! Legislate the thriftless man into ease, whack the stuffing out of the creditors and tell the debtors who borrowed the money

2 William A. Peffer an often-ridiculed, extremely bearded agitator, was a Populist senator from Kansas from 1891 until 1897. He was also a rival editor (of *The Kansas Farmer*).

five years ago when money 'per capita' was greater than it is now that the contraction of the currency gives him a right to repudiate.

"Whoop it up for the ragged trousers; put the lazy, greasy fizzle who can't pay his debts on the altar, and bow down and worship him. Let the state ideal be high. What we need is not the respect of our fellow men, but the chance to get something for nothing…. Let's drive all the decent, self-respecting men out of the state… What Kansas needs is men who can talk, who have large leisure to argue the currency question while their wives wait at home for that nickel's worth of bluing…"

He concludes by repeating the question, this time in utter seriousness: "What's the matter with Kansas?"

Then, for those lazy, greasy fizzles who still may not get it, he provides the answer: "Nothing under the shining sun."[3]

White properly (and correctly) assumed his readers shared that view. Most Kansans still do. By the turn of the century, White and his readers already had more than their fill of lectures from Eastern intellectuals who thought there was something very wrong with Kansas.

Only fifty years before White, "Bleeding Kansas" had suffered as the proto-battleground of the American Civil War—a conflict that erupted in the 1850s, when, as we shall soon see, lots of other people decided to tell Kansans what to do. This stuff was living memory to many Kansans when White was writing, and he and many, many others had grown tired of being portrayed as small-town babbitts with pinched spirits and narrow minds, rural idiots who lapped up the platitudes about God and country and tradition peddled by Populist rabble-rousers and by cynical GOP slicks.[4]

3 *Emporia Gazette*, August 15, 1896. It appears in an appendix to this volume.
4 Some even attribute the defeat of William Jennings Bryan—a Nebraskan, a Democrat and a Populist—by McKinley in 1896 to White's editorial, which was used widely by the GOP as campaign literature. Bryan's "Cross of Gold" speech was the "My Sharona" of late 19th century political oratory, his single hit which he trotted out again and again

And in fact this is exactly the point made by George in his clever essay, in which he neatly turned White's ironic question into a condescending indictment.

George began by recalling that day in the track-side restaurant, especially "the miserable two tiny cuts of bread, not half the size of one's hand, set before me. There they lay, silent and anemic spokesmen of what's the matter with America. Tell-tale symbols of what's the matter with Kansas. And that is: Capitalism.

> ...[T]he farmer has been deceived by countless schemes and schemers, who allure him with promises of what he wants, but without telling him that it is impossible before abolishing capitalism. Indeed, they solemnly warn him against such 'outlaw' ideas."

As a political sell, both George and the apparently progressive editors of *Kansas* magazine must have known his essay wouldn't do much to sway the minds of Kansans. While a lot of leftists were *from* Kansas, there weren't a lot of them actually still *in* Kansas.

But that wasn't really the point, anyway. As these things go, the object was to confirm the political instincts of those who were already part of his constituency. George's essay may have appeared in *Kansas* magazine, but he understood that his readers were people living much more enlightened lives far, far away from the Sunflower State, even if only mentally; George was simply appealing to their overweening sense of virtue and superiority. After all, did anyone seriously think there was anything *right* with Kansas? Just look at the miserable slices of bread on your plate!

---

until what had once been a rousing display of rhetorical genius was an irrelevant and dull piece of theatre.

In the wake of the 2004 election, Thomas Frank's *What's the Matter with Kansas?*, was widely lauded in the media as prescient and insightful. In short order it became the standard reference work for those struggling to understand how so many people could have voted for a guy as obviously dim as George W. Bush when they could have voted for the brilliant junior senator from Massachusetts. Then they turned around, after only eight years of enlightened, liberal rule, and voted for that gargoyle of disruption, Donald Trump.

It turns out, according to Frank, that Harrison George was right all along: it's stupidity that causes this stuff. Indeed, with its portrait of Midwesterners being so moronically blinded by the pyrotechnics of cultural warfare they're unable to make what Frank calls "certain mental connections about the world," and so keep voting for the dark forces of capitalism, his conclusion is nearly identical to George's seven decades earlier.

Those who put "stupid" next to "evil" in the catalogue of sins ascribed by the left to those with whom they disagree loved the book.

And what's not to love? *What's the Matter with Kansas?* is a pleasure to read. It features our favorite colorful devils and a familiar narrative (cynical, rich rightwingers playing on the moral vulnerabilities of the unwashed who, at least until the appearance of Trump, were more properly the property of the left). Nor have hopeful liberals ignored the secondary narrative of Frank's book, in which he is no kinder to Democrats than he is to Republicans. He pillories the "party of [Franklin] Roosevelt" for its failure to reach out and embrace "the class language that once distinguished them sharply from Republicans" and for feeding the image of liberals as a latté-drinking effete élite by, among other things, drinking lattés.[5]

---

5 I'm not convinced Frank would want to be left out of that élite, by the way. His promo blurb for a recent issue of his magazine, *The Baffler*: "Many commentators have remarked that the United States is a nation of rank buffoons. Few, however, have care-

His point—that the Democrats would have won if they'd only run *even more* to the left—sounds better and better the farther from the Republican River you get.

Some locals complained that Frank himself was about as far from the Republican River as you can get. Of course, most of his readers are in New York and San Francisco, so they won't understand that. They presume that, because Frank is from a place called Mission Hills, Kansas, he wears the halo of agrarian wisdom.

The marker on State Line Road. One more step and you're not in Kansas anymore.

In fact, Mission Hills, that most luxurious of Kansas City neighborhoods, is only marginally in Kansas at all: if it weren't for a big country club on its border, the place would be in Missouri—and Kansas City, Missouri, is a place that's been run as a fiefdom by Democrats since before the days of "Bleeding Kansas". As University of Wichita historian Craig Miner[6] put it, "[Frank] knows a lot more about Mission Hills than he does about Garden City—and Mission Hills

---

fully measured our nation's recent and steep tumble into idiocy, much less attempted a unified theory to explain it. In its sixteenth issue, 'Nascar, How Proud a Sound,' *The Baffler* reveals the shocking breadth of American ignorance, and argues that the nation's mental and moral decline-like that of the Roman Empire-is spreading from *the better classes* downward." As one particularly fiery conservative commentator, John Altevogt, remarked to members of a Kansas email list, it is "strange how [Frank] communicates through those great working class political organs *Le Monde Politique* and *Harpers*. Clearly the kind of magazines one finds littering the bathroom stalls of our factories."
6 Miner is the author of a very readable and useful new state history: Kansas: *The History of the Sunflower State*, 1854-2000 (The University Press of Kansas in association with the Kansas State Historical Society).

isn't Kansas." Not that Frank hides any of this; it's not his fault if his readers choose not to know enough to see it or fail to make certain mental connections about the world.

One of the observations in Frank's book about the Kansas side of Kansas City is that the neighborhoods surrounding Mission Hills are filled with rusting cars, menacing Rottweilers and "No Trespassing" signs. And the malls—well, they just aren't what they used to be.

Mission Hills is sure a lot more swank than the part of Kansas City we lived in when I was young, back when I was probably— although I don't remember it—playing in those rusting heaps of metal and dodging runaway Rottweilers. My parents couldn't quite swing Mission Hills. After the war, they lived in a small mobile home parked next to my great-grandmother's house and picked up extra money for a few years by running an ice house and fireworks stand in front of a local feed store on Gladstone. I had my first memorable adventure in Kansas—being held upside down under a faucet after eating the rat poison I found behind the sofa. I recovered.

My old neighborhood was called Welborn. It's not there any more. It's buried beneath a layer or two of Wyandotte County's thick, Democratic sprawl, but even in its heyday it was never Mission Hills, where, in 2000, the per capita income of the 3500 residents was just at $100,000—a stupendously high figure compared to the rest of Kansas— and where, in 2003, there were exactly zero violent crimes. By 2016, the median price for a house in Mission Hills was just at a million.

Then, again, *neither* neighborhood really has much at all to do with the rest of Kansas. Kansas City is home to people who watch major league sports, attend huge universities and work for global corporations. The rest of the state gets by on American Legion games, high school football and jobs involving agriculture, no matter how tangentially.

Nevertheless, playing on the profound coastal ignorance of the heartland — as well as the assumption that something really *is* the matter with Kansas because…well, because it's so very, very Republican — Frank's book became a message of hope for those who either were mortified by being in Kansas or had never been to Kansas and who certainly had no intention of ever going.[7]

Not that Frank is wrong about everything. He is absolutely right, for example, when he claims that when conservative Republicans win, they do so because they have popular views on cultural issues. However, the notion that Democrats would win more often out here by embracing good, old-fashioned class-warfare as a central strategy…well, let's just say that every conservative Republican on speaking terms with God says, "Thank you, Jesus!" for that strategy every night. After all, there's a reason why even smart people voted for George Bush, a man whose rhetorical style is best-suited to a pick-up truck window, instead of John Kerry, a man who was clear and erudite in most of what he had to say. Kansans didn't vote for Bush because they were stupid. While they may not have liked the way George Bush spoke, they didn't like what Kerry said. When they had a chance to redeem themselves in 2008 and 2012, they declined. Then they voted bigly for Trump.

---

7 I don't know if the book made many converts in Kansas. (Although in fairness that may be because not even the choir bought the sermon; in my casual 2005 survey of Kansas statehouse Democrats, I could only find one who had read the book—although several admitted to owning copies. Jim Ward, the deputy minority leader who said he did read it, dismissed it as being "too negative.") Even Kansas Democrats, hearing how they should run on a platform that Kansans abandoned during the Roosevelt years, get skeptical in a hurry. A friend of mine, a hard-working Kansas Democrat, said she'd been to hear him give a talk, but had come away disappointed. "The people who came had open minds, but he lost them early on."

As it happens, I think I agree with almost all of the rest of Frank's contentions about Kansas and Kansans and I often recommend his book. It's his conclusions that need work. Do I think Frank is right that Kansans—like other Americans— play a little game with themselves when they enter the voting booth? Si. Do I think old-money Republicans are keeping those troublesome conservatives in check? I do. Do I think some Republicans put moral principle ahead of self-interest? Oh, yes. Do I think that that they understand perfectly well that in voting for conservative Republicans to solve social problems like abortion and gambling and school prayer they're voting for candidates who invariably will be stymied by liberal Republicans and Democrats and not be able to deliver on their promises?

Well, of course they do.

But I also think they worry that Democrats just might deliver on *exactly* what they promise. In 2004, they didn't want to risk it. In 2006, it was a chance they were willing to take—although it's unlikely that argument was framed just this way. Would the Democrat governor of Kansas be replaced by another Democrat in 2008? Sure, why not? But for Kansans, the governor's one thing. The president's another.

Despite the fact that this book will attempt to explain to people who live on the banks of the Hudson, the Potomac and the Charles, why people who live in towns along the Republican River think the way they do, I suspect that the chances of someone who reads this book not falling into one camp or the other are probably pretty close to nil. There are precious few truly "undecideds" in America today. Besides, most of us know what we know and don't want to be bothered by the rest, so if people vote for A instead of B, what we know about them is that they're either brilliant or they're stupid, depending how we feel about A, whoever, whatever and wherever it is. And the A and B of our country are Republicans and Democrats, red and blue. For most of us, that's all we need to know.

But it isn't true in Kansas and Nebraska, where most people are Republicans, and don't feel they stop being one even when they vote for a Democrat, as they often do.

There's probably a limit to how sensitive about politics people should be allowed to be, anyway. There should be a point at which if somebody's feelings are going to be hurt despite every good intention, you should just say, "So sue me." Trouble is, most of them would. The whole country's grouchy. For example, this book is an amateur anthropological investigation that basically follows the course of the Republican River. Yet, as I wrote in the Preface, in discussing a title for this book, I was told that even mentioning the Republican River would put "some readers" off.

But I guess you know who you are, even if you are from Kansas.

PART ONE

PART ONE

1

OUT WHERE?

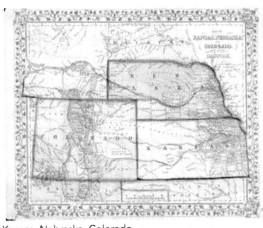

Kansas, Nebraska, Colorado.

I started the first version of this book on November 3, 2004, about 4 in the afternoon. I was on a farm in the hills of Pennsylvania, sitting in an office repurposed (some say unconvincingly) from its previous use as a pig barn. It was of course the day after the 2004 election and I had spent a large part of the morning reading the news on the internet and much of the afternoon talking on the phone about politics. Bush had defeated Kerry.

Aside from a brief conversation with Tom Morrall at the local feed store, there were no "moderate" phone calls. A magazine editor carefully prefaced his comments by saying, "I hope you're not a Republican." I told him I was an independent. He hesitated for a moment, probably calculating the difference between "independent" and "coward" and "liar", then began complaining about the "moronic" voters who'd been seduced by homophobia and lust for war. I reassured him that I feared nothing *but* war. Another guy at an entertainment magazine told me that somebody ought to look into all that vote-rigging in OH and maybe FL, without mentioning a word about the obvious breast-rigging in *O.C.* A surge of grief and disbelief had swept across America's blue states and raced across the water: A friend in Europe emailed to demand to know why the hell Americans had learned *nothing* from *Farenheit 9/11*.

Not everyone that day was sorrowful, however. Neighbors, who long ago asked me to please stop making them into metaphorical silage for "that crazy stuff" I write, were in a good mood. The guy a couple of farms over called with an ag question but ended with a last-minute topic change: "Kicked butt yesterday, bud." A dairy farmer stopped by to gloat: "Hey, *that* was fun!" One duck-out-of-water New York Republican gleefully informed me he'd spent the morning after the election on Manhattan's Upper West Side, "soaking up the gloom." My cousin the accountant called from a dot on the map just south of the Republican River in Kansas. "Hey, what happened to you guys in Pennsylvania?" she wanted to know.

"Happened? Kerry got the Philly and the Pittsburgh vote." The large margins there had been enough to push the Commonwealth into the Kerry column. Pennsylvania had gone to the Democrats by 100,000 somewhat suspect votes from the big city precincts—about the same suspicious margin by which Bush took Ohio, next door.

"Well, that's no excuse," she said. "We've got K.C. and all these newspapers out here—but heck we're on top of the world!"

She obviously didn't read those papers—or scan the 'net or watch TV because heck it may have been the top of the world from where she sat in Kansas, but Kansas—and Nebraska and Missouri and Oklahoma and the whole rest of the middle of the country, and the southern part, too, and also those mountainous regions, plus Alaska—looked a lot like hell to those clinging anxiously to the nation's edges.

But *especially* Kansas.

In fact, to a lot of Easterners, that election was the first in a series of stupefactions. After all, for weeks, months, *years*, since the beginning of the millennium, hadn't the truth been obvious? Had all those thousands of celebrated reporters, editors and columnists, the best writers in America, the best *minds,* just been wasting their time? Had they not worked tirelessly—almost *selflessly,* really—creating a simple narrative that was as easy to understand as the label on a bottle of Saint-Emilion? Left=tolerant. Right=cruel. Al Gore? ☺. Dick Cheney? ☹.

By now everybody should have been on the same page! In fact, the whole effort had been brought to the level of art during the campaign. Even the Boss campaigned for Kerry.

So why hadn't all those farmers gotten the message in 2004? Or, as one British newspaper's headline whimsically pondered, "How can 59 million people be so dumb?"[8]

Anyway, at 4 in the afternoon, I started typing the first draft of this. I thought I should get on this before it all turned around, as it surely must. Over the next days and weeks, the 2004 election was "analyzed"—to put it gently—by journalists, pundits and ordinary leftwing types. As would happen again in 2016, their incredulity

---

8 *The Daily Mirror*, November 3, 2004. Actually, the population of the United Kingdom is closer to 60 million, but the *Mirror* is perhaps allowing for the possibility that a million people may not be so dumb.

blended with hysteria and spread until it was everywhere: Cartoon maps of America with big inland seas of stupid; entire websites devoted to outraged rants; sociological studies. I was on the phone again, this time talking to a New Yorker toiling in the sweatshops of the global lit biz. I mentioned the 59-million-dumb-people headline. "Yes," she enthusiastically, agreed, "that's what I'd like to know. Really, the only reason I can think of that all those people out there vote like they do is that they're *dumb*. Can there be another reason? Isn't what it comes down to is that they're just *stupid*?" By "out there," she didn't mean the pedestrians on 57th Street. She meant *way* out there in Jesusland, the heart of political darkness, that big pile of red states filled with rednecks.

Jesusland (light gray)

"Out there" is a fairly precise measurement describing the distance from where you stand to where all knowledge disappears and all sense evaporates. A smart writer can double that distance: "The village of Holcomb stands on the high wheat plains of western Kansas, a lonesome area that other Kansans call 'out there.'" That's the brilliant first sentence in Truman Capote's novel, *In Cold Blood*, locating Holcomb, Kansas, not only out there, from the viewpoint of a *New Yorker* writer, which he was at the time, but *out there* even to a *Kansan*. That places Holcomb on another planet in another solar system at another time, since as everybody from everyplace else knows, Kansas itself is already "out there."

As it happens my whole family is from out there. Aunts and uncles with names like Minnie and Goldine, Clyde and Chester. I had a great-grandmother named Fannie, a Civil War widow who, according to my mother who was terrified of her, wore black mourning and cut her grass with a scythe in the middle of summer —at age 95. I spent part of my childhood in that vanished part of Kansas City and a good portion of my youthful summers after that even farther out there— in north-central Kansas just south of Superior, Nebraska, on the Republican River. When my mother and father wanted to go "back home" from wherever my dad's job had taken him, they went *out there*, and when they wanted me to go back home for the summer, they sent me out there, because for them, as for me, out there's where home was. When I got older, I became the default eulogist for a time—until they all realized that the guy doing all the uncomfortable sobbing was the guy delivering the eulogy. My most public and indelible failure (and we're setting a bar here) was the inaudible words I uttered at my grandmother's funeral. I made John Boehner look like Seneca.

When I was little, we'd make the trip in dad's incredible '49 Olds convertible or in one of the much less stylish sedans that subsequently did service as a Boylesmobile. I had every tourist trap on Route 66 memorized, from Bagdad, California, east. I'd throw floorboard tantrums because I wanted to sleep in the giant concrete teepees, watch cowpokes rustle rattlesnakes, trade with the Hopi. I actually did get a tom-tom once when my parents weren't thinking. It was made of authentic inner-tube rubber and a hand-painted coffee-can. I saw Paul Bunyon and a huge plaster bronto, the Painted Desert, and a meteor crater, and once, in Gallup, I saw a man's head, lit by police spotlights, sitting under his pickup after it had been hit broadside by a semi. His body was still at the wheel. I was ten. My father had said, "Don't look!" so now of course it's a face I'll never forget.

Sometimes those trips were great adventures. One summer, I rode out there with a couple of ladies in daring sundresses who stopped to rendezvous with a Navajo guy in Window Rock during a big tribal meeting. They put me in a motel room for a few hours, then let me out to look around. Me and many miles of Navajos! A couple of summers I rode the Union Pacific to Grand Island; when I was about 13, I fell in love with this 19-year-old girl who had designated herself my train-sitter. (My clear understanding was that she'd pledged herself to me all the way to Grand Island—*then* one night I find her sitting next to some Pat-Boonealike Baptist *seminarian* character in the Observation Car with her head *on his shoulder.* It took half of New Mexico and the conductor with his keys to pry me out of the washroom.)

The point is, "out there" has pretty much always described my idea of where I came from and who I hoped I really was. I always considered out there to be more authentically home than the little house in Hawthorne, California, where my parents inexplicably moved— or, for that matter, my ex-pig barn office there in Pennsylvania.

And here's something else: I've never thought of any of my relatives, all Out Thereites through and through, as stupid—unless of course I was mad at them for something that made *me* feel stupid. This was usually some sort of variation on a theme of cityboy goes cow-tipping, and was almost always the result of a convoluted plot engineered by my brilliantly wicked cousin Terry who helped me remember that my job was to be the urban idiot and encouraged me to do that job to such a level of perfection that I can still pull it off without much difficulty. In fact, when it came to the things that seemed to me to be useful measurements of intelligence—putting stuff together, taking stuff apart, adapting one of these to improve one of those, knowing when to add some of that; using one of those to catch one of those; really, all the lessons in applied science a kid could drag out of a country shed—I always assumed a rural education, with daily life as its ongoing internship, demonstrably superior to the one I received in crowded suburban schools.

That's largely why, when I had kids of my own, I contrived to find a setting for their childhood that was as close to out there as I could get, without, of course, actually going out there. Hence, the farm in Pennsylvania—bought with sudden urgency (and my new wife's reluctant compliance), when we discovered we were going to be parents and I convinced her to leave our suite of rooms in Baltimore's Hotel Belvedere and move to a remote patch on the slopes of the Allegheny Mountains, where the snowfall measurements are almost pornographic—more, more, harder, harder, deeper, deeper. Sixteen years later, I still hadn't found an entirely reliable drinking buddy, but fine meals were caught from the ponds and the kids lived the way all kids should live when they're young, with the big porch and the dock and without shoes, and acres of fields and woods, a pony! lots of sheep, a three-legged goat, a blind donkey named Jack, Murphy the chess-playing border collie, and the big pit out back where daddy poured all his money. It was life as I'd seen it lived on TV.

Once, in fact, one of the Hearst magazines sent a photographer out to take a picture of me on a cute, old tractor and another one of me talking to the writer who was standing inside my office, marveling over its décor motif, which was the kind baroque rustic look you get if you don't pick up after yourself. His story was about a writer living on a farm. No wonder the magazine went out of business. There are two stories every lifestyle magazine feels compelled to do: the one about the taxi-hailing writer who goes to racecar-driving school and the one about the English major who leaves Manhattan to live in the woods. At some point, almost *every* writer lives on a farm, and I'm sure by now most of us know that "writer on farm"=at least one hoax, and possibly two. A goat, a bunch of hay in an old barn and chickens in the yard don't make a farm, unless you've got the rural philosophy beat for some big-city newspaper or magazine.

Real farmers run agricultural businesses that live or die according to how much common sense is applied to an enterprise that depends on the precise use of large vehicles and proper paperwork, an understanding of basic economics, lots of red-tape, and skill driving an iPad. Real farmers use phenomenally expensive uncute high-tech equipment to farm acres by the thousands, often from an office where they sit phoning their brokers, reading about the weather in other places, complaining about the weather where they are and cursing the EU's damned ag policies with the rest of us.

But for the angry Democrats I talked to that November morning and in the weeks afterward, *nothing* about out there made any sense. They knew what they knew, and they knew it with a certainty that defied argument. It never occurred to any of them that Kansans and Nebraskans would have been happy to vote for a Democrat—just not for ones like John Kerry or Hillary Clinton, thanks. From what we've seen since, many Democrats felt the same way. If you think end-of-the-world hysteria started with Trump's election, try to remember John Kerry's surprise defeat. Populist "revolts" are incredibly easy to predict. Just read a *New York Times* endorsement editorial and look the other way.

In 2004, the sky fell. All red-state residents were morons. Then, only two years later, a miracle! In 2006, places like Kansas were suddenly filled with geniuses. In the wake of the 2006 mid-term elections, which were unkind to Bush and his Republicans, *The New York Times* ran an editorial[9] imaginatively called "What's Right with Kansas". It was the paper's celebration of "a major shift in the nation's heartland"—normally a geologically frightening concept, but to *The Times* an awesome moment borrowed from Darwin: "Kansas — lately considered the reddest of red states — emerged from the election as a bastion of moderation." Right out of the swamp primeval and into a new pair of wingtips. And wait: There was more:

> The Democratic Party posted major gains, including some by former Republicans who switched parties. The moderate Democratic governor, Kathleen Sebelius, received a whopping 58 percent of the vote to secure her re-election. Three moderate Republicans holding statewide jobs also won easy re-election, two of them after beating back conservative challengers in the primary. And two of the four people elected to the House of Representatives were Democrats, a result that would have seemed inconceivable not too long ago.

Only if you believe what you read in the papers. Kansas may be filled with Republicans, but there's a reason why God put Kansas in the middle of the country. It's a political waterbed, sloshing one way then another, just enough to make everybody uncomfortable. Out there is a sanctuary for political wildlife, filled with RINOs who would be liberal Democrats anyplace else; moderate Democrats who

9 November 15, 2006.

would be reviled anywhere east of the Mississippi and west of the Rockies; and libertarians galore, all of whom vote with a cavalier disregard for party loyalty. By 2006, the governor of Kansas had been a Democrat for 33 of the previous 50 years—each of them elected with the hefty support of liberal Republicans (called, disarmingly, "moderates") who'd *much* rather a Democrat than a conservative Republican. It's true that a mildly liberal Republican fought off an Oxford-educated conservative Republican challenger for the all-important post of state insurance commissioner that year, but then Kansas almost never elects a conservative Republican to *any* statewide office. One of the rare exceptions came in 2002, when a seriously pro-life candidate, Phill Kline, surprisingly defeated a little-known Democratic opponent to become the state's attorney general. He lasted one full term but spent most of it in an unsuccessful brawl with Kansas' many abortion supporters, particularly those appointed to sit on the state's supreme court. In fact, it was specifically that 2006 defeat of Kline that provided the real inspiration for the *Times's* discovery of Kansans' sudden political sophistication.

But by 2008, something was once again the matter with Kansas. The whole dang state voted against Obama by 15 points and two years later, with liberal Democratic governor Kathleen Sebelius term-limited and packing to go to D.C. to mastermind the rollout of Obamacare, Longtime Republican senator Sam Brownback was elected governor and became the first conservative Republican to occupy that office since forever.

It did not go entirely well. Brownback attempted an ambitious overhaul of the state government, cutting taxes and making an effort to contain healthcare costs. In this, he was opposed by a very sizable contingent of liberal Republican and Democrats in the state legislature; for his reelection campaign, 100 Republican political leaders gave him a public statement opposing his candidacy. As a result, he was reelected but just barely: the margin was less than four-points.[10]

The left-right conflict in Kansas is an amplified version of the animosity that marks civic discourse. America is at one of its crazy apogees of polarization in which political beliefs have replaced often mollifying religious ones; that is, if you believe people are stupid because they voted for Donald Trump or morally bankrupt if they voted for Hillary Clinton, you're engaging in a kind of faith-based hatred, and Kansas grows anger by the bushel. In a recent speech at Harvard, James Q. Wilson talked about the intensity of the current environment by distinguishing what we see now as something radically, dangerously different from traditional partisanship:

> By polarization I mean something else: an intense commitment to ca candidate, a culture, or an ideology that sets people in one group definitively apart from people in another, rival group. Such a condition is revealed when a candidate for public office is regarded by a competitor and his supporters not simply as wrong but as corrupt or wicked; when one way of thinking about the world is assumed to be morally superior to any other way; when one set of political beliefs is considered to be entirely correct and a rival set wholly wrong. In extreme form, as defined by Richard Hofstadter in *The Paranoid Style in American*

---

10 In 2018, Brownback, term-limited and facing strong resistance from liberal Republican and Democratic legislators, accepted a diplomatic post in the Trump administration. He was succeeded by his longtime friend and political ally Jeff Colyer, whose own campaign for reelection in 2018 was halted by his primary defeat by Secretary of State Kris Kolbach, even as state liberals and Democrats were ramping up to the election. This book will be published just before that 2018 election, but it will take a miracle to get Kolbach past his opponents. *The New York Times* is especially disapproving.

Politics (1965), polarization can entail the belief that the other side is in thrall to a secret conspiracy that is using devious means to obtain control over society. Today's versions might go like this: "Liberals employ their dominance of the media, the universities, and Hollywood to enforce a radically secular agenda"; or, "conservatives, working through the religious Right and the big corporations, conspired with their hired neocon advisers to invade Iraq for the sake of oil."[11]

As Wilson and many, many others suggest, the "disagreement" in national politics is actually a deep mutual revulsion made permanent on both sides by an assumption of *moral* superiority. Not only do Democrats and Republicans not grant good faith to each other's arguments, the divergent views held by each of them are seen by the other as moral madness. Invariably, the most militant on both sides mistakenly see hatred as a valid political strategy, but anger rarely carries majorities for long. At some point, you do need an idea people can actually vote for.

Midwestern political life is much more complex than Manhattan editorialists think it is, as I discovered when I first set out to write about it back in 2004. I thought I knew the territory and that it would take a few months—but I discovered that I knew a lot less than I thought and that it would take much longer than that. I convinced my wife and my three very reluctant daughters it would be pleasant to leave our home in France and spend a few months in a dusty little town near the Kansas-Nebraska border, sponging off the ancestors.

---

11 This version of Wilson's speech appeared in the February 2006 issue of *Commentary* magazine.

But Kansas is sticky, and by the time I was finished, my daughters were being coached by one of the top-ranked fencing coaches in the country and taking music lessons from a fabulous teacher from Fairbury, Nebraska, who, with her students, had toured the world. They had become friends with all the knitting ladies in three counties, spent many afternoons with the concert organist who was our landlady and with an amazing young woman just home from her opera studies in Milan. They had catalogued the rather substantial costume collection at the local museum, studied chess for months with a friend of Anatoly Karpov's, indulged their passion for Gilbert & Sullivan, discovered it was socially unacceptable to put a muffler on your pick-up truck in Concordia, Kansas, and one of them had joined a community orchestra. Finally, a public school anxious to have them as students rigged them up with computers loaded with the state's curriculum and access to teachers and tutors and waved us all goodbye. Soon, we were all back in France, in a charming village, surrounded by museums, great food and beaucoup friends—and for a while the whole family was furious at me for making them leave Kansas, where I still pay taxes.[12]

One thing I did learn was that at least I was right going in: The reason why people in Kansas and Nebraska vote the way they do isn't because they're stupid. A good deal of the evidence[13]

---

12 And where they all went to the state university. And predictably became liberal Democrats.
13 For example, here's a brief report card:

	Nebraska	Kansas	New Jersey	New York
Average SAT score 2004	1145	1169	1015	1007
Instructional expenditure per student ($) 2003	5,151	4,413	7,424	8,213
Operating expenditure per student ($) 2003	8,074	7,454	12,568	11,961

Source: Standard & Poor's.

By 2016 SAT scores had risen by about 50 points in all four states, but expenditure rose much quicker. In 2016, New York spent $22,366 per student, while Kansas spent $9960.
Source: 2016 Annual Survey of School System Finances, U.S. Census Bureau

would suggest that people out there do just fine, brainwise. Best of all, most of them are smart enough to not think all Democrats are stupid, either.

2

WAY OUT.

To many coastal Americans familiar with travel to once-exotic locales, driving across the middle of their own country is more daunting than, say, safariing across the Masai Mara. Kansas, Nebraska, one Dakota or another—none of them seem to have much charm as a tourist destination. In fact, the middle of the country is only perceptible to most coastal dwelling Americans around election time, when they perceive it dimly and suspiciously, like something ironic dreamed up by the Coen brothers.

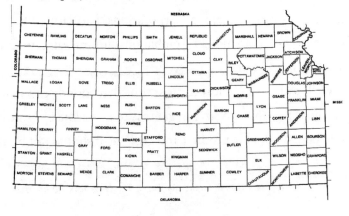

Kansas

The same assumptions that others make about the Midwest are also made by Midwesterners who live in the big, inland cities—Chicago, Omaha, St. Louis, Kansas City. A *New York Times* piece about Nebraska is a more or less typical example: "[I]t's big: over 77,000 square miles (about 10 percent bigger than the six New England states combined) and 450 miles wide, roughly the distance from Boston to the District of Columbia....large parts of Nebraska are arguably in trouble. The dismal statistic that trends lower, year after year, for many of these struggling counties, is population."[14]

That's the takeaway many Easterners have on places like Kansas and Nebraska: it's really big and nobody's home. It's true that as farming practices have changed, some small towns have become even smaller. The urban assumptions underpinning the "dismal statistic" have infected even some small town residents who, often compelled by their own bitter pessimism, see their village and their way of life in some sort of downward spiral. When that happens, the first thing they jettison is common sense, the very fuel that sustains them. The *Times'* writer, for example, was from Omaha, Nebraska's own Gotham, and while he is normally an astute observer of topics farther afield, he spoke for many urban Midwesterners when he looked at the consequences of farm consolidation and the technological revolutions changing global agriculture: "A cynical futurist might see mega-farms, owned by global corporations, and farmed by armies of robot combines, controlled by global positioning satellite technology from offices in Omaha."

Well, call me a cynical futurist, but that sounds excellent to me, especially if the object of the ag game is to grow lots of healthy, cheap eats. Food is a valuable product and growing it should not be a lifestyle

---

14 Richard Dooling, "Nebraska's Nostalgia Trap," *The New York Times*, February 5, 2006.

choice. Even in Oklahoma and Texas, nobody says, "think I'll grow some oil out back this year." City folk might find lunch more picturesque when grown organically by people walking very slowly behind mules, but that's about as realistic as expecting all American motor vehicles to be made by philosophically inclined shade-tree mechanics in backyards scattered across Michigan. Farming is not gardening on a grand scale; it's not a giant-sized hobby. It's a business. If more efficient farming means more nutritious food for more people for less money, who—other than an inefficient farmer hanging onto his federal supplements, or a romantic city dweller hanging onto her pastoral sentiments—is going to say that's *bad*?

I happen to agree however that a culture cut adrift from a respect for agrarian values (and that can be as complex a set as you wish) is lost in the woods. But one of those common sense values is that efficiency=good, so those who want the Midwest to flourish only in bucolic splendor as in days of yore should rent a U-Haul, move out there, plant some boutique crops, join the Rotary and pitch in. Beautiful little towns, charming main streets, very inexpensive housing, idyllic summers, big lakes and boats out the wazoo—it's all yours! You can do any damn thing you want in that part of America, including grow designer wheat. Just *go* there and make something happen. Otherwise, hush.

If you do go, you won't be alone. Blue state folks amazed that a town that once had 1000 people in it now gets by on 700 should probably remember that the exodus from small towns in the Midwest pales compared to what's happening in their own neighborhoods. It takes far less to turn around the population drift in Concordia, Kansas, a lovely town of 5400 that loses a couple dozen people every year, than it does to save most big cities, where the dismal stat that trends lower, year after year, is population. In 2004-2005 alone, New York City's population declined by 21,500—about four Concordias. In the 40 years between 1960 and 2000, Chicago lost 600,000 people, Boston lost more than 100,000, Washington DC lost 200,000, Detroit lost 700,000 and Philadelphia dropped a half million. Large parts of urban America, from Boston to Washington, DC, are in trouble, and not just because cities are losing population. In the same 40 years, meanwhile, the population of Nebraska grew by 300,000, while Kansas picked up as many new citizens as Philly lost. Other middle-American states did even better: There are 11 *million* more (legal) Texans now than there were in 1960. It costs a lot of money to get into farming these days, but not nearly as much as it costs to get into the worst house in most parts of Irvine, California.

Philadelphia may have lost a quarter of its population, but the place still seems kind of crowded to commuting Philadelphians — and to visiting Midwesterners, almost all of whom have a more or less complete knowledge of New York, Philadelphia, San Francisco, Chicago and other blue enclaves, not only because it's the America of TV and movie producers, but also because most of them have been "East" more than once. My grandfather used to tell his tales of Times Square 1918 the way only a farmer-turned-soldier from Formoso, Kansas, could tell them. My grandmother lived through many losses in her life, but few as memorable as the one that took her prized hat off her head and sucked it out the window of the train she was riding East to New York City at about the same time. Eighty years later, that hat was still on her mind. Almost every day, marching bands or drama clubs or debate teams or entire high school graduating classes board busses in Kansas or Nebraska or Oklahoma and end up in Washington, D.C. or Boston or Pasadena. What does Nebraska get in return? Provincialism, ignorance, anger and condescension from *The New York Times*.[15] Since the invention of busses, none has ever carried a bunch of inquisitive New York City students to Alma, Nebraska or Cawker City, Kansas—and too bad for them.

The wheat fields of Kansas roll on mile after mile, crossing an invisible border to become Nebraska or Colorado or Wyoming. It's a very big-picture landscape unfamiliar to many Americans for whom the heartland of their own nation can be strange and even terrifying. It's unknown territory, not just mapwise, but mindwise, with only the most basic of stereotypes to use for navigation. For many who don't know the middle of the country well, it must seem there's a

---

15Here's the *Times's* go-to guy on the Midwest, Timothy Egan who followed up on his November 17, 2017 op-ed "We're with Stupid" with "Blame the 400-pound Guy": "Waiting for Trump supporters to find their hearts, their brains or their patriotism," he writes, "is a fool's errand"; New York Times, July 20, 2018. Two days later, the Wall Street Journal ran a piece by Bob Greene about the town of North Platte, in Lincoln County Nebraska, and the reception the residents gave the surprise arrival of hundreds of soldiers being moved from A to B across the great prairie:

> During World War II, North Platte was a geographically isolated town of 12,000. Soldiers, sailors and aviators on their way to fight the war rode troop trains across the nation, bound for Europe via the East Coast or the Pacific via the West Coast. The Union Pacific Railroad trains that transported the soldiers always made 10-minute stops in North Platte to take on water.
>
> The townspeople made those 10 minutes count. Starting in December 1941, they met every train: up to 23 a day, beginning at 5 a.m. and ending after midnight. Those volunteers greeted between 3,000 and 5,000 soldiers a day. They presented them with sandwiches and gifts, played music for them, danced with them, baked birthday cakes for them. Every day of the year, every day of the war, they were there at the depot. They never missed a train, never missed a soldier. They fed six million soldiers by the end of the war. Not 1 cent of government money was asked for or spent, save for a $5 bill sent by President Franklin D. Roosevelt.
>
> The soldiers never forgot the kindness. Most of them, and most of the townspeople who greeted them, are dead. And now, in 2018, those 21 busloads from the 142nd Field Artillery were on their way, expecting to stop at some fast-food joint.
>
> "We couldn't believe what we saw when we pulled up," Col. Jaskolski said. As each bus arrived over a two-day period, the soldiers stepped out to be greeted by lines of cheering people holding signs of thanks. They weren't at a fast-food restaurant: They were at North Platte's events center, which had been opened and decorated especially for them....

Trump carried Lincoln County by almost 60 points over Hillary Clinton.

perpetual darkness hidden in the heart of America, a moral primitivism wholly at odds with their experience of the world, a place made grim by Republicans and civilized only by populating it with the imaginary Democrats of Brokeback Mountain, handsome lads who dress for beef but keep their eyes on the sheep. Unless the natives of the middle-nation are moved by a bit of electoral unpredictability in 2018, as they were in 2006, "Here be stupid bigots!" is emblazoned across an Easterner's mental picture of middle America.

Buffalo Bill and Sitting Bull

This is not new. In the 19th century, publications like *Harper's Weekly Journal* and *Frank Leslie's Illustrated Newspaper* churned out lurid stories of the exotic outback to big city readers eager to read accounts of Indian war battles, Army scouts, poker-murders, train robberies and other high plains exploits. To Bostonians and New Yorkers, these tales of uncivilized, mysterious mid-America were almost as horrifying as they were exciting; for decades wily showboaters like Buffalo Bill grew rich by selling the whole shebang to city slickers. A half century later, Truman Capote was canonized for doing the same with *In Cold Blood*. While he captured the essence of the high plains at mid-century, the complexities he reported were largely ignored. His book was beloved not for its sophisticated nuance, but for confirming in the minds of readers the flat and banal evil of America's grim prairie. More than a half-century later, Thomas Frank was still at it.

Happily, air travel places one blue coast next to the other. What a relief to not have to drive through Nebraska.

But the cold truth is, even people who do travel that way now travel blind if all they see are their stereotypes. They're certainly missing something. Something big. It's called America, and it's different from how it looks in the papers and on TV or in the imaginations of slightly anxious coastal visitors.

For those heading to west Kansas and trying to choose from a menu of Interstate options, allow me to recommend US 36, one of the country's older federal highways, and one of its oddest. It starts, as close as anyone can tell, just north of the golf course in a little Ohio town called Uhrichsville, before disappearing, after some 1414 miles, near Deer Ridge Junction, five miles west of Estes Park, Colorado, in the Rocky Mountains National Park.

US 36 is a great ride, flirting here and there with I-70, but for the most part going its own crazy way. For the family on the slow-go, it's not a bad teaching aid: the kids in the back seat will like US 36's immense diorama showing how geography and antebellum civic architecture morph on the run west, every mile taking you deeper and deeper into the great red sea — surfacing only to access the ring roads that typically surround the little blue atolls of cities like Columbus and Indianapolis, where machine politicians cling to power by relentlessly milking the goat of urban misery and discontent — then straight across the red belly of Illinois, a state made blue only by Chicago's imperiled voters. Buy the time you hit Missouri, you're on a boy's own highway crossing the Mississippi in Hannibal.

Actually, until just a few years ago, the river bridge at Hannibal was a two-lane, spindly iron thing—slightly worrisome but completely beautiful. The highway dumped you right into downtown Hannibal, where Samuel Clemens' family lived for ten years, until 1853. The captains of local industry here are fictional characters—Tom, Huck, Becky, Jim, Aunt Polly, the Injun—and as a result, every building of a certain age has been pressed into service as the site of something from Twain's tale or as the residence of some character that never actually lived anywhere except at the dendrite end of Clemens' fabulous hair. But Mark Twain is a long time dead, and as a result the annual fence-painting contest does not result in anyone's actual fence being actually painted. Instead, at the peak of the Fourth of July National Tom Sawyer Days festival, whitewash is slapped on eight boards nailed together in the middle of the street, tourists cheer and a valuable point about hucksterism is lost—even while another about Midwestern kindness is made.

Evidence: not long ago, traveling 36 with my wife and three daughters in a minivan, I broke down in Hannibal in the middle of their big Harley get-together—kind of a mini-Sturgis, but not mini enough for a guy in a minivan with a wife and three daughters. The place was packed with colorful weekend miscreants and there were no rooms at the many inns. I managed to find the service manager of the local Chrysler dealer at home. He came down, unlocked the place, took in the minivan and gave me loaner in which to make my getaway west. "At least this will get you out of town and down the road," he said, pointing up westward and into 36's rolling hills, which are fine — and toward the fireworks supermarkets, which are excellent.

Missouri is the home of the Y chromosome: No other state in the Union provides their citizens with access to every class-C firework known to man. This spectacular bounty is sold at gigantic, Walmart-sized boxes perched along the highway. Where California has warehouse-sized crafts shops selling needlecraft supplies, Missouri has fireworks-filled supermarkets selling explosives. Out front: cars filled with sleeping women parked in front of huge "no smoking!" signs. This is shopping for unburdened men: nothing but stuff with wicks arranged in rows like a not-very-Safeway. Push a cart (a built-in baby seat included!) down the rocket aisle, say, with everything you need for that backyard moonshot, from toothpick-sized bottle rockets to missiles the size of Tom Cruise. This aisle is nothing but stuff that makes painful noise. *This* aisle is box after box of crackers, from teensy little pops to mini-bombs strong enough to rule out a pro bowling career for a pyrotechnician fresh out of luck. A rack of cherry bombs the size of a produce section. O what beautiful wrappers are created by the Chinese—and so poetic! Some sound like Oriental paintings: Night blossoms, golden lady, moon raindrops. Some sound like strippers: Ruby storm, jasmine star. Some sound like ex-wives: Midnight banshee, whistling witch.

After a few hundred green and undulating miles, 36 leads you to another bridge, this one across the Missouri River, where you're given two last-chance options: North, to the cheesy casinos in St Joseph, or south, to the rich suburban malls of Kansas City, 50 miles away. But for the undecided, or the persistent, there's a third choice, marked on a sign hanging over the middle lane like a fire exit. It says simply "Kansas." If Truman Capote wrote highway signs, it would read "Out there."

That's the lane that takes you away from the river, right through that hilariously obvious speed trap in Elwood and in no time at all, you're looking at Troy (Pioneer Days in September), then the Walmart on the bend in the highway at Hiawatha (museum with 40 windmills; ice cream social in June), and on into America's huge heartland, passing county seats every thirty miles or so as if they were sitting still and waiting. US 36 is an almost-straight line across the northern tier of Kansas counties—Seneca, Marysville, Washington. Between every town, scores of hand-painted signs—"Choose Life: Your Mother Did", "Abortion Is Not a Choice", "It's a Child Not Tissue"—saying in big, bold letters things people wouldn't say aloud in most places in Manhattan unless they were being, like, sardonic. The highway follows, very approximately, the route used by the Pony Express, so lifesized silhouettes of riders leaning forward over their saddles appear on distant hilltops. They've been cut from sheets of steel and they're all going your way, straight across all those side roads leading from one story to another. Just south of Hiawatha, for example, is Powhattan, home the Kickapoo Nation and the Kickapoo Nation School Warriors (a name offensive to those who think it's offensive to Kickapoos). Buy a souvenir and watch authentic Kickapoo accountants banking the tons of money they're raking in from their Golden Eagle casino.

By the time you cross the Republican River the first time, you realize you're a long way from everywhere—and not just geographically either. It's drier here, harder, more austere. When I was younger, I used to ride the western part of this highway in dad's back seat, reading, then rereading Hamlin Garland's *Main-Travelled Roads*. Garland was a friend of William Dean Howells and an austere American "veritist". His fact-checked fiction is filled with people for whom leisure is unknown and for whom disaster was as common as dinner and never the stuff of drama. Everywhere out here is the sense of make-believe permanence, of unsentimental enterprise surrounded by heartbreaking necessity, a willingness to tear down as quickly as you build up, since the object of the game is survival. Your traveling *Times* writers may have missed a grim truth about the Midwest: It's been hard times out here since hard was invented. Here it is in the 1880s:

> He came at last to the little farm…and he stopped in sorrowful surprise. The barn had been moved away, the garden plowed up, and the house, turned into a granary, stood with boards nailed across its dusty cobwebbed windows. The tears started into the man's eyes; he stood staring at it silently.
>
> In the face of this house the seven years that he had last lived stretched away into a wild waste of time. It stood as a symbol of his wasted, ruined life. It was personal, intimately personal, this decay of her home.
>
> All that last scene came back to him: the booming roar of the threshing machine, the cheery whistle of the driver, the loud, merry shouts of the men. He remembered how warmly the lamplight streamed out of that door as he turned away tired, hungry, sullen with rage and jealousy.[16]

It's the shock you feel when you pass through a town where once you bought pop and prayed for girls but where now cattle crowd through the holes cut into the walls of the broken buildings of a falling-down downtown. The dusty, grim realism of Garland's stories seemed to me to be just as well-suited to the Kansas-Nebraska

---

16 *Main-Travelled Roads* (1891).

border as to his own "middle-border" farther north, in the Dakotas. Besides, out here, as everyone knows, the true borders run north and south—you've got rivers, and then you've got mountains. Everything in between is however many states you need: Those east-west borders that stack neatly atop Oklahoma until you get to Canada mean nothing to God (unless you count State U football loyalties as religion—and many certainly do). Straddle the line between North and South Dakota and you'll get the idea of ironic conceptualism.

The slope away from the great central rivers of the nation is barely perceptible on US 36. But it's there, gently shaping the floor of what Hays State University geologist Mike Everhart calls "the oceans of Kansas,"[17] since what divides the eastern and western US used to be a huge inland sea some 600 feet deep. To drain the plains it was necessary to raise the Rockies, a plate-shifting process that elevated the flat floor of the sea a half-mile: The elevation at the eastern end of Kansas is about 1100 feet. The elevation at the other end is 3700 feet. It's less a plain than a persistent slope.

It's a landscape as purpose-driven as Wall Street's: You can see how people might find charm in a place like Missouri, with its Twain-drawn towns, its woods and lakes and southern mountains. But the high plains at the far end of 36 look deliberate and hard. Nobody comes this far unless they mean agribusiness.

Before you know it, you're passing Cortland and Formoso (the latter is my father's birthplace, the former where his grandparents, Oliver and Fannie, are buried). Then Mankato, then Lebanon—the

---

17 Michael Everhart's *Oceans of Kansas* (Indiana, 2004), beautifully illustrated with charts, graphs and a bunch of speculative paintings of what the monsters that once lived in the inland sea that once divided the north American landmass looked like, is the essential book of charts for a dryland mariner. The book grew from a fabulously detailed from a fabulously detailed website Everhart grew at oceansofkansas.com. Mike teaches geology at Fort Hays State University in Hays, Kansas. website Everhart grew at oceansofkansas.com. Mike teaches geology at Fort Hays State University in Hays, Kansas.

geographical center of the 48 states—then Smith Center, then Phillipsburg, Norton, Oberlin and St Francis, where I once saw a series of spidery twisters along the distant northern horizon, fingering crazily down from the clouds, like the latex glove of God.

Then, at last, 36 disappears into the Rockies. Long before you get there you realize that once you're out here, you really are way out there.

3

MIDWESTERN SCALE.

For a very brief period—the half-century between 1870 and 1920—the flow of America's growing population defied gravity and spread uphill from the rivers and toward the mountains. Railroads, farms and towns appeared on the featureless maps—only to immediately give way to a slow runoff of people and businesses.

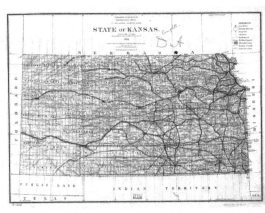
Railways in Kansas 1885

There are modern analogies to this kind of speculative optimism. In the 1990s, huge, overproduced website "communities" popped up anywhere there was a T1 line, the back-in-the-day version of an internet onramp. I worked for a while as the editorial director for a couple of these ersatz villages dodging nerdy salesmen-turned-CEOs who would collar you just before an IPO and with a straight face say, "I'm going to make you rich." The assumption behind these sites was that if you gave people everything they need, if you built a solid online community with lots of "stickiness", they'd never want go anywhere else. Because why should they? Once they landed on your little patch of the web, they'd know they were home.

Railroads were America's first T1. A century or more before the first dot com, developers—often including the railways themselves—convinced everybody that if you built a community next to a railroad track, filled it with libraries, banks, schools, churches, restaurants, Masonic temples and bars, all you had to do was kick back and wait for the 7:13 from Chicago. People would get off the train, fill up your town and never go anywhere else. Because why should they?[18] For a minute, it worked beautifully. Then, in the 1890s, came the first big economic collapse and all those city-builders realized that the main problem with having a railway in your town is that the same trains that come to your community also left it. A series of these boom-and-bust cycles and today you have towns that spell trouble to the people who write for *The New York Times*.

Depopulation isn't a new thing in the Midwest, but it does create some interesting special effects. For example, as cities and towns are reduced by circumstance to a bare minimum, the individuals left behind grow larger and larger. In places like New York and LA, there's

---

18 I've always liked Richard Hugo's explanation, in his part of "The Only Bar in Dixon", a poem he wrote with James Welch and JD Reed, of what makes a place home:
This is home because some people
go to Perma and come back
from Perma and say Perma
is no fun...
The poem appeared as "Three Poems On The Same Theme: The Only Bar In Dixon" in *The New Yorker*, October 10, 1970, p. 48.

one citizen for every 100 square yards or so. In Midwestern states like Nebraska and South Dakota, there's somebody for every 10 *acres*, give or take, so if you want to rub shoulders with your neighbor, you'll have to drive to do it. The old joke about a farmer being a man outstanding in his field works differently out there because as anyone can see it's no joke at all. It's just a normal way of looking at a man and at a field.

Understanding the optics of the Great Plains is essential to understanding how to look at Midwestern politics and the rationale behind local political values. For scale determines everything about the relationship between people and government. You'd think that when the distance from here to there is no longer measured in feet or blocks, but in miles and hours, you'd feel a little smaller; and, indeed, that may be the case when you're flat on your back on a patch of buffalo grass wondering about the meaning of life and all that.

But it isn't at all the case when you consider the scale of a man or a woman to a village or town. When you travel from Mankato's West Street dead north to my grandfather's old farmstead, 12 miles away, there's a long, empty stretch of gravel, and when you get to granddad's old place, you'll find my cousin Bryan. He's hard to miss because he and his wife, Jan, are about the road's only residents. So when the barn catches fire, old Bryan could do what they do in Queens or Marin, and call the fire department and ask the government to send out a little help! in the form of a fire truck. But if he did that, he'd only be talking to himself, since he's the fireman and the township fire truck is already parked out back.

The largely essential distance between citizens and the messy lasagne of layered bureaucracy that makes life possible in big, blue cities is non-existent in the heartland, where taking part in "government" is something most people see as an unpleasant but necessary personal obligation. Bryan's older brother, Marvin, was very greatly annoyed when he had to take his turn as city councilman in Burr Oak, a microscopic (pop. 274) village a few miles away on White Rock Creek, near the Nebraska line. Marvin spent "two years talking about cracked sidewalks" followed by a three-year term on the board of the local bank before he could get back to full-time farming. "It was grueling," he told me.

There may not be much separating many Kansans from government, but that's not to say there's any shortage of the stuff. In every corner of Kansas, you have a school board, a county government, a few city governments and a bunch of township governments, all providing services (including "services" such as monitoring a truly annoying set of liquor laws) that often duplicate each other, and all in a county so small you could evacuate the entire population by just calling a cab, if there were a cab to call and a public phone. It's the one aspect of 19th century[19] overdevelopment that won't go away; it's been like this since day one, and if the state legislature, controlled by "moderate" Republicans and Democrats, has its way, it'll be like this forever . It would be positively French—if anyone actually got paid much for doing any of it. So one person wears many governmental hats out here. Almost all of them look like ball caps with feed company logos on the front.

Take Cuba—the one in Kansas, a town settled by Czechs[20] where the population is just under 250 (from an all-time high of just

---

19 Nebraska's a little better. For the last 70 years, Nebraska has had a unicameral legislature in which everybody gets to be a senator. Nominally nonpartisan, party affiliations are clearly understood.

20 Sondra Van Meter McCoy and Jan Hults, co-authors of 1001 *Kansas Place Names*, say the town "most likely" was named after "the Bohemian capital of Kuba." Kuba's a common name in Eastern Europe. Lots of writers and artists are named Kuba. So's a thick Czech soup made out of mashed barley groats, mushrooms and garlic. And so's a beer. The local story is that a traveler who had once journeyed through the Caribbean stopped in town long enough to tell a Cuban tale ripe enough to impress the locals who founded the town in 1868. Czechs didn't settled the area until the 1870s. Maybe they

over 300), and where the scale of man-to-government has been thoroughly documented for more than three decades by *National Geographic* photographer Jim Richardson. One of his best illustrations of Cuba's tax-dollars at work is a photograph he calls "City council fixing the sidewalk"—or, as he described it to me, "the antidote to *What's the Matter with Kansas?*"

City Council fixing the sidewalk. Photo: © Jim Richardson

Taken in 1977, the photograph shows three guys looking at a puddle of wet cement and says approximately 100,000 words about the relationship between taxpayers and government in red state America and how different the whole idea of government is in blue states. When the photo was published in *National Geographic*,[21]

---

thought "Cuba" was the American spelling of "kuba" as in a place offering beer and soup, two very good reasons to pull over the wagon and stretch your legs.

21 In May 2004. That issue's cover is devoted to the "Heartland" and Jim Richardson's excellent photographs and text are well worth the trouble of finding a copy. If you want a copy of the Cuba photographs, send a note to him at the gallery he runs with his jewelry-designing wife, Kathy, at 127 N. Main St., Lindsborg, KS 67456 or an email to smallworld@ks-usa.net. The day the magazine came out, the citizens of Cuba held a day-long celebration of Richardson's enduring affection for the citizens of the town. They made a video of the event.

the caption read: "Mayor Larry Hinkle, at right, convinced fellow citizens to help him pour a sidewalk, all for a couple of beers."

The guy behind the wheelbarrow is Steve Benyshek, who told me he became mayor the day Hinkle, a school teacher, walked in and said, "I quit, *you're* mayor." The sidewalk repair, he told me, wasn't an unusual situation. "It was an easy job—a one six-pack job." It seems *all* city projects undertaken during the Hinkle-Benyshek administrations were measured in terms of beer consumption. When the "city man", who was the only fulltime municipal employee—in this case, Mike Knox, the guy on the left with, okay, the beer in his hand—had something that needed to be done, he'd round up the mayor and the president of the city council and escort a few six-packs to the job site, and look it over. Then, after a couple of cold deliberations, the city government would spring into action. "Now the senior citizens' center floor, *that* was a two-*case* job," said Benyshek, who served five terms as mayor and for his trouble was paid around $100 a year. The city government—that would be the mayor, the city man, the president of the city council and the three city council members—finally had to pass an ordinance that, while not exactly forbidding a beer assessment for work to be done, did require the work to be done *before* the beer was actually consumed, "because, well, you know."

Cuba, like many small towns, hires a chap like Mike Knox every year to do fix-it jobs around town. When Benyshek was mayor, back in the '80s, the city man made around $500 dollars a month. His job? "He's the city man—the 'works department.' Electrical, plumbing, street repair, you name it, it's him," said Benyshek. The toughest part of the mayor's job was hiring a good city man. "You learned real quick to have respect for somebody's mechanical aptitudes. If the city man didn't know what he was doing with, you know, plumbing, then it was cheaper just to sub it out."

One year, Cuba got a new city man who, it was discovered one frigid midwinter night, didn't actually know much about how the city's water system worked. You only have a few moving parts: a well or reservoir to feed a tank, a pump to lift the water up into a tower and gravity to full your toilet bowl every time you flush. The taller the tower, the greater the water pressure. During winter, water in the small municipal systems used by towns this size is kept in motion— in Cuba's case flowing back and forth between the 30,000 gallon (about the volume of a backyard pool) underground tank fed by the city well and the big, 50,000-gallon tank up on stilts in the center of town with "CUBA" painted on it. In summers, demand keeps the water moving, but in winter, it's essential to keep things flowing, because moving water won't freeze as easily as still water. "But if you *don't* know that," Benyshek recalled, "you just fill up the tank and wait until you need more." One night, mid-January, 20 below, "we lost water pressure all over town. I knew right away what it was. We had a 50,000 gallon ice cube." In seconds the entire town went dry, and not just Sunday-in-Kansas dry either.

Local governmental authorities immediately brought in "a lot of beer *and* whiskey" and built a big tent around the tower scaffolding, then parked a truck with a propane heater on it inside the tent, while emergency water from the city well was provided by an old centrifugal pump from the early 1900s. As town residents began taking turns to keep the pump running 24 hours a day, the municipal employees opened the beer, poured the whiskey, lit the giant propane heater and waited. God was merciful. "We finally got a warm day and the water started going again," said Benyshek. The propane and the beer? "Well, it really didn't do that much," he admitted. Not long after that, a woman ran for mayor and won. One of her first acts was to abolish the beer deal.

You wonder why the citizens in places like this have so little respect for big government? The towns of Burr Oak and Cuba have far fewer residents than a typical apartment building in Manhattan. Yet the citizens of Burr Oak and Cuba have to meet the same set of civic demands that all of New York City meets: Somebody has to run the schools, pick up the trash, plow the snow, patch the roads, fix the sidewalks, make the arrests and throw away the key—all while doing a real job. There's a park in Burr Oak, for example, several churches, a bank, a school, a museum, a small library, a mill, a little grocery, a bar, a very good café and some small businesses. Same thing in Cuba (with the addition of a great little museum-like room in the local antique store celebrating the town's moment of fame in the national press and offering copies of Richardson's prints of the town's residents, past and present). Every bit of it requires the infrastructure of government in order for Burr Oak and Cuba to continue their hardscrabble existence. And, owing to the populist eccentricities of Kansas history, often it has to be done twice-over—once for the city government, and then again for the county government. Imagine a town of 1500 souls. They support a local police department — a couple of cars and a few deputies. The town is in a county with, say, 3,000 inhabitants. And the county also has a sheriff's office, with more cars and more cops. No wonder local politics is taken so seriously.

Thanks to this lasagna-style layering Kansas has as much government as France, yet aside from the local school administrators, to whom we will turn in a moment, there just isn't a professional civic caste in these little towns, as there is in urban areas. It's government by amateurs, just like Tocqueville said, and it works. Every citizen in places like Cuba carries not only the expense of local government but also provides the labor and expertise to make things work well enough to get from one year to the next. Imagine running the government of, say, Newark, NJ, on a spare-change, time-and-materials basis.

To maintain their tiny town's park and other civic attractions, the residents of Cuba hold an annual "Rock-a-thon" to raise money. "Usually, it's a marathon in most cities, but not everybody here can run," Richardson told me. "So it's a Rock-a-thon"—seven straight 24-hour days of riding a rocking chair right out there on Main Street. "This way, everybody can be a part of it." Over the last 25 years, Richardson estimated the Rock-a-thon has raised between $300,000 and $400,000.

Burr Oak, like Cuba and most other small towns up and down the Republican River valley, has just one full-time employee. Everybody else working for local government is a casual. If you want to visit the Burr Oak parks and recreation department, talk to the teenager with the summer job cutting the grass around the town's swing set and slide. He's it. Just as the women serving lunches in the café are two-thirds of the local school board and the guy running the welding shop is the highway department. Next year, they'll all change, a couple of people will move away, and life will carry on.

Even in bigger towns on the Republican River, such as Concordia, you walk past a street repair site and you'll hear, as I did, one of the workers call out to a pedestrian, "Hey, would you call my wife and tell her I'll be a little late?" The pedestrian just nodded, gave a little wave, reached for his cell and kept walking. At the motor vehicles office in the Cloud County courthouse, a guy named Jeff will help you figure out why Maryland is still looking for you for that parking ticket you got twenty years ago, the one he verified you'd already paid. Lynn Scarrow, Jewell County's treasurer, told me the funny story about the people who came from someplace else, bought a house and asked the county to send around somebody to see how much of it was up to code. "I just laughed," he said.

Quite simply, out here government is a do-it-yourself project, which is how it started in this country a couple of centuries ago. So while it's efficient and well-run, mostly, it's extremely minimal. The inhabitants of this giant inland sea understand the realities of this kind of scale instinctively, both from experience and common sense. That understanding of what government should be and how it should behave is pervasive in red America. A few days after Hurricane Katrina struck New Orleans, a woman named Lisa Mikesell stood up in her church and suggested using an empty nursing home for New Orleans flood victims. That was in the morning. By the afternoon, the place was swarming with people cutting grass, mopping floors, getting rooms ready. Word of mouth and an announcement on the local radio station—not an intervention by the government, of which there was none, did the trick. "Some of these people, we didn't even know," Mikesell told me when I stopped by late that night to drop off a few supplies. She was exhausted—but the place was ready. "The Red Cross said they might be here by two this morning."[22]

In America's bluest precincts, meanwhile, calling for government help is as normal as calling for food. Got a fire? Call the fire department. Got hunger? Call WIC or some other human services-type office—or, if you've got the money, call the corner pizzeria. Relying on all this stuff, provided by a faceless government and other people you really don't know at all, is a blue-state way of life. In the most populous parts of America, "government" is a conceptual thing, an invisible machine that keeps urban life ticking. You're allowed to pay for it, but you're not allowed to get in the way of it.

---

22 They never arrived; the Red Cross found most of those bound for Concordia places in shelters further south.

For years, I lived near the corner of Lexington and 28th in Manhattan. Every time a truck rolled down Lex in the middle of the night and hit the permanent pothole halfway between my place and 27th Street, the sound of steel banging against steel echoed up and down the avenue while I clung to the cheap chandelier. I called the pothole hotline on Monday mornings. This went on forever; the pothole (or another exactly like it) was still there when I moved away. If I had wanted to fill the pothole myself, I'd have been arrested. I wouldn't have been able to do the city's work if I had wanted to, and certainly nobody in City Hall came around during lunch hour and asked me to pitch in filling the thing, or for that matter, to help out sweeping the streets or lend a hand fixing the sewers. In fact, if I'd volunteered to do anything beyond tossing trash in a can or persuading the dog not to dump on the pavement, they'd have thought I was nuts.

I could have lived my whole life in Manhattan and never once would I have had to perform any of the tasks associated with the survival of the *polis*, beyond paying my giant taxes. At night, I ate dinner with friends who told me how uncomfortable they felt every time they left Manhattan. They meant they missed friends and their jobs, of course. But I think if they were anything like me, what they really missed was the feeling of living lives that were richly, deeply upholstered to protect them from the hard realities of what is, after all, a precarious, unnatural existence on a big granite rock surrounded by cold, cold water.

Take away all that government, close the restaurants and what you've got is a very different perspective. As they put it Out Here, things get *different*.

INTERLUDE: SUPERIOR PEOPLE 1.

I *f you divided the great red sea of American voters that stretches from one blue coast to the other and stood on the dry ground in the middle, you'd be looking down the wide, dusty main street of Superior, pop. 2055, the biggest town by far in Nuckolls County, Nebraska.*

At one end of the street are the Burlington Northern's tracks, along with a few rough warehouses and sheds and a liquor store with lots of warning stickers on it to scare away the kids. At the other end, a neighborhood of fashionable Victorian houses, all done up with new gingerbread and fresh paint. In between, the dime store, the Crest theater, the bank and a bunch of beauty parlors, antique and appliance shops, hardware stores and a clothier. Superior has a newspaper, a park, a pool, a library, a couple of supermarkets, a crafts shop, and the BPOE—the Benevolent Paternal Order of Elks, where everybody goes for Sunday dinners. If you want a fancy meal, you can go to Evelyn's. There's a winery outside town, but nobody seems to know what to think of that.

In the middle of it all, the old Leslie hotel, where I once had to paint the lobby a sickening green in exchange for a room after my grandmother tossed me and a couple of high school friends out of the house for smoking a cigarette in the attic. We had driven out to Kansas right after graduation. Jim Wilde and Bob Wurster were both folk singers, and I wasn't. It took them from LA to Colorado to get me to hit the right last note of the Beatles' "I Want to Hold Your Hand." I don't know what we had in mind: There were no summer jobs we wanted out there, for sure. Wurster, president of our class and Princeton-bound in the autumn, was especially unkind about the hot, dusty landscape. Sitting in granny's stifling attic he wrote a little parody of Malvina Reynolds' "What Have They Done to the Rain." He called it "What Kansas Needs Is Just a Little Rain" and he sang it while Wilde sat next to the window smoking a Parliament and promising me granny would never notice. He underestimated my grandmother's olfactory powers, refined by a lifetime of Nazarene purity. She threw us out with 30-seconds' notice.

We forgot to bring money because we had forgotten to get jobs so we were desperate for a place to stay. Finally, we drove into Superior, where there was a ball game in progress. Wurster, a very handsome blonde boy, promptly chatted up a local girl who got us the lobby-painting job. It wasn't until Bob's obituary ran in the Superior Express 20 years later that I discovered his mother was from Superior and had gone to high school with my father. We could have freeloaded there, but Wurster had never mentioned it, a nagging mystery.

South of town, on the Kansas border, is the muddy Republican River, the giver of local life, where you can see farmers standing on the highway bridge watching the river go from trickle to torrent and back again, knowing that if it stops, everything else does, too. Beyond all this is the distant, uninterrupted horizon—what New Yorkers see as the endless flatline of a dying middle America, but which the rest of us see as the reasonable limit of a normal man's ambition.

Superior's where dad got his enlistment papers for World War II, like two of his brothers, one of whom, Gerald, survived Iwo Jima. It's where two more of my uncles, Delmar and Neal, died after coming home from the service to face decades of emphysema caused by smoking cigarettes and huffing wheat chaff in the cab of a combine. It's where my friend Bill has run the local newspaper since the day his dad closed the Sinclair station south of town that gave him his first job. ("That green in the hotel lobby? That was Sinclair Green. It was from a shipment Sinclair Oil had sent by mistake. It was a whole carload. We painted everything in town green for years. I think there's still some left.")

Superior is also the town where I spent many of my summers growing up, sweating through the week from one Saturday night to another. At

13, I learned to steer down the dirt roads that went from Superior out toward Burr Oak, Kansas, in my uncle's old Studebaker pickup (the silhouette of the naked lady on the steering wheel knicker-knob is embedded in my noggin as if I'd encountered it head-on at 60, which I nearly did more than once), with my cousin Terry—a year older and consequently full of himself—and Uncle Neal all jammed into the front seat, offering suggestions in that white-knuckled but casual way that says, "For God's sake, don't scare the boy." Though I tasted my first beer in a pool hall in Beverly, Kansas, and got in my first serious fight in a field near Burr Oak (with a kid named Davey who never seemed to have to wear shoes), I also got my first real kiss in Superior, from a girl at a street dance.

When I began thinking about this book, I was going to make the whole thing about Superior. I thought if I could make Superior comprehensible to friends in New York and elsewhere, my job would be done. But even a town as big as Superior couldn't contain all the things that turn voters out here crimson, so I went up and down the river. Superior's at the center of that river's arc, however, and at the center of my Midwestern history, such as it is.

After telling my friend Harry, in New York, so much about Superior people, he decided to come out and meet some of them himself. So, relying on Bill and my cousin Gloria for names and unaware of whatever political convictions they may have had, I invited what I thought was a pretty broad (well, if five people can be "broad"—I was picking up the tab, after all) cross-section of townsfolk to lunch at Evelyn's, at the time the best restaurant in Superior, and traded them a free meal for an hour or two with Harry and a tape recorder.

Here's our table:

Bill Blauvelt. Owner and editor, *The Superior Express*, and one of the most respected men in the county. In addition to the *Express*, Bill had also started a singles' publication for rural lonely hearts called

Country Connections through which he met his beautiful, smart wife, Rita. For years, most of us thought Bill had been a genius to start that thing just to meet a wife, but, he told me, "It was a commercial decision." (The newsletter, that is.) It was just a coincidence that Rita was among the first to send in an ad looking for an honest man. "She was letter number 37," he mentioned casually one day.[23]

Val Heim. Retired farmer, avid golfer and for a while in 1942, a White Sox outfielder.

Rich Nelson. Banker.

Pat Richards. Widow and grocery store owner.

Stan Sheets. Local amateur historian.

Stan: One thing I think a lot of people on the coasts don't understand about Midwesterners is how independent we are. Most of us sitting here are the offspring of pioneers, and pioneers are pretty strong-willed people.

Pat: It's true, the independent streak is powerful out here. But, really, I don't think they give us much thought at all. West of the Mississippi, you just sort've drop off the face of the earth.

Stan: I think they kind of lump us all together…

---

23 It's still going strong, despite the Internet. A recent *Express* ad: "GOOD TIMES await! A subscription to Country Connections helps country-loving people meet new people. Reputable, confidential plan. Free details. Write Country Connections, PO Box 406, Superior, Neb. 68978." Or try superiorne.com.

Pat: Right. Not very bright, and not very interesting... (laughs)

Stan: You know, words like 'provincial' and 'backward' get tossed around a lot, but those things cut both ways. I remember back in 1947, I was back East, and was dancing with a girl from Wellesley College. I was wearing my cowboy boots, and she asked about the danger from Indians. I explained they're pretty well settled down by now.

Bill: I used to know a fellow in college whose family vacationed every summer in Colorado. And he told me they'd always drive all night, because to be caught on the western Kansas plains in the daytime was sure death, it was so hot. He had never been west of Manhattan [Kansas, home of Kansas State University] in the daylight, and he didn't have a clue what Kansas or Nebraska *looked* like, so I decided to bring him out here to Superior. On the way, I blow a tire, and he goes into a panic. "What's wrong, what's wrong? Are they shooting at us?"

"No, we just blew a tire."

"What are we gonna do?"

"We're gonna change it."

"Is it safe? Is it safe?"

So we changed the tire, and it worked out fine. The Indians never attacked, and nobody died of thirst.

Stan: The very term Midwest is confusing to people back there. If you say "Midwest" to someone in New York City, they're thinking "Ohio." Nebraska? I don't know *what* we're supposed to be.

Bill: I was on a boat trip in the Bahamas one time and one night the fella across the table from me asked how long you had to stay with my company before you got to be promoted to New York City. He'd just been promoted there, and was saying how wonderful that was. I said "My company would never promote me to New York City, but I'd quit if they did." He was amazed, he just couldn't understand that.

Rich: No, he wouldn't.

Bill: It's not really so hard. I walked to work this morning. I like that.

Pat: And when you left home, did you lock your doors?

Bill: No.

Rich: I was back East not long ago, in New Brunswick, New Jersey, outside New York, and I'd go into the city with some bankers from Texas. One day one of these guys says; "You ever notice what happens when to try to have a conversation with someone on the subway?" I said, "What do you mean? They seem all right." He says, "I mean, how they'll never look you in the eye." So I started looking for that, and he was absolutely right.

Pat: I think that's self defense—you don't want to bring anything into your life that day that might hurt you.

Rich: But can you imagine *living* that way?

Stan: Just knowing there might be people around you with criminal intent! In a rural community, there's not that same anonymity factor—and the criminals know that all those farmers out here have rifles.

Me: I think the setting makes crime—especially murder—even more threatening. *In Cold Blood* couldn't be about a murder in Brooklyn.

Pat: That's true. Here, everybody knows everybody. If you come to this community, your privacy is no longer entirely yours. But you are respected as an individual, and you can be sure the community will care about what happens to you. If you're ever in need, there'll be hundreds of people who'll step forward to help you.

Bill: To give some indication of the crime out here, and what's valuable: A few years ago, I was at the lake, and, as is my practice, I left some money and my driver's license unlocked in my vehicle. I came back, and the money was still there, but the driver's license was gone. (Laughter.) Evidently some young fella wanted to buy some beer.

Stan: It's flattering to you, Bill. They never steal my license.

Bill: Well, it was an older photo.

Pat: That's the thing, there's something deeply rooted about coming from the Midwest. We hang in there, we're tenacious. And we know how to work.

Rich: No question, that comes with the territory. It's second nature.

Bill: I started at two years old, literally. One day Granddad lifts me over the fence in the yard and says "I need you in the garage to help me fix tires," and I was there every day after that. Val knows, he used to come in there and buy gas.

Val: It's true, I remember it well.

Pat (laughing): Couldn't happen today— "Child endangerment.

Bill: But, you know, it didn't do me a bit of harm. To the contrary, it gives you a sense of responsibility and importance in the world. They tell me that when I was six, and supposed to start school, I said "Well, maybe in October, but we're too busy at the gas station in September." You really felt that the family would starve if you weren't there to help.

Pat: A lot of that is still alive and well out here. When our kids get up in the morning, they know there's work to do, you've got to put your shoulder to the wheel if you're gonna get by.

Bill: That's just a given. One time when I was ten, I was helping my dad tear down a barn a few miles away. There were just the two of us, and we had a truck and pick-up, and we had to get back home. So he said, "Well, son, I'll take the truck and you take the pick-up." And I did, no problem.

Pat: More child endangerment. But that sort of thing gives kids a sense of identity in the family, and the understanding that they're important. I'm not sure that's as true in other parts of this country. I have a niece who worked for a while in New York City, and she said that, in her experience, employers were glad to get kids from the Midwest. They speak well, they're respectful, they're mannerly and they get their work done.

Rich: I don't doubt it.

Bill: You hear on the news last night that they had a coyote in Central Park?

Stan (laughing): That made the news, did it?

Rich (laughing): I hate to even estimate how many dollars it cost New Yorkers to catch that thing. Probably involved several municipal departments.

Stan: Instead of one farmer with a rifle…You want to talk about the difference between people on the coasts and people here, that's it right there. I know you can't have people shooting coyotes in New York, but I mean the principle of just taking care of things on your own. They pretty much believe government should handle everything. From cradle to grave.

Bill: It's easier here to see how the money that gets wasted, and the incompetence, and the red tape. I had a personal experience lately that highlights that. For the past couple of years, I've printed envelopes for a couple of government agency offices, and the arrangement has worked out very well. They've been delighted, because my prices are so much better and my service is so much faster than what they're getting elsewhere. Well, I delivered some to them the other day, and afterward they called and said 'We're sorry, but we can't buy any more envelopes from you. We have been reprimanded pretty severely because you're not a General Services Administration contractor and we have to buy our envelopes only from them."

Rich: That's government for you.

Bill: So I went on the web to see what it would take to become a GSA contractor, and it turns out you have to sell a minimum of $25,000 a year before you can even be considered, and *then* you have to give a kickback on every order to the General Services Administration. And you have to be willing to accept orders of any size, and do a series of reports – some annually, some quarterly, whatever. And you have your affirmative action reports, your this, your that. I suspect that even if I was willing to do the $25,000 a year, they wouldn't accept us. We're not a union shop, we don't have any minority employees…we don't have a very large minority community. So we're out of it, even though we're cheaper and better.

Stan: And I don't see how anyone could *not* see that kind of thing as a problem? But it seems like a lot of people in other parts of the country just don't. It looks like common sense to us but they simply accept it as normal and natural.

Pat: Well, you know, we talk about why we in different parts of the country don't understand each other better— maybe that's the wrong question. There's a book that sub-divides the United States into nine distinct regions, each with its own unique culture and ways of looking at the world. Culturally, they're almost as different as the nations of Europe. Why should people from New York or Boston appreciate our ways, or vice versa? Do you ever hear the French or Italians wondering why they don't have more in common with the Germans or the Danes? We're just different, that's all.

4

THE RIVER.

The map of the Republican River valley is a battle map. In addition to corn, wheat and milo, the river also irrigates a bountiful harvest of interstate judicial fights over rights and agricultural policies; the landlocked states through which it flows are engaged in a perpetual war over water.

The Republican rises in a far corner of Kit Carson County, Colorado, slips across the northwest Kansas border near St. Francis, then arcs gently across southern Nebraska, where it passes through Willa Cather's hometown of Red Cloud. It re-enters Kansas in Jewell County, south of Superior, and cuts across the northeastern quadrant of the state, ending as it joins the Smoky Hill River to form the Kansas (or Kaw) River. Here's the map:

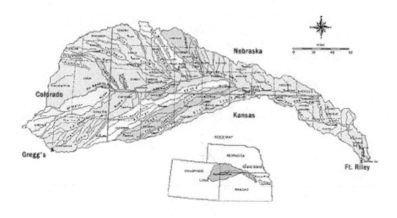

In other words, if you spill your beer in Kit Carson County, Colorado, where it's really needed, it will eventually end up in New Orleans, where it's not needed at all.

The rivers meet just outside Ft. Riley's Grant Gate. Where most American towns have a happy-face sign welcoming you to The Home of Sublime Tranquility, Ft. Riley has a huge water tower on which is painted three words that let you know you're a long way from Pleasantville: "America's Warfighting Center." You can park just outside Grant Gate, cross the busy road leading into the fort and pick your way through the brush and trees to see the exact point where the Republican ends.

Finding where the Republican River starts however is a little trickier. I'd been looking for the spot for most of a morning, and finally found myself in Flagler, Colorado, about 12:30 in the afternoon. The whole town was closed—even though "open" signs were everywhere. The few shops were locked, and so were the library and city hall. Only the post office was open. A woman standing in the middle of the main street chatting with a friend explained that everybody was home eating lunch. Except for the post office, it was like a schoolday in Italy.

The postal clerk looked at my very detailed, highly expensive map with me but couldn't figure out where the river started, either. "Maybe over toward Arriba?"

Maybe. So I finally drifted back down to the interstate, to the co-op gas station-pizzeria, and annoyed some people—a big, extended family from the look of things—eating lunch. We all looked at the map again.

"I think it's over toward Greggs. Probably Greggs is what you're looking for."

I studied the map closely. "I don't see 'Greggs'."

"I'm Gregg," said Gregg Lukenhimer, smiling. "Try going south about six miles or so. You'll cross the Republican a couple of times. It's dry." And so I did and it was. I drove six miles down a dusty gravel road into rolling, treeless grasslands and never was sure I'd finally found the exact spot. I tried the same stunt later from Arriba, and got the same result, but

without the Gregg. I finally decided to ask the Colorado Department of Natural Resources. I received an email from Ken Knox: "It is difficult to identify the exact location of the Republican River

71

headwaters due to the flat topography and the point of flow origination changes in response to rainfall or other precipitation events," he wrote. "For descriptive purposes, the headwater of the South Fork of the Republican River begins on the northern high plains of eastern Colorado, approximately 3 miles south of Arriba, Colorado."[24]

Wherever it starts, it doesn't run for long. The Republican River is only about 550 miles long. And while it wasn't named for the GOP—it took its name from the "Pawnee Republic," a description early traders gave to what they thought was the tribal structure of the original residents—it does provide an irresistible cartographic trope for this kind of grand theorizing about Midwestern political and cultural values. Every single one of the 19 counties through which the Republican flows voted overwhelmingly for George W. Bush in 2004, and in even greater numbers than voted for him in 2000, when we only guessed he couldn't speak English. A Democrat may sneak in every now and then thanks to Kansas City and Lawrence, but along the Republican River what you have mostly is lots of Republicans.

This is to say, relatively few Democrats have ever so much as laid eyes on the Republican River, and it's a good bet that those who have, at least in recent years, have done so with some smirking. That's because the Republican's no longer a little Big Muddy the way it was when I was small. Back then, you could wade and play in the Republican. The Republican loved to flood and did so with regularity, as every old-timer loved to recall. There were major floods in 1870, 1906, 1935 and 1951.

---

24 Your red-state government in action: I sent my inquiry at 8:30 on a Saturday morning of a three-day weekend. I had my reply from Mr. Knox by 2pm Sunday afternoon. I saw from his reply that at least two other people—Marta Ahrens and Jim Hall—were involved in making the reply.

The floods of 1935 were most spectacular. Twenty years later, they, and the Dust Bowl they so rudely interrupted, were still the daily topics of conversation in towns all along the river. In the space of only 20 days, four floods swept through the valley, the biggest one a killer surge following a storm that dumped 24 inches of water in six hours between Flagler and the Kansas line. "We'd had five years of drought before that flood," Mrs. Verylron Williams told me one afternoon sitting around a table in the municipal museum in McCook, Nebraska. "And then after it we got another five years of drought. So over the ten year period, we got average rainfall. We just got it all at one time." What she remembered most, she said, was "how hard it was to believe something could come so quickly and be so terrible."

She was 15 at the time, the youngest by far of four girls, and the only one still at home on the farm—"right on the river"—outside Culbertson, where the river makes a slight feint to the north, just west of McCook.

"It had been raining for weeks," she said. At first, it seemed like a blessing, dampening the huge drifts of dust and grit that had been blasting across the prairie for years, daily reminders of Depression and drought. But the rain didn't stop and then the river rose and then the ground became saturated, and her mother warned her father that water was starting to flow across the flat surface of the earth, not just down the gullies and washes. She started out to take care of the livestock, and watched, shocked, as the river snatched a group of calves. "Then," she said, "it came for the cows, too."

By five in the morning of May 30, 1935, the river was at the door of Verylron Williams' parents' home. "I was sleeping upstairs when mother and father came to get me. They said, 'We have to go now.' But when I went down the stairs, the water was already in the house. We waded through water up to here"—she indicated her waist—"and got up to a neighbor's. It was on top of a hill. There were already nine people there. Then right after we got there, a man came riding up from the south and said he couldn't go any further, so that made 13 of us."

They were on the highest ground around, so the small group thought they might be safe. But suddenly, as they watched, a wall of water eight feet high roared down the valley. The flood's increase caught them by surprise and sent them sprinting across the farmyard. "You had to run if you were going to stay out of it," Mrs. Williams said.

By now, the river was in full flood, the water level rising uphill in some places at 10 miles per hour or more, faster than most men can run. Houses, cars, wagons, barns, sheds, livestock, people, whole towns washed past them. The group dashed from the farmhouse to a barn and finally up to a granary. "It was the only building bolted to its foundation," she said. "It was just a little building with a wall dividing it down the middle." The water followed. "So we all climbed up into the rafters, the men on one side and the women on the other." It was about 11 in the morning.

Her perch was next to a small shutter. Looking down, she could see the river slowly climb the walls. They all knew that if the water rose high enough to reach them, there would be no place higher to go but heaven. From time to time, one of the rafter-clingers would ask her to open the shutter and take a look. She would open it a crack and peer out across the valley. "It was like an ocean." By then the river was four miles wide, and the plains had become the turbulent sea it had been in prehistoric days. Below her, the little wooden building swayed and groaned. One wall went, then another, leaving behind just the timber frame to which they all clung desperately. "We just didn't know what we'd do if the water went any higher."

But it didn't, and at 8 the next evening, they came down out of the rafters and into the mud. When they finally went back to their farm, the house had floated "a block or two" downstream. For farmers already hard hit by calamity after calamity, "it was complete devastation," she said.

"It must have been like New Orleans," I said. We were meeting a few weeks after hurricane Katrina had struck the gulf. "Did Mr. Roosevelt send some help?"

She looked at me like I'd just put on a stupid party hat. "Oh goodness, no! The government? We never even thought of that. We just went back to work."

The summer of 1935 was a disastrous year elsewhere in America—including Florida, where on Labor Day one of the strongest hurricanes on record struck the Keys and wiped them clean, killing more than 400 people. But in the American Midwest, the Republican River flood was the big deal, permanently changing the towns, jobs and lives of the people who live there. As another farm woman, Bernice Haskins Post, recorded in her memoirs, "Yes, The Flood. I had lived on the river bottom all my life [and] I have no desire to write this story. To those who were victims of the flood, no words are adequate to describe it. To those who see the valley now, or read about the flood, it is hard to realize what the flood did."[25]

The river had been a problem since forever, of course, and after a little more of this sort of thing, two vast reservoirs were finally built in Nebraska—one, Swanson reservoir, is near Trenton, and the other,

25 There are many accounts of the 1935 flood. Most of the towns along the Republican have a collection of flood-related documents, newspapers, photographs or journals in their municipal museums. Mrs. Post's account is from the Nebraska genealogy website maintained for Franklin County by Patti Richter Simpson at http://www.rootsweb.com/~nefrankl/.

Harlan County Lake, is near Alma and Republican City—one in Colorado, and several more in Kansas. It's the kind of government activity locals understood: "We needed the government for that," said Mrs. Williams. "We can't do things like that by ourselves." Blue-staters can see the reservoirs by simply looking out the left side of the aircraft approximately halfway through their flight.

Maybe from up there you can even see the towns submerged at the bottom of some of those reservoirs. If you're closer to the ground, though, you can take the main street in Wakefield, for example, and head east toward downtown—but you'll never get there because Wakefield's old downtown is under Tuttle Creek reservoir. The town museum has pictures of what you've missed (including several floods): A town settled by English people whose stout little Anglican church was rescued from the rising water and much of whose population descends from a boatload of orphan boys rounded up off the streets of London in the 1870s and sent to break sod and put down roots in Kansas. A former Kansas Governor—John Avery, a nonagenarian who guided Kansas through the Brown v. Board of Education trials—lives just north of town.

Over years, the network of reservoirs has expanded until it now stretches into Colorado. Today, the river's cycles are regulated fairly well; local floods, like one in Scandia in 2003, are still a problem, but farmers and small towns milk a steady living out of the Republican all along its course as it trickles through prairie grasses and wheat-fields until it joins the Smoky Hill to form the Kansas.

Aside from the reservoirs, for most of the way, the Republican, the Smoky Hill and the Kansas rivers are what Karl Mueldener, who runs the Bureau of Water for the Kansas Department of Health and Environment, described to me as "pretty native—pretty much they way they have always been, very pretty."

This natural beauty lasts until the Kaw reaches the discharges of the only two areas in Kansas that voted against Bush in 2004—the faux-New England college town of Lawrence—home to the Kansas Chapter of the Sierra Club, the Kansas Green Party, the Friends of the Kaw and Save Our Kansas River and the Kansas Wildlife Federation—and Kansas City, at the Wyandotte County line, just inside I-435, where the river finally loses in sewage, dredging and levees whatever's left of its wholesome upstream charm. "From that point on, the river is like a half pipe," Mueldener said.

5

GONE WITH THE WIND.

Two of the largest towns on the Republican—McCook, Nebraska, and Concordia, in Kansas—have populations of 7700 and 5400 respectively. I should say "had" since this is the agricultural heartland, and that was last year; every year twenty-five to fifty people in both places pack up and leave. It doesn't seem like a lot, but the population decline actually started not long after the towns were founded — Concordia in 1866, McCook sixteen years later — with the cycle of agrarian economic collapse and depression that's swept the region since the 1890s.

In fact, that these towns continue to exist at all, with their schools, churches, libraries, speaks to the remarkable sense of optimism with which they were built and which, for most citizens, remains a permanent state of mind. Still, there were always those who saw things more darkly – or, perhaps, simply more realistically. Perceiving the economy in collapse almost as soon as the paint was dry, they moved on farther west or went back to their eastern hometowns. The population boom never happened, but for more than a century, through one cycle after another, the slow, painful drip-drip of resignation, sometimes becoming a rush before slowing again, continued on.

It continues now. The last great economic disaster hit in the early 1980s as a consequence of bad agricultural policy, high interest rates, tumbling commodity prices and a collapse in land values. By 1985, the entire Midwest was languishing; the oil boom skidded and crashed in Oklahoma and Texas and agriculture took a beating in states farther north. I'd see it on my periodic visits. Closed cafes and stores—even big places that always had that sense of near-institutional permanence, like the Dreilings store and the JC Penney in Mankato. All closed. Farm sales outnumbered church services in some places. Main streets that had held on through decades of tough times yielded as this latest wave of depopulation swept the region.

Concordia is typical. One of the toughest jobs in town these days belongs to a fifth-generation Concordian named Kirk Lowell. A reformed farmer with a charming pattern of avoiding obscenities ("My cow!" is an apparent favorite), he is the director of the local economic development bureau. That is perhaps the most thankless job in Cloud County, Kansas. He's charged not only with raising a crop of opportunity in rocky soil— i.e., reviving the main shopping district, the four blocks along Sixth Street—but also with holding back the coyotes of pessimism that populate every small town, greeting every new idea with howls of derision and charges of fraud.

Far better than any distant bureaucrat, he knows what's at stake. When Concordia started suffering, Lowell suffered too. "My cow! You were in the middle of the farm crisis and you had a lot of closures downtown," Lowell said. "We had 17, 18 empty storefronts on Sixth. I called it 'Tumbleweed Alley'. I used to say you could commit suicide by laying down in the middle of the street on a Saturday, but you probably wouldn't die until Monday. There were just no cars." His cousin, who runs the local paper—a daily, no less—was trying to keep it afloat, but, if anything, Kirk had it even worse; he was trying to pick up a little extra money at the time, selling ads to local businesses.

Same story in McCook, if somewhat less colorful: In the ag disaster, said Muschi Mues, a German-born artist who arrived in the McCook area in 1972, "farmers were hurt, yes, but it was the main street that had the hardest time. When I came we had a men's clothing store, two women's clothing stores, shoe stores, all kinds of stores. But then [in the mid-'80s] it was just sort of dead."

Mark Graff is chairman of the board of the McCook National Bank. Its big, brick-solid building on the town's main street, Norris Avenue, provides a not-so-subtle hint that come hell or high water—and both come calling from time to time—McCook would somehow survive. That's perhaps why Graff, a native McCooker, or whatever hey're called,[26] refused to go as far as Mues. "We never quite *died*," he told me. "But it was bad." Even the Keystone Hotel, a 1920's project of a local "Kan-Do Club" to stimulate downtown business, gave up welcoming newcomers and instead became an old-folks home before finally closing completely.

To Easterners, the population density of the high plains is bizarre, even frightening. The fact that it's necessary to drive 30, 40 miles or even more between towns is dizzying to people whose sense of these distances is experienced as commuters. In the New York metro area, forty miles equals a long time in tight traffic or in jammed trains and

---

26 The otherwise entirely estimable McCook *Gazette*, a very good small-town daily, uses "McCookite" but that somewhat stationary term seems to me to lack the feeling I saw there of a whole community that had a lot of work to do and was busy doing it. The place is definitely cooking, in the best vernacular sense.

busses. In Nebraska or Kansas, it's a couple of commercial breaks on Rush Limbaugh – something else that, to many who live far from out here, may never be quite comprehended.

It's been a couple of decades since the last great ag-economic crisis, and while some towns have failed, plenty of others are today getting by quite nicely, thank you, by their own standards if not those that predominate among accountants and tax attorneys in places like Beverly Hills or Manhattan. Genna Hurd, the co-director of the Center for Community Economic Development at the University of Kansas, told me of her ambition to study the high plains towns that are growing "for no good reason." Frankly, it doesn't seem all that complicated. Some people simply like living in places like these pretty, uncrowded smallvilles, with their bargain housing, good schools and decent commercial infrastructure. Weirder things have happened: I used to live in what only a few years before been a sweat shop on 25th Street in Manhattan and I thought I was the luckiest guy on Earth for having the privilege of doing so. A little town with a little park, a little café and rather modest prices doesn't seem so odd compared to that.

Besides, living in small-town Nebraska or Kansas isn't exactly camping. The nicer the town, the more people want to live there, of course, while ugly, unfriendly towns tend eventually to blow away, evaporating like huge chunks of downtown Detroit because they're unpleasant places to be.

Change doesn't always mean disaster, demographically. In fact, often change is necessary for improvements to take place. Just a couple of decades back, lots of people were sure that when the steel mill closed, Bethlehem, Pennsylvania, would become a ghost town. I used to own a condo in Bethlehem, in the old bank building on Main Street, just when gentrification was setting in; I wish I could afford to buy it back now. Thinking the plains will be completely depopulated because of a changing farm economy is the same kind of thinking has pronounced cities dead, from Seattle to Baltimore.

Few have been as exhaustive in their civic obituaries as *The New York Times*, which has pronounced the Midwest dead many times, usually in melancholy features like the one called "The Vanishing Point: Life in the Emptying Great Plains."

My favorite in the series is the 2003 profile of Reydon, Oklahoma,[27] a map-speck near the Texas panhandle border, where, as you might suspect, "the plows of depopulation and decay slice through the Plains;" yet where miraculously "a turtle crosses Main Street unscathed;" and where reporters harvest insights like this one: "To make it in Reydon, people rely on one another" — and where paradoxes sometimes seem to be fuelled by 'shrooms: "Empty roads and pickup trucks are a common site around Reydon." The reason for all this overwriting? It seems Reydon "is running out of people!" I checked and sure enough, the proof was in the numbers: The plow of depopulation and decay certainly did slice through Reydon. In 43 years, from 1960 until 2003, the number of residents dropped from 183 to 166. But by 2010, the population was at 210, the biggest jump in population in 70 years, so now all those Main Street turtles will be scathed for sure. Call the Times and hold the servers, presses no longer worth holding.

"Bonds among families and neighbors supply the economic energy that used to come from small farmers, big employers, government offices, Main Street services and stores and, ages ago, streams of new settlers." What the? None of those things were *ever* in Reydon, Oklahoma. There hasn't even been a liquor store in Reydon for half a century. Thousands of square miles dotted with Reydon-sized

---

27 "Bucking Trend, They Stay, Held by Family and Friends," December 2, 2003.

hamlets is a terra so wildly incognita that big city reporters don't know what they're looking at even when they go to see it.

So maybe it's not very surprising that curious ideas about what to do with this part of the world keep getting generated by people who live far away from it—and whose minds are totally blown by the idea of a turtle crossing a Main Street anywhere anyway. Many of these people are Eastern academics, profs who read studies about dwindling populations and big, empty fields. They look at maps and charts and what they see it is a vast, empty canvas upon which their creative vision might be fingerpainted.

Among the most strangely imaginative of these ideas is the one put forth by Deborah Popper and her urban-planner husband Frank, a pair of professors from Rutgers University in New Jersey who in 1987 famously championed the "Buffalo Commons" concept.[28] Their idea: the best thing to do with the Great Plains was to return it to the Manufacturer. Just let the grass grow and let buffalo eat the grass. It seemed a timely proposal; the economic collapse of the mid-'80s was just ending and prairie towns were looking at a future made bleak by recent events. Looking back on the proposal, the Poppers wrote:

> We conceived the Buffalo Commons in part as a literary device, a metaphor that would resolve the narrative conflicts --past, present and most important, future-- of the Plains. In land-use terms, the Buffalo Commons was an umbrella phrase for a large-scale, long-term restoration project to counter the effects of the three cycles. We wrote that in about a generation, after the far end of the third cycle had depopulated much more

---

28 In "The Great Plains: From Dust to Dust," *Planning*, December 1987.

of the Plains, the federal government would step in as the vacated land's owner of last resort…

One academic's literary device however is another family's hometown. So no matter how nuanced the Poppers' proposal was, it was received by most Midwesterners with the sort of insincere smile specially reserved for people who come from the coasts to the middle of the country, look for a Starbucks and then start every sentence with the phrase, "What you ought to do out here is…"

> As we traveled the Plains, it became clear that we did not control the meaning of our metaphor, nor did anyone else. For some the Buffalo Commons was only about bison, for others about wildlife in general, for others about raising cattle to more closely mimic bison behavior. The metaphor might mean getting the people out of the region, encouraging their coexistence with wildlife, or promoting economic development based on wildlife. People variously interpreted the metaphor as a general assault on their way of life, an evocation of a fabled past, a vision of a feasible future, or a distillation of what they were already doing. Many Plains people intensely disliked the commons portion of the metaphor, associating it with collectivism and lack of choice, but even so the strength of their reaction helped achieve some community-building.

Implementing the Poppers' project is the goal of the Great Plains Restoration Council, where Frank Popper sits on the board. The GPRC is a "multicultural, multiracial non-profit organization building the Buffalo Commons step-by-step by bringing the wild buffalo back and restoring healthy, sustainable communities to the Great Plains…. The Project will rescue prairie animal nations out of the current emergency-room situation."[29]

In April 1990, the Poppers showed up in McCook to explain to the citizens of the town their good idea about the prairie animal nations. It's hard to overstate the disinclination Midwesterners had to accept the Poppers' idea—or how quickly environmentalists and think-tankers quickly claimed and adapted it for their own purposes. In McCook, the reaction was to launch the Buffalo Commons Story-telling Festival every June "just to thumb our noses at the Poppers," as 82-year-old festival co-founder Mary Ellen Goodenberger explained to me. What started as a modest local storytelling-morale boosting session now fills the town's old Fox Theatre and other venues. People come all the way from New Jersey to hear musicians like Jay Ungar and Molly Mason and other musicians, cowboy poets and storytell-ers. If it keeps growing, they'll have to send out somebody from the Buffalo *News* to cover it.

There's no shortage of Popper-type plans, usually advanced by organizations with clumsy but evocative, romantic-sounding names, like "The Wildlands Project's Heart of the West Wildlands Network" campaign. Among the WPHof theWWN's goals: stopping oil drilling in Wyoming and "assisting Utahns in the assimilation of naturally recolonizing wolves into Utah, through science-based planning and education." Okay. More wolves, less oil. Bonus for Democrats: Less Utahns, too. I remember reading a few years ago—probably another *New York Times* op-ed, I think, but I can't seem to locate it—about

---

29 From the organization's website at www.gprc.org. The organization recently seems to have decided to spare McCook. According to their website, the new plan is to create "a stunningly beautiful new Refuge for buffalo, prairie dogs, pronghorn antelope and more that is larger than Manhattan on the shortgrass prairie of southeastern Colorado, about 200 miles from Amarillo, TX."

a wilderness-making proposal that would essentially close the High Plains off to all visitors except those making excursions by rail. Maybe environmentalists could hunt buffalo from the train windows, like back in the day.

The latest greatest idea is from a team of mad scientists led by C. Josh Donlan, a biologist at Cornell University. Donlan's idea, published in *Nature*,[30] is "Pleistocene re-wilding" of the Great Plains by turning feral horses and Bactrian camels loose in the backyards of Kansas and Nebraska in order to replace the species scientists say were killed off by those rapacious invaders from Asia some 13,000 years ago.

And that's when the fun starts:

> The second, more controversial phase of Pleistocene re-wilding could also begin immediately, with the maintenance of small numbers of African cheetahs (*Acinonyx jubatus*), Asian (*Elephas maximus*) and African (*Loxodonta africana*) elephants, and lions (*Panthera leo*) on private property. Many of these animals are already in captivity in the United States, and the primary challenge will be to provide them with naturalistic settings, including large protected areas of appropriate habitat and, in the case of carnivores, live prey.... The obstacles are substantial and the risks are not trivial, but we can no longer accept a hands-off approach to wilderness preservation. Instead, we want to reinvigorate wild places, as widely and rapidly as is prudently possible.

---

30 August 18, 2005.

Cheetahs! That's what they need out there. Drumming up support for his idea, Donlan explained to NBC News his idea for a "vast ecological park in the Midwest with free-roaming carnivores, free-roaming elephants, and the other large biodiversity that we once had." This sounded more Jurassic than Pleistocene to many Midwesterners. Donlan, writing in Slate, seemed aware that there may be some pushback from the locals:

> Sure, the costs and risks of bringing back the megafauna are significant—they include angry ranchers, scared passersby, and unanticipated effects on other plants and animals. But without rewilding, we settle forever for an American wilderness that is diminished compared with just 100 centuries ago. And in the event of global climate change that affects Africa in particular, or economic and political strife there, we risk the extinction of the world's remaining bolson tortoises, camels, elephants, cheetahs, and lions. Safari trip to Texas, anyone?

Most of my friends gave up their Pleistocene re-wilding just after college, but about 15 years ago when I was writing a book about lions[31] I spent a long day with a guy who ran a "safari ranch" near Houston. His plan was like Donlan's I guess, but with a private enterprise twist that gave a more humane ending for all those "rewilded" lions released on pension. He bought old lions from circuses and zoos when they got too old to roar convincingly. Then he'd turn them out on his 2,000 acres of savannah-like Texan prairie, where the largely

---

31 *Man Eaters Motel*, Ticknor & Fields. Highly recommended.

toothless beasts would find some shade and just go to sleep. Then a dentist from New Jersey—maybe the guy who does Frank Popper's root canals!—standing in the back of a pick-up would ride up and shoot the thing. Only cost a few thousand. Making the skin into a nice rug for the doc's office, that was extra.

It's not quite clear how Donlan's cheetahs and lions are going to go down with the GPRC's prairie animal nations already suffering in that emergency-room situation of theirs. There are also a few prairie humans in actual bedrooms across the region to worry about. Prof. George Packer from the University of Minnesota told a reporter that the problem he sees with Donlan's plan was that "once [lions] have figured out that humans are food they will go into houses and drag someone out of bed." So, yes, there's that. What would we do without professors?

When I told Bill Blauvelt about the Pleistocene rewilding idea, he told me about the circus lion that got loose someplace north of Superior not long ago. "They asked me if I wanted to go up and take a picture for the paper. I said, 'No, thanks.'" Bill allowed that it might be more interesting to rewild Ithaca, New York, where Cornell University lives.

Donlan, the Poppers, the defenders of the prairie animal nation, The Wildlands Project's Heart of the West Wildlands Network enthusiasts—none of these are the first people to take a look at the big, open, extremely unpopulated expanse of Kansas and Nebraska and decide that the people living there have it all wrong. Along the Republican River, people have been listening more or less politely for years to the big plans visitors from deep blue precincts have for the Midwest. Since the 1850s, Kansans and Nebraskans have been told where they should live, where they should work—and, especially, how they should vote—so many times it just doesn't matter any more. They know that when city people start asking questions like "What's the matter with Kansas?" the last thing they want to hear is William Allen White's simple answer.

INTERLUDE: SUPERIOR PEOPLE 2.

Pat: I read something on the internet this morning—I think it's been making the rounds—about a terrible category 5 blizzard last winter in North Dakota, and how the neighbors came out and helped each other, but no one in the rest of the country paid any attention. No FEMA, no nothing. No one shows up to report it And I really do think that's part of the Midwestern mentality: When it's good, we share, when it's bad, we share, and help each other out. When there's a disaster in one of the coastal areas, we all rally, but (laughs) I don't see anyone rallying to North Dakota.

Stan: Probably because they think nobody's there.

Bill: No one that *matters.* (Laughter.)

Pat: When the blizzard was coming, the front of my grocery store was lined with expensive pick-ups, all with engines running while people ran inside to get a few things, and they know no one's gonna jump in and take it.

Rich: Of course not. It wouldn't even cross anyone's mind.

Bill: You rely on people to do the right thing, it's just the way things are. Like, for instance, there was the time four of us got into Alliance late at night, and couldn't get a motel room, either there or in Valentine—no place in the inn. Around midnight, I go into a convenience store to see if I can buy an air mattress to sleep in the bed of the truck, and there's this railroader in there. Never saw him before. But he's headed home and he says 'I've got a spare bedroom, and we can set up a tent in the backyard. A couple of you can sleep inside, and the others in the tent – I'll leave the back door open Just let me call my wife and alert her you're coming home with me.'

Pat: Oh, of course—men volunteer their wives all the time. (Laughter.)

Bill: But I just don't know if that would happen in a lot of other places in this country? We have friends from Delaware, I've been to their house, and they have a whole series of locks on the front door. Well, they came to visit us here, and one day we're sitting in the living room, and there's a knock at the door. My father calls "Come in," and in walks someone we've never seen before. I tell you, these people are scared to death, they can't believe we just let this stranger walk into the house. (Laughs.) It was just someone looking for directions.

Stan: My family got here in 1934, the Dust Bowl era. The dust would fly by so heavy you couldn't see across the street. And of course those were also the Depression years. And, boy, how people helped each other then!

Pat: There was no other way. There might've not been much else, but people saw to it no one starved. Everyone had eggs for breakfast....

Stan: ...And a new pair of overalls in the fall to go to school in...

Pat: ...And there was always flour for bread. Farmers never lacked for that.

Bill: I was at a church pot luck in Lincoln, Kansas, not long ago, where people brought all kinds of good things to eat. And one older gentleman said, 'I remember one pot luck in the 1930's where we had only two things to eat, cottage cheese and chicken. Everybody brought what they had at home, and that was all there was."

Stan: We fed a family of five on six dollars a week. (Laughs.) And if some stranger knocked on the door and walked in, we'd have fed him, too.

6

A LOCAL HISTORY
OF DEMOCRATS.

One of the many easy conclusions most people reach about places like Kansas without actually going there is that somebody's political party reveals their place on a left-right spectrum that seems to have only two positions, like a light switch. "Republican" means conservative. "Democrat" means liberal. And in most parts of the country, that's simply quite true. There are not many blue-dog Democrats in Manhattan for example, and while the number of liberal Republicans is still significant in many parts of blue America, they're a dwindling number, holding onto power in places like New England, California, Alaska and New York City, usually by appearing to be militantly palatable in their politics and more practical in their application of Republican values than their Democratic rivals.

But in the Midwest generally, and in Kansas and, to a lesser extent, in Nebraska, the situation is a little different. There just aren't many Democrats around. The result is a confusion of the labels most of us use for convenience. In Kansas, you have the same range of ideological beliefs you have anyplace else, but you have most of them shoehorned into one party. In Kansas, conservative Democrats aren't particularly unusual, and until 2004, the Kansas GOP was a living museum of Eisenhower Republicans. The state is as divided as the rest of America, but in Kansas, liberal Republicans and their Democratic allies have always held sway until very recently.

The two factions function more or less like énarques, France's odious ruling class despised especially by the French themselves; they are less interested in party ideology—a pleasing departure from the usual political bloodsport—and more fascinated by protecting each others' interests—a decided disadvantage to those interested in democratic expressions of popular will. For more than a half-century, they have tossed power back and forth, usually keeping it well over the heads of leaping conservatives.

The state's former governor, Kathleen Sebelius, was a celebrated Democrat, supported by Emily's List, wildly pro-choice, and otherwise banner-waving for the familiar positions of liberal Democrats everywhere. Unkind cynics even observed that her hairstyle was a replica of John Kerry's famed gray helmet. She entered the 2006 campaign with $2 million in the bank and then added to it—including far more money donated by Republicans than gave to the Republican party's actual candidates. She enjoyed the support of previous "moderate" Republican governors like Bill Graves and Mike Hayden, both of whom joined her administration. Her lieutenant governor, Mark Parkinson, was, until just before the 2006 election, the state chairman of the Republican party.

So what was going on there? Actually, a lot less than meets the eye. Or, to put it more precisely, pretty much the same thing as when Massachusetts elects a Republican governor, or California, or New

York. Voters cast their ballots in state-wide races with a different mindset than they do in national contests, based on very different, and more parochial, concerns. Indeed, in many ways Sebelius resembled no one so much as New York's charmless George Pataki. Her political style – reactive, almost passive, and given to platitudes about the importance of community and booster car seats for kids – was calculated, above all, to not alienate significant numbers of voters and to give the docile local press as little to write about as possible.

It is in presidential, congressional and senatorial races that, to the consternation of liberals, Kansans show their true colors, which tend toward the scarlet. Wandering through much of the state, it was as hard to find a Moveon.org Democrat as it is to unearth a card-carrying NRA enthusiast ordering a pastrami on white at Zabar's.

Until Brownback, Kansas' ruling class agreed on most things— big, expensive school systems and buckets of tax revenue to support them, for example, and a generally hands-off attitude toward most social issues, especially abortion and gambling. But the thing they agreed on most heartily was their shared hatred of conservatives. It's not a casual hatred, either. They actively despise them personally, and the feeling is mutual.

Slowly, though, as conservatives gained more strength, the parties started a belated realignment, something conservative Republican strategists like Kris Van Meteren thought was a very good thing. "We've gotten lazy," he told me a few years ago. "In 2006, the state Republican party acted like it was 1972. They raised very little money for our candidates. They mailed out a couple of flyers and a fund-raising letter or two and that's it. Instead of ripping the Democrats, the party's chairman [former state house speaker Tim

Shallenberger, who was defeated by Sebelius in 2002] attacks conservatives for being divisive."

Over time, the effects of this kind of stranglehold on power became increasingly evident. For example, the Kansas Supreme Court is one of the most activist in the Midwest, perhaps in the nation, because Kansas, until Brownback's victory, had never elected a conservative governor, and so no opportunities for giving the court ideological balance (or even representation) have ever presented themselves. Instead, the court was seen even by journalists sympathetic to the "moderates" as a nest of political cronies. While this situation is no doubt pleasing to Kansas liberals, many felt it was probably not the best way to insure widespread respect for the state judiciary. The closest Kansans ever came to electing a conservative governor was in 1991, when they voted in Joan Finney, the merrily eccentric, populist Democrat who shunned the statehouse Democrats and instead preferred the company of Native American lobbyists and affable legislative Republicans.

Democrats were routinely elected in the most conservative, rural districts of Kansas and Nebraska, so long as they aren't overtly liberal—or overtly Democrats. Most Democrats outside the two areas that faithfully elect them—Kansas City and the university town of Lawrence—wouldn't dream of campaigning as Democrats. Once they reach Topeka, they become reliable votes used by Democrats to thwart the conservative Republican agenda, an agenda that lived in a perpetual state of frustrated thwartedness. Conservative leaders in Kansas kept saying the electorate is with them, but the party isn't.

This all frustrated activists like Van Meteren. He looked at states like Missouri where there is a real balance between the parties in terms of registration, where Republicans mount vigorous campaigns and sometimes win, and he saw in the defection of liberals a long-term advantage for Kansas' conservatives Republicans. "People don't want bitter politics, but they do want a good debate on the issues," he said. "To have that, we need to have a little realignment and let Democrats run as Democrats—not as Republicans."

Running as a Republican, no matter where your loyalties lie, is a regional habit shaped by a history that started about the same time Kansas itself started—in the mid-1850's, as the nation was descending into Civil War. There were no Republicans when the Kansas-Nebraska Act of 1854 was passed as part of a plan designed, so its cynical sponsors maintained, to save the union. Two soon-to-be states were carved from the vast Nebraska territory with the expectation that they would maintain the delicate balance between North and South: Nebraska would enter the Union as a free state, Kansas as a slave state. The catch: this meant repealing the terms of the previous arrangement, the Missouri Compromise of 1820, under which slavery would have been barred in both territories. The solution: the magic words "popular sovereignty." If Kansans wanted slaves, argued the Democrats who held sway in Congress, then they should be able to have them. So put it to a vote, they said. It was Kansas' first exposure to a genuinely libertarian formulation—unless of course you were a slave, in which case it was just more slavery.

There were several immediate consequences to the Act. One, of course, was the formation of the Republican Party as an explicitly anti-slavery party, which made almost certain that the political divisions in the country would be irreconcilable.

Another was to make Kansas the first battlefield of the Civil War. Indeed, "Bleeding Kansas" was soon a byword and a rallying cry for those on both sides.

Free-staters, those who opposed slavery in Kansas, held a clear numerical advantage in the territory, but in short order pro-slavery Democrats began flooding into Kansas from neighboring Missouri, determined to ensure another slave state by stuffing the ballot boxes, then going back home to Missouri. This soon led to an eruption of spontaneous violence that shook the nation to its core, with real fighting breaking out all along the banks of the Missouri River and deep into the hills of Kansas.

Even as Republicans met to organize a national party, "Free-State" Kansas partisans organized to defend the territory against pro-slavery incursions from Missouri redoubts and from Democratic towns on the Kansas side—Atchison, Leavenworth, Shawnee Mission and Lecompton. The pro-slavery faction spawned local guerrilla bands with Klan-like names like "Sons of the South" and the "Blue Lodge"[32]

Operating from Topeka and other, smaller towns, The Free-Staters brought in plenty of outsiders of their own, including twelve hundred New Englanders, armed by newspaper owner Horace Greeley and other anti-slavery leaders, along with radical firebrands like John Brown and James Henry Lane, who were ready to take up arms to abolish slavery not just in Kansas or Missouri, but everywhere. These were regarded by the Democrats with the kind of special loathing reserved only for those enemies who would presume to occupy a higher moral perch.

But it was impossible to staunch the tide of "border ruffians" from Missouri. Indeed, at one polling station, in a vote held in 1855 to elect a territorial legislature, a mere twenty of the six hundred

---

32 The idea, apparently, was to give the pro-slavery faction the aura of Masonic association. However the relationship, if any, between the pro-slavery Blue Lodge and the Masonic movement has been debated for a very long time. See The Builder, January 1924, which is available online at phoenixmasonry.org.

who cast ballots were found to be legitimate Kansas residents. As a result, the Kansas legislature was delivered safely into the hands of Democrats. As Samuel Crawford, who would soon become governor, wrote, "Proslavery people resorted to every means, fair and foul, honest and dishonest, to establish slavery in Kansas... [they] swarmed across the border into Kansas and committed crimes most brutal and barbarous. They came in squads, companies, and regiments, and...elected citizens of Missouri as members of the [Kansas] Territorial Legislature—a Legislature, the majority of whose members committed perjury when they took their oath of office... and enacted a code of laws for the territory of Kansas by taking the statutes of Missouri [which permitted slavery] and striking out the words, 'State of Missouri'...and inserting in their place the words, 'Kansas Territory'"

In the wake of the vote, violence spread. As a pair of Democratic administrations, those of Pierce and Buchanan, presided over national policy and lent support to local pro-slavery forces, the opposition, operating as militias with names like the "Free State Army of Kansas" gathered public support and fought pitched battles across the territory.

In 1858, a new referendum was held, and the decidedly anti-Democrat result gave Kansas a political compass that pointed the way for a century and a half. When Kansas finally joined the Union in January, 1861, on the eve of the Civil War, it was as a free state, passionately embracing Lincoln, the Republican party and a deep commitment to end slavery. As Crawford later put it, "From start to finish, it was a red-hot fight, with justice, humanity, and the heavy artillery on the Republican side." In the Civil War that followed, Kansas would lose more men per capita than any other Northern state.

While "Bleeding Kansas" is not really the grist of most American kids' education, it certainly is in Kansas, where every child learns that the Civil War was previewed right there next to the football field. The state's seventh-grade curriculum requires that Kansas children be able to "analyze the importance of 'Bleeding Kansas' to the rest of the United States in the years leading up to the Civil War." They learn about the Kansas-Nebraska Act; about Brown and Lane and about Quantrill's raid on Lawrence, where the pro-slavery men burned newspaper offices and ransacked homes. They're told what happened to anti-slavery Republican Sen. Charles Sumner after he delivered a scathing speech called the "Crime Against Kansas" attacking the Democrats and "the harlot, Slavery." (He was beaten nearly to death by a furious Democratic congressman.) And students are asked to be able to answer this question: "Why was [Kansas] a free state when it's next door neighbor Missouri is a slave state?

It took Sumner nearly three years to recover from the attack, but in Kansas, the Democrats never did.

"[The events of the 1850s] had a big effect on Kansas," historian Craig Miner explained to me when I asked him why there were almost no Democrats on the property. "I think you'd have to say [Bleeding Kansas] is one big reason." The state's schools teach kids about Roosevelt and the New Deal and LBJ, Martin Luther King and civil rights, but they're also taught about a homegrown conflict that was not only a shooting war, but also a political one with certain modern parallels. It involved upstart Republicans facing off against establishment Democrats. And no one is sorry that Democrats lost.[33]

---

33 To become smart as a Kansas schoolkid, I suggest Miner's *History* (op cit.) and David Donald's *Charles Sumner and the Coming of the Civil War*. I plead guilty to grossly oversimplifying a highly complex historical period, but the bottom line here is not at all unclear—those who wanted Kansas to become a slave state and were willing to use force to get their way were southern Democrats, not only the southern Democrats of 1854, but also the southern Democrats of a century later.

That what it meant to be a Republican—and a Democrat—was permanently fixed for so many generations by events in the 1850s may strike many Blue Staters as absurd, but, given the issues involved, it is at least understandable. What's far harder for them to grasp is the degree to which much that's followed has only served to reinforce that political affiliation and to put off until now the emergence of Kansas Democrats as a serious political force.

True enough, Republicans were briefly voted out during the Dust Bowl years of the 1930s, when the New Deal offered the prospect of better times. But by 1940, Kansans had turned away from Roosevelt. "You know when things really went wrong for us?" 85-year-old Mitchell County Democratic party central committee-man Charles Hackett told me one evening after a local party meeting in Beloit, "With Roosevelt. When we needed government help, he was fine. But when we didn't, we were left with all that government red tape and regulations, telling you what you could and couldn't do. That was no good. Farmers hate to be told what to do."

As a result, in 1940, Kansas went for Wilkie—and for every Republican after that with the exception of 1964, when Kansans, along with the rest of the country, bought into the Democratic claim that to elect Barry Goldwater meant nuking the kids playing in the front yard.

Even Truman, from just across the river in Missouri, couldn't break the Democrats' losing streak. Few in Kansas identified with him. As Kay Thull, a lifelong Democrat from Cawker City, told me, if it hadn't been for Truman's involvement with Thomas Pendergast and Kansas City's corrupt Democratic machine, he would have remained an Independence haberdasher.[34]

---

34 Tom Pendergast, a saloon-keeper, had started his political involvement in Kansas City's working-class 10th Ward, but he soon came to control not just Kansas City politics, but Missouri politics as well. Introduced to politics by Pendergast's nephew, a war buddy, Truman was installed as a judge in Kansas City and in 1934 elevated to the US Senate in an election rigged by the Pendergast machine. Pendergast finally died in

"We knew all about Kansas City and Pendergast. We didn't want to be identified with *that*," said Thull.

After Truman came Eisenhower, who was a legitimate Kansan, a son of Abilene, a solid Republican and a genuine military hero with a style of governance that appealed to Kansans' general disdain for political theatrics—although his use of federal troops to end the racist policies of southern Democrats fit nicely with the way Kansans felt the world should work.

Nothing has fundamentally altered Kansans' formal political affiliations over the half century since. Until recently, the extremist rhetoric from both sides in the ideological civil war that's taking place in the country today has left Kansans—and Midwesterners in general—happy to be a long way from places like New York and San Francisco. That's all coming to an end, of course, as conservatives, who draw a parallel between being anti-slavery and anti-abortion, lambaste "pro-aborts" while liberals attack "crazies" and "fundies." None of this is very persuasive, of course.

Real moderates are becoming as rare in Kansas politics as they are elsewhere in America, not least because of the way the word "moderate" has been repurposed by the press for use as a lead pipe with which to bash conservatives, including even moderately conservative conservatives. You'd think "liberal" wouldn't need a euphemism; Nelson Rockefeller lived a long and politically happy life as a "liberal Republican."

Only in the newspapers of Kansas can somebody be described as a "moderate" because he or she supports bigger government, gambling, high taxes, over-bloated education budgets and unrestricted use of a certain type of late-term abortion procedure

---

1945. "When Truman attended that man's funeral," Thull said, "we Kansas Democrats were just *disappointed.*"

that shocks even the ostensibly liberal populations of countries like France, Germany and elsewhere in the European Union, where such things are seen as not just illegal, but disgusting (and where other litmus issues in Kansas and Missouri, such as embryonic stem cell research, are seen as morally indefensible, too[35]).

In Kansas in 2004, all you needed for a partial-birth abortion is five grand and an appointment with Dr. George Tiller, the owner of America's number-one partial-birth abortion clinic. Women (and girls) in very advanced stages of pregnancy flew to Wichita to call on Tiller from all over the world, since most of the rest of the planet frowned on the grisly procedure. But not Kansas. Although the state notionally forbade post-viability abortions and requires reporting cases involving children brought to the clinic for abortions, there was no mechanism for enforcement without effective monitoring. The state even subsidized flights to the Wichita airport.

Occasionally, a young woman died at one of the area motels Tiller used as ad-hoc post-op facilities; the death of one teenager with Down Syndrome who was given an abortion in her 28th week was the basis for a grand jury investigation of Tiller. Sebelius, meanwhile,

---

35 A Missouri billionaire named James Stowers, founder of the Stowers Institute for Medical Research in Kansas City, pumped lots of money into that 2006 election—as much as $30 million in Missouri (under the banner of The Coalition for Life-Saving Cures) and, according to one state legislator, another $12 million or so in Kansas. His Institute is heavily invested in gaining approval for embryonic stem cell research, so he targeted local political races and was successful in both states. Missouri Sen. Jim Talent, a Republican who opposed Stowers' ambitions, was defeated and a bill to allow the research was approved.
Stowers targeted conservative Kansas legislators whom he thought might pose a risk: One Kansas City-area legislator, Mary Pilcher Cook, was defeated by a Republican-turned-Democrat who was supported by a well-funded organization called "Kansans for Life-Saving Cures." The science must have been a bit complicated. As Pilcher Cook complained to me at the time, "She keeps talking about 'nomadic stem cells'." Unfortunately for Pilcher Cook, the Bedouin vote was not sufficient to carry the day. She lost her 2006 state house race by 150 votes. Two years later, she was elected to the Kansas state senate and re-elected in 2012 and 2016.

raised even a few "moderate" eyebrows when she vetoed a bill passed by the legislature requiring health inspections of clinics. The bill sailed through after a TV news item showing rats infesting a Kansas City clinic was broadcast. "The place was so filthy you wouldn't want your sister to go there," one statehouse journalist told me, drily.

Kansans knew all that; before the 2006 election, the rightwing airwaves were filled with news about Tiller, Sebelius and the abortion mess in Kansas. The intended beneficiary of all this was at the time one of the few conservatives in a statewide office in Kansas: Phill Kline, who was locked in a struggle with man named Paul Morrison, the Johnson County DA who had been re-elected four times as a Republican but who switched parties to run as a pro-choice Democrat.

So the voters got to decide. What they decided, by a large margin, was that if they had to choose between listening to Phill Kline and being the partial-birth abortion capital of the world, they'd take the abortions, thanks. It was less embarrassing, and nothing moves the Kansas vote quicker than being laughed at by people who have never been to Kansas, as William Allen White knew. It was also Kline himself and his earnest shrillness—"a little too intense" is how one sympathetic conservative legislator described it to me—that put people off.

Kline infuriated the Topeka press corps and his political adversaries not only because of his dogmatic religio-conservatism, but, one suspects, because of his lengthy, complicated but extemporaneous defenses of his views. When *Esquire* magazine sent a writer out to nail Kline on his anti-abortion opinions, all the guy could do was run paragraph-long quotes of stuff Kline said between bites at dinner. He assiduously avoids the empty-headed Trump-speak journalists and pundits hope for when they quote conservatives. For example, when I asked him about Kansas's oft-misunderstood status as a conservative red state, he told me, "The challenge is deep rooted in the failure for us to teach, learn, understand and apply some basic principles of governance in a culture that even denies that there are principles worth protecting." Right. But…

"In a culture of moral relativism, everything is pragmatic and therefore the foundational principles and the importance of those principles is lost in the immediacy of the moment," he continued.

In 2006, a golden year for Democrats running in mid-term elections, Morrison swept not only the usual blue precincts around Kansas City and Lawrence, but counties all across Kansas, places where Democrats hadn't won an election for years. Suddenly, it seemed the range was filled with donkeys.[36]

Thus did Kansans finally earn the praise of *The New York Times*. Gone was the mortifying gloom that came with all those liberals wondering what the matter with Kansas was anyway? Kansans had finally made those "mental connections" that critics said were supposed to result in economic benefits, somehow.

But it was just a moment. Another one was on the way: In a state as divided as Kansas, there'll be something the matter again soon enough. Despite *The Times'* claim, the 2006 election wasn't "a major shift in the nation's heartland" at all. Here's what happened that year: The Republicans' best candidates for governor[37] didn't run. Barnett campaigned broke, and many thought Rep. Jim Ryun's defeat by Democrat Nancy Boyda was long overdue. Ryun wasn't exactly a charismatic figure. In fact, one of his opponents

---

36 In retaliation, the Johnson County Republicans voted Kline into Morrison's old job
37 The underfunded Kansas House speaker, Doug Mays; the paralytically indecisive Rep. (now Sen.) Jerry Moran, who kept everybody guessing about his gubernatorial plans until funding for other potential candidates dried up; and the unrealistically ambitious Sen. Sam Brownback, who apparently thought he could be president, if only anybody outside Kansas knew who he was.

confided in me that "his best campaign events were the ones he didn't attend." Most observers felt Boyda had taken advantage of Sebelius' successful run for re-election as governor and didn't expect the congressional seat to remain with the Democrats for long, and sure enough, in 2009, Boyda was soundly defeated by Republican Lynn Jenkins.

But in 2006, the biggest defeat for the Republicans was the one most Republicans apparently wanted most: the ouster of Kline. The modest gains made by Democrats cost them millions of dollars: Kline was outspent two-to-one by Morrison, who raised more than $1.25 million, and the issue-oriented campaigns for things like embryonic stem cell research that aligned themselves with the Sebelius-Morrison effort piped in many millions more.

The composition of the state house wasn't appreciably changed, and remains about the same today. So *The Times'* endorsement of Kansas notwithstanding, nothing much changed in Kansas after 2006. The pendulum that had swung a notch to the right, now swung a notch to the left. It's the 21st century, after all, and Kansas is in the middle.

7

PRAIRIE COMPANIONS.

A s a '60s romantic. I always thought I understood the appeal of lost causes. After a high school career as a Republican, I became an English major—a sure-fire way to avoid future employment while justifying a political position designed to perpetuate unemployment forever—edited an underground newspaper, sold ads to head shops and started a local SDS chapter (the then-private university I attended simply prohibited "SDS" *anything*, however, so we called our chapter "American Pie"). I marched on Washington lots of times, and not just because my girlfriend at the time so happened to be lodged in George Washington University's famed "superdorm"—137 floors[38] of women, stacked! I helped other guys get arrested. I managed a folk group and went to a Youngbloods concert; I dug the Fugs. I was clean for Gene, then betrayed by Bobby. I served ten years active duty as a poet in Europe. I have always thought I knew the face of trench activism during heavy bombardment.

---

38 Factually, this is an exaggeration. Emotionally, figuratively and aspirationally, it's a gross understatement.

Then I went to the 2005 annual meeting of the Mitchell County Kansas Democratic Central Committee (2004 results: Bush 2600, Kerry 700, Nader 25). Me and seven people roughly my age—including of course the woman from the local paper—in a bank's community room in Beloit, Kansas, plus one other guy in his late thirties. Old business: Cash on hand: $200 and change. New business: "We're going to turn Kansas blue," Fred Karlin told his Democrats. Everybody agreed. The obvious solution: A fund-raiser! They figured on a cook-out in the park with an auction in which a George Foreman Grillmaster would be sold to the highest bidder. The guy in his thirties asked, "What are the chances we can get younger people involved? I mean…" he looked furtively around the table. "Well, you know, I mean people my age." Everybody laughed and the business part of the meeting ended. Then I was invited to ask questions.

"This is Kansas. Why are you all Democrats?"

I expected the synaxarion of liberal saints and their causes and something about justice for the workers of the world. But they all said they were Democrats because their parents had been Democrats, back during the New Deal. "Here's a story," Karlin said. Then, looking around the table, asked, "Should I tell him the story?"

Everybody said no.

"Okay, I will. When my grandfather was dying, he called everybody to his deathbed and said, 'I've been a Democrat all my life. But I'm converting.'

"'Why?' everybody asked. 'Why would you do that?'

"'Because,' he said, 'When I go, there'll be one fewer Republican left alive.'"

We all smiled.

"Have you read *What's the Matter with Kansas?*" one of them asked. "He really lets them have it, doesn't he?"

I agreed. "He does. Did you read the book?" Pause. "Well, what do you think of his advice to Democrats? Think you'd do better if you ran to the left?"

Startled looks. A double-barbershop quartet of Democrats replied in absolutely perfect unison: "No!"

A big, affable man in T-shirt and shorts, said, "The problem is, people back there" – he gestured vaguely in the direction of the East Coast – "they think that because we're Democrats, we don't go to church, that we don't believe in God. Hey. We're pro-life. We're not agitating for gay marriage. We don't go for *any* of that stuff."

The others all nodded.

So Frank's wrong on that? You should just skip the social issues and focus instead on economic issues?

"I'd say Mr. Frank's way wrong on that one," said another man.

"What we do think is that people should be easier on each other—spend a little more when we have to help out other people," said Karlin. "That's what I was taught, anyway."

The fact is, when it came to "values" issues, economics and national defense, most Kansas Democrats were far more at home with Zell Miller than with Howard Dean. Not surprisingly, outside the tiny blue precincts of Wyandotte county and the liberal university town of Lawrence, very few Democratic candidates even use the word "Democrat" on their signs and flyers. "Why give people a reason to vote against you?" observed former Kansas House minority leader Dennis McKinney.

From a very heavily Republican district himself, McKinney voted pro-life, pro-gun and supported the amendment to the Kansas constitution that prohibited gay marriages. (He went on to become state treasurer; Democrats foolishly voted against him in the 2017 special election in the 4th District primary.) Another Democratic legislator—in fact, the most liberal member of the state senate, according to Doug Mays, the former speaker of the Kansas House— State Senator Janis Lee, explained it to me this way: "On my signs, no 'Democrat' and no donkeys. It's just not worth it." Instead, she pounds pavement and presses flesh. A few years ago, when I was holed up in a little house on the northern edge Mankato to work on a book, Janis Lee came by not once, but *twice*. I saw her more often than the guy next door. Lee escaped electoral politics in 2010 and was appointed chief hearing officer for the Kansas Court of Tax Appeals.

I n the Midwest, most non-urban Democrats know that the only way they can win anything is to run just slightly left of the conservative Republican candidate, thus capturing "moderate" Republican votes. In fact, many don't bother with the D-word at all, registering and running as Republicans. "My family have always been Democrats," Bill Light, an extremely affable state legislator from a very rural, conservative southwestern district, told me one night over a beer. "But you know what the first thing I did when I decided to run for the [state] house? I registered as a Republican. It would have been pointless to run if I didn't do that first." In 2006, Light was re-elected, unopposed, and served in the House until 2010. He was replaced by Steve Alford, from tiny Ulysses, whose political career looked a shaky after he told a crowd of locals (in an appearance carried on youtube, even) that legalizing marijuana was unwise, since African-Americans were prone to using it as a gateway drug. They were, he said, "basically users and they basically responded the worst to those drugs just because of their character makeup, their genetics and that." In January 2018 he was basically stripped of his legislative posts — but not his legislative seat — after issuing an apology.

If Republicans in Kansas suffer from self-inflicted injuries more often than expected, it may be because there are so many of them. At the same time, the problem of what it meant to be a Midwestern Democrat only intensified as the country became ever more closely divided. In 2006, Ted Kennedy, Barbara Boxer, and Hillary Clinton spoke for vast elements of the national party, but they didn't sound much like anyone from Kansas, where people hate talking politics, even with their politicians. "That Josh Svaty! I'd vote for him," said a cousin of mine who will here go nameless. This was one afternoon after meeting a very young, very liberal Democratic representative from Salina at some rural organization's annual get-together. I rattled off Svaty's support for one liberal agenda item after another. "Well, what I mean is that I'd vote for him if he'd keep all that to himself. He's really funny!" After winning three elections in a district where Republicans outnumbered Democrats by a ratio of 2-to-1, Svaty finlly went down to defeat in the 2018 Democratic gubernatorial primary despite visiting all 105 counties and running a pro-life campaign and —perhaps more tellingly — receiving endorsements from Kansas ex-GOP moderates such as former governors John Carlin and Bill Graves and former GOP US Senator Sheila Frahm.

Where Kansas had Josh Svaty, the rest of the country has cut-ups like Patty Murray and Chuck Shumer. "We'd do a lot better if it weren't for [the national party]," McKinney told me one day, standing in front of Dan's lunch counter in the Topeka statehouse. I had just watched him guide his Democratic House caucus with a light touch through a day of education funding. All around us were John Stuart Curry's fantastic murals, showing, among other things, a really furious John Brown on the rampage. The Kansas statehouse was in the process of being restored, an acre or so of ugly blue paint has been removed, and the result was stunning: re-discovered huge painted ceiling panels running around the House chamber and, above the transoms, the emblazoned names of famous Free-Staters and proto-Republicans. These kept watch on McKinney's small band of Democrats who huddled together for safety along one of the chamber's walls.

"The national party just makes it a lot harder for us," continued McKinney, who readily noted the contrast between the civility he finds in Kansas politics and the ugliness coming out of Washington. "In southern Europe, the Serbs and Bosnians still hate each other over atrocities that occurred over 700 years ago," as he wrote in a Dodge City newspaper. "But these atrocities were no worse than the crimes committed by pro- and anti-slavery forces in eastern Kansas and western Missouri from 1856-1864. Why was our country able to rise above this, while others persist in hatred?" You would answer this question one way if you were a faithful reader of the *San Francisco Chronicle*. You'd answer your own question this way if you were a Kansas Democrat like McKinney: "[Because] we regularly reaffirm our Christ-taught values of love and forgiveness. Second, we regularly affirm those values and ideas that make democracy work. We work hard to instill these values and ideas in our children. [The national party] has a lot more to do with New York than it does with Kansas," he said. It's certainly true that voters in Kansas and Nebraska are far more unpredictable than voters in, say, New York City, where no shame is too great for voters to bear so long as they get their Democrats in office. Articulate, wry and honest, McKinney's was a politician who seemed to his many supporters to live the beliefs he preaches. I myself was more than a little surprised when out of the blue he brought up the guy a cousin of mine was dating when she interned for him several years ago; he wanted to be sure she hadn't married him. "He was kind of..." He wrinkled his nose. But she hadn't and McKinney was visibly relieved. And weren't we all?

Many blue-staters readily dismissed Democrats like these for putting so-called "social issues" ahead of what people like Frank perceive to be their economic interests. But, aside from the fact that most of those issues have little to do with the actual lives of Midwesterners, such a view vastly underestimates the importance of values in all people's lives. In fact, what's truly bizarre is the concept that people should be comfortable voting for candidates who *disregard* the social issues they hold dear.

INTERLUDE: SUPERIOR PEOPLE 3.

Stan: People wonder why we elect so many Democrats in this part of the world. Well, it may sound strange to those from outside, but out here Democrats and Republicans can be almost identical on the issues.

Bill: What that also means is there's not the same level of partisan animosity you find in other places. I've been a Republican all my life, and I think most Republicans would think I'm was a pretty fair Republican. But the two Democratic county commissioners are both farmers, and a few years ago, when the Democratic lieutenant governor was out here campaigning, it was milo season. One of the commissioners said, "Bill, we've got to be in the fields, harvesting milo. Will you take her around and introduce her to people?" I don't think they gave a thought to the fact that I was a registered Republican – I just didn't have any milo to cut that day. (laughter)

Pat: Basically, you vote for someone who shares your values.

Rich: Exactly. Some of us are bothered a lot by some of the things we see happening these days— all the latch key kids with both parents working, rising divorce, declining education, all the junk that you see when you turn on the television. To me, that's one of the biggest differences between the thinking here and on the coast. It seems like people there aren't quite as concerned about those things. They think conservative values are boring, they lack color, they lack *pizzazz*. I even read an article that said that for a lot of people, integrity is not an issue anymore. Well, I sure think it still is.

Stan: I'm with you all the way on that.

Pat: I guess we do come across as conservative – which, for the most part, we probably are. Fundamentally, most of us have deep conservative values . But on an issue by issue basis, a lot of people would be surprised at how liberal some of us are. Take the issue of gays, for instance – the image in some parts of the country is probably that if you're gay, you'll be shot if you come here. It's not true at all. There's a lot of sympathy and understanding and compassion for gay people in our neck of the woods.

Rich: Even those who hate the practice, they have compassion for the individual. And you can run down a whole list of issues—we think *our* views are the compassionate ones. Because to our way of thinking, they're the ones that make for a better life for children and families, a stronger economy, a better world…

Pat: Take the issue of illegal aliens…

Rich: Which as far as a lot of liberals are concerned, you're not even supposed to call them. You're not allowed to call the thing what it is.

Pat: I think most of us are kind've torn. Because you do feel for these people…

Rich: On the other hand, how much are they costing us in social services?

Stan: But they're also giving back. They're buying things, paying taxes…

Pat: And taking service industry jobs that Americans don't seem to want.

Stan (laughing): If we made them citizens, and they got stuck with as many taxes as the rest of us, then they'd be sorry.

Rich: The whole multi-cultural thing is part of it. If they really wanted to *become* Americans, and made sure their kids learned English and our history…

Stan: That's right, then there'd be a lot fewer objections. Because a lot of them already have a wonderful work ethic.

Bill: They sure do. I remember one year we had a booth at the fair, and a little boy, maybe ten or twelve, used to come down every day for the helium balloons we were giving away. So after a while, I start objecting to how many balloons I'm giving to the kid, and he says 'Listen, I run the ring toss game at the carnival, so you come up, and you'll be a winner.' So one night I have a little time, and I wander over to the carnival and find his ring-toss booth. He looks up at me and shakes his head no. The next day he comes down and says 'I saw you last night, but I had to be careful, I had customers. You come down when I have no customers, and you'll be a winner.'

(Laughter.)

Stan: There's a kid that's gonna go far in this world.

Pat: If he works hard.

PART TWO

8

THE SUPERCENTER
OUT THERE.

Kansans and Nebraskans by now should be the most cynical people on Earth. Everyone who crosses the state line from somewhere East or West has something to tell them about how they could do it all better if they'd just listen up, stop being hicks, and especially learn how to vote right by voting left, as the New York Times, Thomas Frank et al. have been telling them for years.

It's not that they just don't listen. They just don't care. For those who live out here, the concerns that interest most people don't have a lot to do with national politics. From Ft. Riley to Gregg's place out there in Colorado, the issue that compels attention most is water, which is related to weather, which impacts agriculture, which determines income and the profitability of local businesses, which affects greatly schools and other government services, which is where politics is on the list of local priorities. For most Kansans, the recipe for Midwestern success is simple: Just add water.

As I write (and the years doesn't really matter), the plains are in the midst of yet another drought (or another year of one very long drought, depending on how you look at it and who's talking) and, again, ag policies, including those which have nothing to do with rainfall—and barely qualify as "policies" at all, given their arbitrariness—are in flux. This year, more farmland will be taken out of production and put into conservation programs—just another way to write the subsidy check. Malthus was wrong, wrong, wrong. The problem isn't too many people. It's too few trains.

Less than a mile from where I sat in Concordia was a huge elevator where summer after summer the wheat harvest overflows capacity as farmers arrived with semi-loads of the stuff, dumped it, and waited for the check. Most of the guys I knew when I was younger all still go out and help harvest wheat from Texas up to the Canadian border; last year, one of them came back after spending a couple of hours sitting out an Oklahoma rainstorm talking with Gen. Tommy Franks who happened to own the farm down the road. His brother swore that if the government would just get out of the way and let farmers do what they do best, the whole planet could be fed by Kansas. Maybe that's a bit of hyperbole—and the global farmers' market isn't quite that simple—but even now, with completely nonsensical ag regulations in the way, there aren't enough rail cars on the planet to be able to cart it away all the wheat grown here, and even if there were, there aren't enough ovens in hell to bake it all into bread: One bushel of wheat contains more than a million kernels and yields more than 70 loaves of bread; in Kansas alone farmers produce enough wheat every year to make more than 36 billion loaves. The BNSF and the UP practically have to plough their way through the mountain of wheat in thousands of places like Concordia. But national railroads don't like getting into the grain-toting business, given its wild seasonal fluctuations, and while smaller regional railways, such as the Kyle here in Concordia, try to move the stuff, it's an overwhelming task. In fact, it would be an uphill task if it weren't in Kansas. So the wheat just piles up higher and higher, until something happens to make it profitable to move it somewhere else. That surplus is now so predictable that the Concordia elevator finally had to do what many, many others did: they built a permanent shelter over the mountain of wheat. If history is an indicator, soon it will be a range of mountains, and given time, maybe skiing will finally come to Kansas.[39]

A couple of blocks away is Sixth Street, Concordia's shopping

area—always called the 'business district" out here, no matter how little business is done there. It's a very fragile environment, economically. "Main street is an easy place," Milan Wall, co-director of the

Sixth Street, Concordia

Lincoln-based Heartland Center for Leadership, told me. While small prairie villages like McCook and Concordia are still slowly recovering from the last hard time, other small towns are slowly dying despite

---

39 This isn't the book to read if you want to learn anything about the crazy world of ag policies. It's a huge welfare scam, not just for indolent corporate rice farmers in Louisiana or conceptual wheat producers in North Dakota, but for everybody who buys the cheap food this country produces. Can we fix it? Not easily, because farms are everywhere; if France or China or Brazil subsidize crops, we have to, too, or face the threat of not being able to grow enough food to feed ourselves. City-dwellers have no idea what it costs to grow food (not even many farmers do, for that matter). The violence all this does to a free market system that, if left alone, could feed the world most cheaply is the fascination of James Bovard whose book, *The Farm Fiasco*, is still helpful (if somewhat dated) reading for anyone interested in an overview of America's idiotic agriculture policies.

a fairly buoyant agricultural economy. "It doesn't take a lot to make things harder," Wall said.

A lot of people in cities far away will give you a short-hand explanation as to why main streets have failed in so many places out here recently. They'll talk ominously of a gray-and-red disaster that descended upon those faraway communities like a swarm of economic locusts, leaving once-idyllic small towns empty and broke. They'll tell you it's called Walmart.

As it happens, Concordia has a Walmart. A Supercenter, no less. And if you ask people like Kirk Lowell, the director of that economic development organization in Concordia, about the effect Wal-Mart has had on the community, he'll tell you that getting Wal-Mart to open a Supercenter in Concordia was "a very big deal."

One reason why blue-state people don't go to Walmart, and why some red-state types wish there were an alternative, is that sometimes just visiting a Walmart is a melancholy, radically purgatorial experience. I am telling you nothing you don't already know. As soon as you walk through the door, a giant blower blasts you, as if you were being deloused. Inside, the place looks like a massive welfare office with shopping carts; there are people shopping there in *pajamas*. Huge pallets of stuff clog passageways and warehouse workers come at you with even more stuff, shoving you off into a pile of rubberized boots next to some plastic shoes featuring genuine leather uppers made in the exotic Orient; everything is cheap and something about the whole thing suggests corners were not only cut, they were hacked, chopped, sliced and torn. All men's clothes are made by George or Dickie, Hanes or Fruit of the Loom. Did Walmart really think "plus-sized" women would feel good buying cheap clothes marked "Faded Glory"? No wonder that house brand has been morphed into something mysteriously called "time n tru". Also where's the hardware guy to tell me how to use a thingie? This surely is what the East Germans had in mind for proletarian retail.

In fact, simply getting to the front door of the one in Concordia is daunting for the town's aging population. The place was built on a hilltop where the Kansas wind wails without mercy across the lot. "They don't like trying to push a cart through that," Rod Imhoff, who runs a rival grocery sheltered in the downtown business district, tells me, with a note of satisfaction.

Wandering aimlessly in a Midwestern Walmart Supercenter is like looking into the Kansas sky at night: you realize that once you're in Walmart you're part of something much bigger than anything you could possibly understand. It's not particularly comforting to know that the sheer size of the company is a reflection of how vast the middle- and lower-classes are in America. In just Kansas, the numbers are staggering: Wal-Mart employs more than 20,000 people, paying most of them more than $13 an hour—much more than most main street retailers—along with a benefit package that can deliver as much as five dollars an hour more. Every year, the company collects $368.5 million in taxes and pays $81.4 million in state and local levies and more than 8$8 million to local organizations; they pay $3.2 billion to 644 Kansas suppliers, and, according to Dun & Bradstreet figures, by doing so help create jobs for another 67,295 taxpayers. Nebraska's figures are about half those of Kansas (except with donations, oddly, where the company gives away some $10 million). Walmart measures profits the way China measures Chinese people: By the billion.

Nationally, the stormy campaign against the retail giant is the perfect caricature of coastal politics, the result of a perfect confluence of elitist disapproval of working-class taste and blatant union self-interest. Far from McCook and Concordia, many blue-state politicians score points by beating up on the supposedly voracious company. These self-serving rants have almost no significance in most of the Midwest, where concerns about Walmart have nothing at all to do with class warfare or chumming for unions or a dislike of Walmart aesthetics, if you'll pardon the oxymoron, and everything to do with local economics. In smaller, more conservative communities, where politics is blogless but deeply personal, growth and the things that compel it are much more volatile topics. In that respect, Walmart is a hot issue on main street.

It isn't about the things that the press finds fascinating—the big, gray footprint outside town; the anti-globalization stuff; the unions. After all, to the extent they care, most Midwesterners—really, most people everywhere—know, that to unions, Walmart must be the most coveted of all prizes: For more than two decades, big labor has been trying to organize Walmart workers, for reasons that are obvious — and have almost nothing to do with Walmart workers in places like McCook or Concordia: Capturing Walmart's workers would represent a huge membership bonanza at a time when unions are struggling harder and harder to remain relevant in the face of worker-stockholders and gig contractors. And because it would pump millions and millions of dollars into union PACs, it would also be good for liberal, blue-state politicians.

The hitch is that despite all that pressure, Walmart workers have said no. In one contest after another, Walmart employees have persistently refused to unionize. After all, their salaries and benefits already compare favorably to those doing similar jobs in similar companies in the same area, and many own stock in the company: You can't leave the Walmart in Concordia without first passing a huge sign displaying the current price of Walmart stock. No wonder most Walmart workers don't think a union would be good for the company's profits. Judging from the long lines of people who show up to apply for jobs whenever a new Wal-Mart opens, many, many others don't object to working in a non-union shop, either. A Rasmussen poll taken in the summer of 2006 showed that even after several years of union-inspired agitation, 69 percent of Americans had a favorable opinion of Wal-Mart. Among those who had actually worked for the company (or had a family members who did), the favorable rating rose to 79 percent. A more recent study, published in January 2018, by *Morning Consult,*[40] showed that most Americans still prefer Walmart over rival boxes, such as Target, but that preference is as polarized as the rest of the country: Walmart pulls red while Target goes blue. According to the survey, based on more than 17,000 U.S. consumer surveys showed "Walmart's favorability leans Republican by 14 points, with a 69 percent net favorability, compared to 55 among Democrats."

I've got no local science to go on, but I'm willing to bet those favorable numbers are even higher out here in Kansas and Nebraska.

Not that this stuff matters to those who Wal-bash as a way of life. Since they can't make their case with workers, the unions have been trying an end-run, folding their campaign into a political-action effort to force Walmart workers to do what apparently they don't want to do.

The frustrations of the unions are understandable. As big as organized labor is, it's nothing compared to Walmart. The retailer is its own economic planet, really, with its own unique ecosystem—one that depends on microscopic margins and huge volume. Naturally

---

40 At https://morningconsult.com/2018/01/25/walmart-vs-target-a-political-divide-among-shoppers/.

any increase in what Walmart pays for goods or labor is passed immediately on to the consumer.

This creates a dilemma: While activists of the left and the elites may hate anti-union, downmarket Walmart, the dog they're kicking is another man's best friend; i.e., the hard working, blue-collar American whose interests leftists so tirelessly claim to support. I don't know if it's true in San Francisco or Manhattan, but in Kansas and Nebraska, as in most of America, Wal-Mart not only offers "the low price," as its slogan goes, but also provides the best regional retail jobs in a job-hungry sector of the economy, often paying well above minimum wage, adding benefits and making part-time schedules that work for students and for their moms. These are jobs not otherwise very plentiful in places like this.

In Concordia, not surprisingly, the Supercenter is one of the biggest employers; almost everyone in town has a vested interested in the success of the local store and in seeing that its prices stay low. They realize that any increase in price hurts working class people—consumers and company employees both. If prices rise, the amount of stuff Walmart's primary customers can buy will diminish. Stores will close and people will lose their jobs—plus they won't have a Walmart to go to when times get even tougher. So Walmart's "problem" is also its genius.

In fact, every argument made against Walmart ends with the same elitist imperiousness: People should pay more for the stuff they buy.

Such a conclusion is of course buttressed by all sorts of well-intentioned arguments. For instance, workers in Bangladesh are making a tiny fraction of what workers in Illinois are making and face just as much governmental corruption (and never mind that they're doing a lot better than all those otherwise employed Bangladeshis, not to mention *un*employed Bangladeshis, of which there are many). Plus, some of the processes used by factories owned by greedy capitalists in the Far East to make things for Walmart have nasty effects on the environment, as factories do—although the world's worst environmental messes are to be found still unattended in the ruins of formerly socialist and community countries. Plus, Walmart workers are denied low-cost benefits (and so what if they're *never* given to other retail workers anywhere in America, either?). Above all, it is asserted that slowing the Walmart juggernaut is essential to saving the small businesses which are the backbone of thousands of American main streets.

Maybe a cozy main street paradigm would make sense if the average household income in Concordia were $71,300, as it is in Marin County, where people are happy to pay extra for the pleasure of buying bread and milk in artificial old-fashioned environments (with props and sets inspired by people whose traditional values they despise, incidentally) and where they hate Walmart and all that it stands for. But in Concordia, the average household income isn't $71,300. It's less than half that: around $31,400. In Concordia, unlike San Mateo, people *need* a Walmart.

In fact, lots of blue state folks in the same fix could use Walmarts, too. But it can be tough to get that message out if it has to be filtered through urban media outlets where the mainstream narrative presupposes that people who work for Wal-Mart are exploited and where a lot of attention is devoted to pamphlets, books and TV shows explaining how to "defeat" Walmart in your hometown, as if it were something the liberal, upper middle-class finds as sinful as a Mormon missionary.

In 2006, there were five times more Walmarts in Kansas (35 for a population of 2.6 million) then there were in California (7 for

33.8 million). When the city of Inglewood, a deeply impoverished pocket of the LA basin, decided against allowing the construction of a Walmart Supercenter in their community, Wal-bangers trumpeted it as a victory, of course. But what it meant was higher prices for basic commodities for low-income people, a few hundred fewer jobs where jobs are desperately needed and less tax revenue for a city with more than 20 percent of its population living in poverty. And to preserve what, exactly? Take a drive through Inglewood some time and note the quaint and charming business district — just make a right out of LAX and left at the second strip club.

Chicago is the Midwest's big, blue melanoma, and there so successful was the wall of rhetoric erected to block the opening of a Walmart Supercenter, that the company moved the store to the other side of the city line and opened it there. Twenty-five thousand applicants showed up for jobs, and all but 500 were from Chicago, which won't see a dime of the hundreds of thousands in tax revenues the store will generate.

Walmart has its own competitors of course. Target is discussed above, while Dollar General and a raft of regional discounters, like Duckwall/Alco and Pamida here in the Midwest, are nibbling away at the edges of its market—and doing their own nasty work on small local businesses.

But the guy whose family owns Target, Mark Dayton, didn't give all his money to help displaced cashiers and stockboys; he used his wealth to become a liberal Democratic senator from Minnesota. At Costco, where the execs endorsed John Kerry and donate heavily to the Democrats, employees aren't retiring rich either. Kmart...is nearly history.

Walmart has defeated all of them, apparently while keeping their employees on the edge of happiness. So Walmart is the sole victim of America's red-blue split. Red-state realists shop there because it's dumb not to. Blue-state elites wouldn't be caught dead in the place.

*

Walmart is also an example of how the modern Midwestern main street works. This can be confusing to people who live along the coasts, for nothing makes blue blood boil like the havoc they see Walmart wreaking on their Rockwell-perfect fantasy of small town America. To them, main street should be a place that looks red but thinks blue. The reality may disappoint visitors from the edges: Gone is the friendly general store, the cheerful grocer, the haberdasher and the dressmaker. In fact, so firmly implanted is this view that even people who live in small towns like to believe it, since it explains their nostalgic melancholy—never mind the fact that these sentimental emblems of village businesses vanished long before Wal-Mart showed up.

Still, to understand modern Midwestern main streets, you have to understand how Walmart fits in, so stick with me here while I toil just a little longer in Walmart's shadow, since every food chain has a big predator perched at the top and it's unwise to pretend the retail ecology is any different out here than it is anyplace else. Yet people who would gladly loose lions and tigers on the Great Plains recoil at the very idea of unleashing a Walmart or two out here. They know that given the right conditions, Walmarts can reproduce like retail bunnies—big, meat-eating, blood-sucking, vampire bunnies.

And so they do. In fact, as middling-sized rural communities in Kansas and Nebraska were shrinking a little, more than 100 Walmarts—including Walmart's supercenters, discount stores, "neighborhood markets" and Sam's Clubs—had moved into the void left by departing merchants, aggregating the lost inventory of hundreds of evaporating small hardware stores, groceries and variety stores.

True enough, there is generally high anxiety the first time a community hears the words "new Walmart Supercenter"—as there should be, since for most small towns, a new Walmart means that everything that has characterized a community's commercial life for a century—including failure caused by market loss—will almost certainly change. If you're a small town merchant running your gadget shop the way your daddy did and his daddy did, your kids will be looking for a new line of work faster than you can say "cheap gadgets," because Walmart will be selling exotic Bangladeshi versions of your gadgets for less than it cost to have me to type the word "gadget". Those small merchants still clinging to life when Walmart shows up either disappear almost overnight or make big, positive changes in the way they do business.

Walmart arrived in both Concordia and McCook at opposite ends of the Republican's wide arc, in 1985, back before it was regarded as quite the monster so many see it as today. Thirty-odd years ago, the company still carried the faint aroma of Arkansas, with all its "Made in USA" signs and smiley faces. The original Walmarts were about the same size as the other regional discounters and carried much the same merchandise at about the same price. "Walmart [in the mid-'80s] didn't have the connotation it has now," McCook National Bank's Mark Graff told me one afternoon. "It was just another discount store." There certainly was no surge of alarm in Concordia. "One day," recalls Lowell, "there was a big sign [on an empty anchor box in a small strip mall] out on the highway that said, 'Wal-Mart – Coming soon.' That was it."

Except it wasn't. Walmarts don't just show up. How the company sites its stores is mysterious to most of us, but even more so to those who find one in the middle of their town. I remember when a Walmart opened in the little Appalachian settlement near our farm. Most of county's residents figured the thing had fallen off the back of a truck. "Never thought I'd see *that*," my neighbor Keith Dibert told me one day. Concordians apparently felt the same way: Walmart? Here? There must have been a mistake. In Concordia, the story circulated that Beloit, a rival market town 30 miles away with a population of just over 4000, had *tried* to get a Wal-Mart in their town. In fact, the "Beloit people" wanted a Walmart so badly, Kirk Lowell told me, that they sent representatives all the way down to Bentonville, Arkansas, to beg for one. Sam Walton himself listened to what they had to say, then flew up to Beloit to go to a town meeting—but *certain citizens*, newly infected with anti-Walmart fever, were so fervently opposed to the company's plans that Walton said the heck with this, got back in his private jet and went home. As he took off, he looked out his window, saw Concordia down there on the old Meridian Highway, and ordered his pilot to land at Blosser field, the municipal airstrip located on Route 81. On his way into town, he spotted an empty building, called the owner and rented it right then and there. And "that was it."

Except the part about the sudden appearance of the Walmart in Concordia, the story is completely apocryphal. I talked to Dean Haddock, the man in Beloit who was in charge of the community's somewhat whimsical economic development effort back then. "Oh, no, no. Sam Walton never came *here*," he protested. "What happened is, I just used to sit around sometimes and call up different people I thought might help the town, so one day I called Walmart. But they never called me back. Personally, I think they had already made their mind up about Concordia." And of course they did. Walmart's market research is peerless. Down there in Bentonville, they don't often throw darts at a map and hope for the best.

Still, for Concordia, as for McCook, the story has resonance, for there was something both lucky and bizarre about Wal-Mart's coming. It was like a scene from *The Gods Must be Crazy*, the film about a rural pedestrian in Africa narrowly avoiding being hit by a Coke bottle that had miraculously fallen out of a small plane; economic revitalization for the town seemed like it literally fell out of the sky. Walmart gave both towns a standard-issue gray-and-red 40,000 square-foot box—the kind of building Walmart calls a "neighborhood market." Their inventory of cheap hardware and plastic laundry baskets hit some local retailers harder than others. The smaller stores that sold that kind of stuff, mostly locally-owned variety stores and the like, closed—only to reopen as Dollar Generals, beating Walmart's prices by selling a similar inventory of even more inferior quality in even smaller towns. Then, in the late '90s, Walmarts across America inflated themselves from their little boxes into giant supercenters, tripling their already big footprint to a dino-track more than three times larger than before.

In middle America, this is nothing new. Not long ago, McCook's and Concordia's main streets not only sheltered mom-and-pop shops, they also were home to huge national retailers such as Sears and Montgomery Ward and local merchants figured out how to compete around them, rather than against them. Fifty years ago, you had to be in a very small town indeed to not have a local JC Penney store selling dress shirts and Boy Scout uniforms. But Walmart is not just another new chain store in town. It's retail at an evolved state, with a DNA manipulated by a half-century of mutation and struggle followed by more mutation. If capitalism's a jungle, Walmart's the king of it—and if you're a main street merchant going head-to-head with the beast, you're a three-legged antelope.

Smaller sized Walmarts were one thing, but the appearance of the Supercenters caused considerably more anxiety, said Graff. "Walmart [in the mid-'80s] didn't have the connotation it has now," said Graff, a cheerful and welcoming chap in charge of what seemed, at least on the day I visited, to be a very friendly, unbuttoned sort of local bank. In fact, the employees were all wearing polo shirts and Dockers; the place looked like a clubhouse full of golfers trying to deal with an inconvenient day job. "You know, the empire-builders. It was just another discount store…There was more community reaction [to the Supercenter], I guess you could say," he added slowly in the careful, qualified, understated cadences of a man who knows how loudly words echo in a small town. "There were some people who were very concerned."

We call those people "grocers", since one of the more intrusive hallmarks of a supercenter is a big supermarket area filled with cheap chow.

In McCook, the Supercenter was enough to almost instantly drive the community's four supermarkets out of business. As for Concordia, once a regional headquarters of Kroger and home to several grocery stores, once the Supercenter opened and the IGA closed, the town was left only with a food distributor's outlet store and a single independent full-service grocer—Rod's, whose feisty owner, Rod Imhoff, greeted Walmart's expansion with a $1.2 million expansion of his own store, moving into what had once been a Montgomery Ward next door.

It was a gutsy move. "Did I bite off too much," he asked one day as we sat chatting in his little office near the busy check-out area. "Maybe. I'd be making a lot more money if I hadn't expanded, but this was a run-down store that needed attention." So far Rod's has continued in business by doing what the local Walmart can't do—helping people to their cars with groceries, delivering orders, remembering names, operating a full-line bakery and a brilliant deli counter. Still, Imhoff said, it's not like the good old days before Walmart showed up. "I'll never set foot in there and neither will my family," he declared adamantly.

In McCook, the Schmick family—Bob and Debbie and their sons—opened a new grocery in December 2005, years after the local Supercenter had put the last local grocer out of business. More than a decade later, the Schmicks are still there — and in three other Nebraska locations — flourishing by providing the kind of service that Supercenter manager Tom Lambing says, "We just can't offer." What are the longterm chances of succeeding against Walmart? Bob Schmick, who once worked for Walmart, was afraid to venture a guess, at least to a passing journalist. "What you say can come back to hurt you," he told me in refusing an interview. The guy who has successfully run a Ben Franklin store on a sidestreet in McCook for 25 years was also worried about antagonizing the ogre on the hill. When I asked to talk to him about the secrets to competing with Walmart, he simply said, "I don't want to visit on that topic" and returned to his work, which happened to be counting money.

Norris Avenue, McCook

So, yes, if you're a grocer in either McCook or Concordia, Walmart was the last thing you needed when your other problems were ready to swamp you. You would either fail or surprise everybody by succeeding. The Schmick family, for example, started a small grocery empire alongside Walmart competition, or perhaps because of it. In both towns, the appearance of the Supercenter on the edge of town has had an unexpected and mostly positive effect.

In fact, to those most intimately involved with the McCook's economic problems, Walmart, as the 'sixties' adage had it, has been part of the solution. In 2004 alone, the Concordia supercenter put $750,000 of revenue into the city's tax receipts, a sum that, had the city on its own sought to offer the services it produced — everything from new streets in an economic development area to the demolition of derelict buildings — would have required a property tax increase of 35 mills, according to local estimates.

At the same time, a restructuring allowing the tax revenue created by Walmart's expansion to go into a local tax area, rather than into the county general fund, was put to a vote in 1999. According to locals, the vote amounted to a referendum on the whole idea of a Supercenter in Concordia. It passed by 70 percent. Then-Concordia city manager Larry Paine ticked off a long list of infrastructure (in addition to the new business list) projects—including everything from new streets in an economic development area that just saw the completion of a $4 million Holiday Inn Express nearby to the demolition of some derelict buildings to make way for a new, locally-owned four-screen movie theatre on Sixth Street. "This is because of Walmart," Paine said.

Far from seeking to destroy local businesses, the manager of the Supercenter, Roy Reif, retired in 2013 after almost a decade. He had been an active booster of Concordia's main street, promoting the idea of late-night openings and circulating a local shopping guide to main street businesses that encourage people to drive 50 or 75 miles to get here, so that when they do, they know there's more here than just the Supercenter.

"We've seen Walmart studies that show people coming to Concordia from all over the area," said Paine. "In fact, people even come here from Salina [a growing city of 40,000 an hour south with its own Supercenter], because the Salina store is too crowded..."

McCook's economic development planner is an ex-farmer named Rex J. Nelson who created a way of measuring the economic vitality of a rural community[41] by determining its ability to stem retail leakage by measuring its "trade pull factors"—the size of the town, how much money people have got, how attractive and healthy the retail environment is, how close the town is to a major highway and how far it is from other towns its size or larger. Generally speaking, the smaller the community, the greater the leakage. Nelson could find only one instance where a rural county with a town smaller than 5,000—Valentine, Nebraska—enjoyed a positive trade pull factor, probably because it's many miles from there to anywhere else with stores and shops. Even so, it's an iffy thing: I once interviewed a lady lion-tamer in Valentine. She wore a sparkly swim suit and worked for a circus, of course, and when the circus left, I did too because frankly, without her there just wasn't enough positive trade pull factor to make me want to stay.

In 2002, Nelson's study had McCook ranked at number two. By 2005, it was down to number 7. Were others doing better? Or was McCook stumbling? Nelson thought the data he used had a certain amount of inherent volatility. By and large, McCook appeared to be

---

41 Rex's findings appeared in 2004 in his thesis written in support of his Master's degree in agri-biz from Kansas State. Its full title is "Causes of Retail Pull in Nebraska Counties and Towns" and if you're a Midwestern economic development officer or a chamber of commerce director in a small town—that would be less than, say, 10,000 citizens—you really need to know about Rex. His study excluded Lincoln and Omaha, and ranked Grand Island as the pullingest retail community in Nebraska. He resigned as economic development planner in 2016 to move East to be closer to his children.

able to supply whatever most residents could want, but, as Nelson said to me, "the expectations of shoppers change. They don't mind traveling as far as they used to."

While there are indeed many problems that face places like Concordia, Walmart just doesn't seem to be one of them. In fact, when I mentioned to one community leader that, aside from Rod the grocer, I couldn't find any main street merchants willing to tag Walmart as a liability, I was told to talk to Verletta Moon, who operated a uniform store in Concordia for 15 years, until Walmart did her in. "She'll tell you what Wal-Mart did to her."

So I called Verletta Moon to ask her what Walmart had done to her.

"Actually," she said, correcting me, "it was my suppliers. They were undercutting me and selling to Walmart. They [Walmart] could sell uniforms for less than I was paying for them. They weren't as good as mine, but they were less expensive." Though her own business may have suffered at the hands of Walmart, she told me she didn't want that to color my view of the Supercenter's overall role in the town. "I was chair of the retail committee of the Chamber of Commerce for five years," she said, "and I'd have to say that Walmart has been good for the community, not bad. It's attracted a lot of business."

Lowell agreed. "The only thing worse than having a Walmart in your town is having a Walmart in a town 20 miles away."

I'm standing in the courthouse square of what was once the pleasant downtown shopping district of Belleville, Kansas, the seat of Republic County. In the middle of the square is a WPA oddity built to replace one of those elegant Victorian gems you can still find in nearby county seats such as Clay Center or Beloit. The Belleville courthouse caught fire on April 1, 1938, but the local fire company, thinking reports of a burning courthouse on April Fool's Day were pretty rich, didn't turn up until too late. The fire remains an unsolved mystery; the new courthouse is a Deco block.

The ring of interesting storefronts and curious architecture that surrounded the courthouse is still there: On the south side, the old Blair theatre soldiers on; a local effort to restore it is underway. On the west, a block of storefronts leading to what remains of the old Republic Hotel: a café and a sewing shop provide the most exciting sign of commercial life. An old Masonic hall boasts some of the most beautiful brickwork I've ever seen—but only on the upper floor. The detail that once graced the street front is now covered with something functional and efficient and uninviting. On the other two sides, a scattering of metal buildings, empty wood-frame stores and vacant lots. Down a side street, a grocery hangs on. The presence of that Walmart Supercenter in Concordia, 15 minutes to the south, has had a predictable effect on Belleville. The town isn't down and out yet. The excellent local paper carries on and so do many local businesses. But that so-close/so-far Walmart has its effect.

"It's hard on us," Melinda Pierson, the director of the local Chamber of Commerce, admitted. "Having a Walmart brings people to your community—and you reap the tax rewards."

Belleville missed its chance for that. About twelve years ago, Walmart started thinking about upgrading its Concordia store and replacing it with a Supercenter. There were already two on either side of Concordia along US 81, the highway that stretches from Laredo, Texas, to the Canadian border, and crosses the Republican River just north of Concordia. One was in York, Nebraska, 93 miles north, and the other in Salina, Kansas, 52 miles south. The midway point, approximately, was at the junction of US 81 and US 36, on the southwestern edge of Belleville. Walmart gave the location a lot of consideration, but Concordia got the Supercenter. Along with it came traffic from towns and villages, especially including Belleville, in a hundred-mile circle.

To make it possible, Walmart had wanted concessions—Brad Lowell, the editor of Concordia's local paper, called it "blackmail"—and to make those concessions possible, Concordia wanted concessions from the rest of the county. The supercenter would be built just south of the city limits; its taxes would be used to create the infrastructure the store needed, and a tax district was established to funnel taxes derived from Walmart into infrastructure and support for a narrow district with a commercial focus—largely along the highway and along Sixth Street.

I sat in Lowell's office and discussed the trials and tribulation of Sixth Street. "I'm not somebody who particularly believes we can save main street," Lowell told me. He thought a business coming to Concordia would do better out on the highway ("closer to Walmart") than in the downtown area. Ironically, Roy Reif, then the manager of the Concordia Supercenter, had been an important booster of Concordia's old downtown, promoting the idea of late-night openings and other activities designed to help his ostensible adversaries, and circulating a local shopping guide promoting main street businesses. Ask for something the Supercenter doesn't stock, Marsha Doyenne, a Concordia shopkeeper, told me, and the chances are very good you'll be sent to a downtown merchant.

With a market area even bigger in area than Concordia's, Tom Lambing, McCook's Walmart manager, also experiments with different ways to convince people to make the long trip to his town. A few years ago, he brought in the Kentucky Headhunters to play a free concert in the Supercenter parking lot, which attracted

5,000 people to McCook. "They said, 'This is like a Denver crowd,'" he told me proudly. But even on a regular business day, "We pull people from 120 miles away to shop in McCook," he said.

Banker Graff tried to calculate for me how many people were employed by Norris Avenue businesses in the good old days and couldn't break 200; the local Walmart employs about 300 people and pays them enough to shop on main street in McCook. The same is true in Concordia, where a nice three-bedroom house costs less than $60,000—what it would cost to buy about an eighth of the cheapest house on the market in San Rafael, the seat of Marin County.

There are two ways for small town merchants to take advantage of Walmart. One way is to exploit the presence of a Supercenter to the greatest extent possible. Concordia city manager Paine recalled the animosity of some residents to change of any kind, let alone lots of change imported from Arkansas. "I had one person come up to me and say, 'Larry, this town is dying. Why don't you just let it die gracefully?'" Paine told me. He handed the man a page listing 60-odd new businesses, expansions, new streets, drainage and commercial district redevelopment projects. "I told him, 'Here's what we're doing instead.'"

I looked at the list and asked Paine how much of this new activity had anything to do with Walmart. "Some of it, directly, indirectly a good lot of it," he said.

"The fact that a Walmart exists in your town does not mean diminished competition," Dr. Carl Parker, the chairman of the economics and finance department at Kansas' Fort Hayes State University, told me. "It could mean increased competition." Parker pointed to the presence of the big-retail steel-cage tag-team, Walmart and Home Depot, in Hayes, Kansas. "We draw people from all over the area. In small communities, yes, stores may not be able to continue, but they may have closed anyway." Other merchants, Parker said, can compete "for years and years" with Walmart. He pointed to his own experience owning an archery shop near a large Supercenter that also sold archery supplies. "I could compete with them on service and on knowledgeability—and I found I could even compete with them on price."

The bigger concern for small town merchants, he said, was from competitors using new technology to bring a world wide web full of choices to people who live in tinytowns everywhere. The new competition for main street, Parker said, is going to come from the predators in a different corner of the retail jungle: "It's going to come from the amazon.coms." On a drone.

9

OLD-TIMERS AND NEWCOMERS.

Stage, Brown Grand. Photo: concordiaks.org

E conomically, Concordia is still far from getting over the slump of the mid-'80s. A beautiful and charming place, situated within striking distance of Kansas City, Wichita and Omaha, its citizens maintain a lovely park and (at great expense) a public pool and they have restored an elegant, turn-of-the-last-century opera house, the magnificent Brown Grand Theatre, opened by Col. Napoleon Bonaparte Brown in 1907 as the town's *second* opera house (the first is still there, on Sixth, above a thrift shop), and a regular stop on the vaudeville circuit that ran from Kansas City through Concordia and on to Denver. After a half-century as a movie theatre, the community restored the Brown Grand to its original condition.[42] Lately, Concordians have devoted themselves to the creation of a National Orphan Trains museum and a project to restore parts of Camp Concordia, a World War II installation that once housed thousands of German POWs.

That's a lot of civic activity for a little town. As is the case in most small towns, where one person can make a huge difference, that means a lot of work for a small cohort of energetic optimists. In Concordia, it's people like Susan Sutton (theatre, orphan train museum, community college), Everett Miller (community college, POW camp, theatre), Eric Johnson (architectural preservation and community development stuff) and Kirk Lowell, the farmer who has turned from the uncertainties of agriculture to the even greater uncertainties of Midwestern economic boosterism. All of them at one time or another have been targets of local animosity, anger that stems largely from what some call 'realism" but others would call "pessimism"—the one fatal cancer to which many small towns are vulnerable.

Experts like Milan Wall and Genna Hurd point to civic pessimism as a kind of death sentence for most communities. "You can see it when you pull into a town," my cousin Richard, a community economic development manager for the USDA, told me. "It's the worst thing of all."

Fighting pessimism is critical to a community's survival. As every small-town resident knows, the polarization of the nation is a genteel debate compared to the viciousness of local politics because

42 The first time I went to the Brown Grand, it was to see the local theatre troupe perform a great spoof on the eccentricities of the Kennedy clan. But Concordians are nothing if not open-minded. The theatre is also used for visitors brought in as part of an annual lecture series. Among those either on their way or just leaving Concordia: Thomas Frank and Kathleen Kennedy Townsend.

so much that is so close and so personal—your old neighborhood, your old school, your old life—is at stake. In Concordia, very few citizens are registered Democrats. But almost all of them are on one side or another of an economic divide almost as old as the town itself, one that stems from the days when north-siders were working-class stiffs and south-siders were the snobs who employed them. To this day, the wealthier citizens of Concordia feel much more comfortable spending money than the rest, where concerns about local taxes are supremely important. On the spectrum of political passion, compared to this, red-state/blue-state and liberal/conservative conflict is at the sweet end. In Concordia, the north, south, east and west quadrant often defines political views far more than the debate about Trump's last tweet. A political reorganization years ago brought an end to ward representation and replaced the familiar city council-and-mayor arrangement with a council elected city-wide and a city manager hired to keep everything running, putting Concordia on the long list of Midwestern towns that have adopted the city-manager model of government.

Predictably, this has caused lots of problems in Concordia. Some of the neighborhoods that were part of the old wards lost their council seats while others gained one or two. Even in a town of 5400 people, the idea that a person from the other side of the street represented people on both sides of the street was anathema. One local man, Melvin "Bud" Kennedy, kept finding anonymous accusatory documents mysteriously left on the seat of his pick-up. His letters to the editor of the local paper, often based on the stuff left in his truck when he wasn't around, became a kind of alternative history of recent civic events. People who had donated time and effort to various citywide efforts were accused of dishonesty and worse. One cynic suggested that maybe a lot of problems would go away if Bud would just keep the door of his truck locked. I mentioned it to him, but there was no humor in this for him. He was angry. "I don't like what this town has become," he told me. He recited a kind of mental graph, showing declining population and rising taxes. He spoke with the melancholy passion of a guy who doesn't feel he has been heard: he didn't know why he'd stayed in Concordia as long as he did. He didn't know how things could have gotten so far out of hand. Then he told me how his wife had died right here in this room, the one in which we stood chatting.

He had been a cabinetmaker for most of his life. His furniture and other projects were in half the homes in town and I couldn't find a soul to say anything bad to me about him; every query was met with a look of sorrow, not anger. Some of his civic adversaries told me how proud they were to have a piece of Bud Kennedy's work in their homes. When I told him this, he softened for a second; it shook him—but only for a moment. His anger was all one-way, fed by a group of disappointed fellow citizens, altogether numbering maybe 400 or so. His blood pressure was high; he was often red with anger; people worried about him. I worried about him.[43]

Kirk Lowell was another one whose task in making Concordia attractive for business drew him into conflict with his more dubious neighbors. As head of the economic development organization, it was his job to bring business to Concordia and the rest of Cloud County. His office downtown was shared with the town's Chamber of Commerce, so optimism was everywhere. And it was always busy—especially on Thursday mornings when the local movers and shakers met for coffee and looked for good news. Lowell was good at finding it, even if he had to go out and wrestle it to the ground.

---

43 We should all have Bud's big heart. He turned 90 in September 2018 and his daughters threw a reception for him at Our Lady of Perpetual Help Catholic Church hall.

I stood one afternoon in 2006 in the lobby of the Majestic, a four-screen cinema that had opened the day before amid much fanfare in a pretty, new building on Sixth Street. Lowell had gone to Topeka and hired one of the big World War II-era civil defense searchlights from Boyles Joyland and had it parked in the middle of the street. "They tell me you can see that beam of light from 50 miles away," he said. "Fifty miles! My cow!"

The cinema was a pure-Lowell piece of work. When the Brown Grand reverted to being the opera house it was meant to be, a small two-screen movie house had opened across the street in a dilapidated set of storefronts. That lasted about 20 years. When it closed, it meant that Concordia's movie-goers had to drive to Beloit, where the community had built its own two-screen cinema and which was unfailing in its ability to get the best first-run family films, or down to Salina, where there was not only an 8-screen multiplex, but a genuine art cinema where you could go see obscure films unsuitable for children every day of the week. That meant Concordians were taking their money to other towns, something the economic development guy inside Lowell couldn't abide.

So he contacted the region's biggest operator of small-town movie houses, B&B Theatres, a Lexington, Missouri-based family business that not only runs movie theatres in small towns throughout Kansas, Missouri and Oklahoma, but also provides film distribution and logistical support to tiny movie houses, like the one in Beloit. "At first, we just said, 'No,'" recalled Bob Bagby, B&B's president. "But Kirk, he just doesn't understand that word."

"I was sort of persistent with them," he had told me earlier when I first asked about the new cinema. I was dubious that the new building would fill the hole on main street that the old store-front movie house had occupied. Lowell had shown me the architect's sketches and explained that local businessmen were putting up half the $1.4 million investment required to launch the new theatre and that he had been successful in getting B&B to put up the rest. "Isn't it neat?" he asked.

It opened big. And a line of local citizens from Concordia and surrounding towns waited patiently to see *RV* and other cinematic gems. "This is the smallest town we've ever opened in," Bagby continued. "Normally, our smallest town is around 20,000—and, well, you know this is a long way from that." He looked across the crowded lobby. "Still, this is a very good opening."

I asked how Lowell had persuaded them to make the commitment. "It was the bus," Bagby said. I didn't know what he meant. "Well, we're all sitting there at work when somebody comes in and says, 'There's a bus outside. They want to see you.' It was Kirk and a bus full of business people from Concordia. They had chartered a bus and come out to convince us to put a theater in Concordia."

But across the street and down the block, the stress of survival shows only in a few empty storefronts, but one of them again belongs to Sears, at least for now. One big department store-sized housed a community church for a while, until a more commercial enterprise moved in and some of what the dust and the Depression an ag policies from Washington didn't destroy was done in by the architecture of the '70s and '80s. For the first decade of this century, once-beautiful buildings were sheathed in garish metal grilles to create a pretend modernity that was at once ridiculous and unbecoming, until good taste and commercial good sense reclaimed the best. The mistakes made in Concordia were perhaps similar to other regional missteps, but perhaps less serious: The astonishing Barons Hotel, whose Oasis bar is said to have been the inspiration for Garth Brooks' country hit "Friends in Low Places," was demolished, and so was the town's elegant, Victorian county courthouse. It was replaced by a bland, modern block that looks exactly like bland, modern blocks everywhere. Several times the city has suggested demolishing the Victorian bank at the corner of Broadway and Sixth and where Delmar Harris used to make playground equipment in the basement, in favor of a parking lot, perhaps as a quick fix to address a claim made by one potential retailer's study that said there weren't enough parking places in downtown Concordia. But the place hangs on, improved, even. Some people even worry that the grandest, most extraordinary building of all, the big, brick Victorian motherhouse of the Sisters of St Joseph—whose magnificent stained glass window has enabled Concordia to cling somewhat dubiously to the sobriquet of "The Stained Glass Capital" of Kansas—might one day follow suit, but that seems unlikely, so far.

The most common explanation for why so many once-grand mini-metros would shrug off their most precious possessions—the old school, the old courthouse, the old everything – is as simple as it is trite: "She was just too far gone." It's probably more accurate to say that, in the end, towns in the Midwest die for the same reason teenage marriages fail and the Roman Empire fell: It's just too much trouble and too much money to keep it all together. "This town is gone," Kennedy had told me. "Those people [who invested in the theater], they might as well have thrown their money away." Bothe Kennedy and the theatre are doing just fine, however.

Besides, that kind of pessimism is dog stereo, simply inaudible to people like Kirk Lowell or Concordia's former city manager, Larry Paine. In a town like Concordia, it's the city man and the economic development guy who are paid to ignore pessimism, since to give in to it is to walk into your office and say to yourself, "You're fired," and neither seemed particularly interested in unemployment.

I remember once going to New York's Washington Heights with a college roommate of mine to visit his elderly aunt. She lived quietly in an old apartment block. In the hallways, you could smell a million burned dinners, listen to invisible dogs yapping from floor to floor and hear a dozen muffled conversations at once. Sitting in her apartment, we were interrupted by a shout and a loud thump on the wall.

"Those people!" she said, irritated but resigned.

"What are they like?" I asked.

"I should know? I've never met them."

You want to know about the culture of small Midwestern towns? Start with this: they're the *opposite* of that. The minute a car door closes and a stranger's shoe hits the gravel, the news echoes up and down main street, stirring conversation in the local cafés and bars.

That's a cliché, of course, both the part about big cities and the part about small towns. But so be it. As another cliché rightly observes, clichés exist because they convey fundamental truths. Those that apply here are that if you want loneliness, move to a city of 8 million, and if you want everyone around to know all about you before you've even met them, move to a farm community where neighbors can live miles apart.

It's a simple matter of scale. In a metropolis, even the most ambitious and dynamic newcomer has close to zero impact on the social and economic ecology of the place. In a small town, the right newcomer – or the wrong one – can change everything; bringing unexpected prosperity to a town whose obituary is already half written or, occasionally, helping finish the job of writing it.

Take lovely Alma, Nebraska, which is a lakefront village — with a missing lake, since the Midwest's persistent drought has shrunk the reservoir to near-invisibility. That didn't discourage Joseph and

Dusti Torrey, who graduated from college then went back to Alma, Joseph's sleepy hometown, and opened Joe Camera, a coffeehouse with an informal folk music venue out back. They started out doing photo-processing, until they were ambushed by technology, changed direction, added caffeine and conversation, and just carried on. The day I called in, Republican Adrian Smith, who represents Nebraska's 3rd District in Congress, was meeting his constituents. It's a tiny main street in Alma, with a locally-owned movie theater, the Parrot, and a modern, locally-owned grocery, Hogeland's, and down the street, Joe Camera. It's busy, which seems somehow surprising, but one of the first things you notice is that a newcomer with enough optimism to open a new business can make a happy difference to a small town.

Which brings us, in a discussion of the newcomer effect, to Lindsborg, Kansas, in 2005. An uncommonly pretty town several miles off US 81, south of Salina and way north of Wichita, the dot on the map now called Lindsborg is as far north as Francisco Vasquez de Coronado got in his search for the seven golden cities of Cibola in 1542.[44] The town was founded a few hundred years later, in 1869, by a handful of hardworking, stubborn immigrants from Sweden, all of whom had names that started with "Lind"; and twelve years after that, the citizens went into debt to build an "academy"—now called Bethany College—in the town.

Home of some 3,500 people, Lindsborg calls itself "Little Sweden USA" and not in an ironic sense at all. In fact, it touts its Swedishness aggressively, loudly and biannually, with lots of crafts and folk dancing and Swedish signs and symbols everywhere. A herd of colorful, wooden Swedish Dala horses are scattered on Lindsborg's

---

44 Some historians however suggest that Lyons, Kansas, some 30 miles southwest, is the real turning point. Fr Juan de Padilla, who accompanied Coronado, was killed there. His roadside memorial is four miles west of town.

porches and lawns, while the shops sell clogs and herring. Throughout the year, a series of unpronounceable Scandinavian festivals is held, with a big, biannual Swede-do called "Svensk Hyllningsfest" headlining the calendar in October of every odd year; and the century-old Swedish pavilion from the 1904 St Louis World's fair—the one from "Meet Me in St Louis" — was moved to the college in Lindsborg in bits and pieces for use as an art classroom.

Lindsborg had long been lucky in its newcomers. Back in 1894, not long after the college opened, a 23-year-old Swedish artist named Sven Birger Sandzén came across a book written by Bethany's founder, Carl Aaron Swensson, and wrote him asking for a job. Sandzén stayed on in Lindsborg, painting and teaching, for the next 60 years, until his death in 1954, helping create a distinctive local style, heavily influenced by his heavy brushwork and bright palette. Along the way he attracted other artists to the town, including such relative luminaries as Lester Raymer, Robert Walker and Louis Hafermehl, helping lend Lindsborg an identity unique to this part of the plains.

Between all the Swedish stuff, the college and its artistic heritage, in the wake of the most recent economic downturn, Lindsborg was certainly better off than many other towns. Still, times being what they were, it was more than ready for an economic and cultural booster shot. Local factions had formed around the usual small town issues, like main street development, and Lindsborg's civic equanimity was increasingly often under a sullen, passive-aggressive cloud.

Enter quiet and unassuming Irwin "Wes" Fisk. Fisk had left his hometown of Byers—an even smaller town some 90 miles southwest of Lindsborg – the day after graduating from the local high school in 1956. In 1997, after a forty-year career as a private eye and fraud investigator in L.A., he returned, settling in Lindsborg with his wife, Susie. "We didn't really have a connection here," he told me, "it just seemed like a nice town." They moved into the old house once used by the president of the college and started fixing it up. Their arrival would eventually have as much—perhaps more—effect on Lindsborg than a dozen Swedish painters.

As it happened, Fisk enjoyed two things in his retirement—chess and writing about chess, usually for *Chess Life* magazine. So, as much to give himself something to write about as anything else, Fisk organized a Lindsborg Chess Club. "I enjoy the game, and I thought it might be good for the kids in town, too." Over the next year or so, Fisk attracted a few dozen members, staged a few local tournaments. By 1999, the club had sought and been granted US Chess Federation recognition, unusual for a club so small and so remote.

Enter a second newcomer – a Russian émigré from Voronezh named Mikhail Korenman, hired by the college to teach chemistry. As it happened, Korenman once had ambitions to become a great chess master, so one day he wandered into the Fisk's club and said hello in that funereal way Russians have. The two men became fast friends; the *Kansas City Star* would later term[45] the meeting a "harmonic convergence."

"I liked him from the very start," Fisk told me. "He wanted to make [the club] grow and promote chess and I thought that was fine because I just wanted to play." So while Fisk happily stayed in Lindsborg and ran the club, Korenman started traveling around the US drumming up interest in Lindsborg, while playing in tournaments. Before long, Korenman met a young Belorussian grandmaster named Yuri Shulman and convinced him to help organize a summer chess camp for kids in Lindsborg. Twenty kids showed up.

"Lindsborg is a small town," Shulman told me, "so I was surprised there could be a camp. That was the first step. I didn't think

---

45 "Chess Fever Hits Lindsborg," by Lisa Guttierez, *Kansas City Star*, September 9, 2004.

there would be a second step. But Wes Fisk, he's brilliant. He's the one who started everything."

Fisk and Korenman decided the second step should be a grandmaster-level tournament in Lindsborg—a scheme roughly the equivalent to holding the PGA Open at the local pitch and putt. Bringing a bunch of chess masters to a small farming community in the heartland is an expensive proposition, and the Lindsborg Chess Club wasn't exactly rolling in dough. So Fisk and Korenman starting going around Lindsborg door to door, asking people to contribute—ten dollars, twenty, whatever they could afford.

Fisk was a charming, slightly debonair character when we met in 2005, and I could imagine him knocking on the doors of depressed Swedes and asking for support for the local chess club. But Korenman? For starters, in his demeanor Korenman is as tragic as the most dour figure in any Russian novel, wearing his melancholy like body art. I tried to put together the image of a big, sad Russian guy on the front porch saying, "Give money to me for chess" in that cheerful way of his. I couldn't do it. Yet, here he was. There must be an explanation. "Is the town a big chess-playing community?" I asked.

He looked at me as if I were mad, then looked over his shoulder, apparently at the floor. "No no. No. They know *nothing* about chess."

Still, the local businesses and the college chipped right in. So did a group of town boosters called the Dala Wranglers, along with the local Rotary. When things looked like they might grind to a halt, Kathy Malm, at the time the chamber of commerce director, took to the phone and started cold-calling for donations.

"Not that I know much about chess," Malm told me. "I just thought, 'Oh, it'll be like a little basketball tournament.'"

But it kept getting bigger, the plans more ambitious. Pretty soon the Russian chess master and the chamber of commerce lady found themselves trying to one-up each other. He would walk in and say, 'Get me $1000,' and I'd try to do it. Then I would say to him, "Misha, get me the best chess player in Sweden—and he would do it." In the middle of all of this, 9/11 happened. Nobody in Lindsborg blinked.

By December 22, 2001, the first day of the Lindsborg Rotary Open, just six weeks after the terror attacks on New York and Washington, seventy-five of the world's top players had descended on the town, including a number of mercurial, temperamental chess grandmasters. To most people in Lindsborg, a small basketball tournament would have made a lot more sense, but the town was nothing if not game. The chamber kept the books and helped with press relations and registration, and when it turned out there wasn't enough restaurant capacity to feed the participants, the townspeople made casseroles and salads and delivered the food to the players. Of course, international chess masters tend to be a finicky lot; they insisted on lots of fresh fruit and dark chocolate – never mind that this was Kansas and it was late December. "It couldn't be milk chocolate, which is what we had," said Scott Achenbach, the town grocer, who runs Scott's Hometown Foods, a business he and his wife started in 1994 after buying an old Thriftway store. "It had to be *dark* chocolate. They seemed to think it had some mental enriching—well, I don't know, it was new to me. So okay, I got a hold of some Hershey's dark chocolate."

The whole thing proved a big success. The Associated Press, trying in vain to convey a sense of scale and perspective, called it "The Super Bowl of Kansas chess." The wire service was so excited they forgot to report who won.[46]

---

46 That would be John Donaldson, a popular international master, chess writer and director of the Mechanics Institute Chess Club in San Francisco. "Lindsborg? Surprising? Yes," Donaldson told me. "And even more surprising to me because I beat several

But, as the AP and Lindsborg would soon discover, the Super Bowl of Kansas chess was nothing. As Malm put it, "Really, we didn't know how big it could be until the *next* year."

It seemed Anatoly Karpov, seven-time world champ and one of the game's most enterprising grandmasters, was casting about for a place to stay while warming up for a match against his arch-nemesis, Gary Kasparov, a man he hadn't beaten for 12 years.

Korenman: "I told [Onischuk], 'Remember, Lindsborg was a good town for chess and maybe Karpov would like to come to see it.' He said, 'We'll see. I will call him.' And he did and Karpov said, 'Sure! Why not?'"

Korenman clearly enjoyed telling the story; he nearly smiled. He seemed to relish the fact that Karpov was willing to come to Lindsborg, sight unseen—certainly something most New Yorkers, for example, would never consider doing. Karpov, Onischuk and a Chilean grandmaster named Ivan Morovic spent 10 days preparing for the match. As the *Kansas City Star* reported, when he won and journalists asked him "how he had prepared, Karpov told them he'd gone to Kansas…. the media roared with laughter. They thought the Russian champion was joking. But the joke was on them."

That would soon change. Karpov. who has 30 chess schools in 15 countries throughout Europe and the Middle East, so loved the place that he decided to launch his first American chess school on Lindsborg's Main Street.

As Malm told me, "When we got Karpov, that's when we thought, hey, this could be big."

Korenman promptly asked the Kansas Department of Commerce and Housing for $261,000 "to develop chess"—and "they gave it to me."

---

grand masters there."

In 2004, the US Chess Federation made Lindsborg its "Chess City of the Year," putting the town on a list with places like New York and Seattle. That year, Korenman organized a two-day, six-game "Clash of The Titans" between Karpov and four-time Women's World Champion Susan Polgar, a Hungarian and the first woman to ever win a men's grandmaster rating. Chess masters from all over joined hundreds of local children in a big parade, the two chess masters battled to a 3-3 draw and overnight Lindsborg was on the global chess map. Where once Lindsborg was all about wheat and Lutherans, it was now about wheat, Lutherans and the Najdorf opening. On the main street, there were kids in overalls who could tell you how to do no-till *and* how to *fianchetto* your bishop.

Just a few weeks before his next big chess event, Korenman and I sat face-to-face next to a chess set in a converted storefront in Lindsborg, the one with the big sign out front that reads, "World Champion Anatoly Karpov International School of Chess." Surrounded by oversized chess pieces used for displays, Korenman, in a T-shirt, trousers and flip-flops, looked exhausted. He summarily dealt with two women who were in charge of tickets for the upcoming event, then joined me with a huge sigh of resignation.

I thought maybe I could stir Korenman by giving him a little flag to wave, so I asked him if he thought he could have done this anywhere else—like in Russia, maybe. I was struck by the easy opportunity Korenman had found in a Kansas farming town, their unquestioned support and all that, and I thought he would be, too. I tried to get the "Kansas has been berry berry good to me" line, but it was tough: "I mean, what if an American kid went to some small Siberian village and set up a baseball camp. Could you imagine..."

"Oh yeah. Russia is no problem because *everybody* there likes chess."

Okay, so what about a bigger American city, like, say, Chicago? Word was around town that Korenman would soon decamp to Chicago to join his wife, who had found a teaching job at a university there. "How would you have do if you tried to set up something like this there?"

"Well, now I can do anything because of my portfolio [of successes arranging tournaments in Lindsborg]. So they will listen to me." He smiled, sort of, for the first time in our interview.

But what about Lindsborg? He sighed, then reached down deep for a drop of charity: "It's a very nice town." As for the school after he leaves, "Wes Fisk or somebody will take care of it."

Korenman kept stifling yawns; he's done this interview so many times, he couldn't smile his way through another ten minutes. In his mind, he was already in Chicago, maybe doing lots of TV. He certainly wasn't in Lindsborg talking to me. He was bored and it was highly contagious. But at least he was talking about himself. I was talking about *him and chess*. I asked him if he played checkers, ever. He didn't answer, so I said so long and left. He didn't appear to notice.

Later, I asked Fisk if I was seeing Korenman in full flower, as it were. "He's just exhausted now, after all of this. He's just got his wife settled in Chicago. And this Gorbachev thing—it's *horrendous*."

Lindsborg's downtown; Karpov's chess school's large white sign is on the right.

A few weeks later, I was standing next to Jim Richardson, the National Geographic photographer who, with his wife Kathy, a jewelry designer, has a gallery on Lindsborg's Main Street. We were watching a parade the town was holding to celebrate yet another chess event, this one the biggest yet. The theme was "Chess for Peace." Yes! I was all for that, and so was everybody else: The chess titans and Jay Emler, the state senator, passed by in old cars, waving, followed by a few informal, chess-related floats; there were large contingents of kids from local chess clubs in team T-shirts. The middle school band, dressed like turn-of-the-century Swedish farmworkers, preceded the Smoky Valley High School marching band, who were dressed like Blues Brothers, in black suits and shades. Lots of people were strolling on the sidewalk parallel to the parade, doing what all red-staters do: smiling and saying hello to everyone they passed.

Suddenly I realized one of the passers-by, heading right for me, was Mikhail Gorbachev, surrounded by a small cluster of security guys who were cleverly dressed exactly like members of the high school band.

"Hello," said Gorbachev, nodding pleasantly, smiling.

"Hi there," I replied, nodding back, staring at the famous birthmark on his forehead, as if he were Harry Potter. Richardson's smile widened. Gorbachev kept on walking, saying hello, hello, hello, as people, startled, smiled back and returned the greeting.

I followed along to town's big main intersection. I had been there before to watch Kansans dressed in Swedish costumes do Scandinavian folk dances. Today, a spindly reviewing stand had been set up. On it: Gorbachev in the center, his ubiquitous translator—the dapper guy with the bald head and little mustache—next to him. Just behind him and off to either side, were Korenman, Gobrachev's daughter, some other Russians and Susan Polgar, a Hungarian chess master.

If you're over the age of, say, 45, and you see Mikhail Gorbachev and a bunch of Slavs on a reviewing stand, the rest of the mental image comes unbidden: missiles on trucks, lots of tanks, soldiers with caps the size of manhole covers with the Red Army goose-stepping through Red Square. Not this time. Gorbachev stood impassively surveying the combined forces of Lindsborg's middle school and high school bands, tons of kids from other Kansas chess clubs, and a float that was originally a wheat-wrapped *julbok*, a traditional Swedish Christmas goat, but, having fallen victim to match-bearing kids so often, now looked like a wad of mesh fencing. It was often a part of local celebrations. "It's kind of a joke—something about being burned out," Fisk said. Those crazy Swedes!

Gorbachev, through his translator, explained how he'd ended the Cold War. A few spectators exchanged that who's-he-kidding look, but most just smiled and applauded. It did seem like the wrong time and place to quibble about the last century's details. I started to ask a question about Ukraine, but cleared my throat instead. The kids in the chess clubs—from towns across Kansas and some from faraway Nebraska—all waved happily.

At a speech that evening in Bethany College's auditorium, Gorbachev delivered a mildly leftish rebuke to Bush and retold the story of the attempted coup in 1992. The event had fallen under the patronage of former Kansas senator Nancy Kassebaum, who had invited her friend Alan Murray, from *The Wall Street Journal*, to emcee the speech, something he did *gratis*. The conceit was that Murray would move a chess piece while asking Gorbachev a penetrating question. Murray instantly admitted he knew nothing about chess. Gorbachev agreed, but answered a few easy questions about Reagan, whom he seemed to admire; Iraq, of which he did not approve; and America's national debt: The country, he said, was not only in debt to other nations, but also "to the future." Then he told the story of the failed Russian coup for what must have been the millionth time. At the end, Murray thanked Gorbachev and the president of Bethany College, along with some other dignitaries, including some of the chess masters who had shown up.[47] Finally, as we all stood to file out, I spied Fisk and his wife, Susie, about halfway back in the auditorium. They stood, smiling at each other and walked out hand-in-hand and into the night, unnoticed by almost everyone else.

Later that night, when the streets were finally quiet and empty, Gorbachev slipped into the town's bar with his daughter, translator and security detail, *sans* journalists. The barroom regulars gave him a cheer and a table. The next day, the owner, Mark Lysell, told a local journalist how he'd exchanged vodka jokes with the security guys while Gorbachev sat around signing autographs and sipping Absolut and cranberry juice, just another new guy in town.

---

47 For *Wall Street Journal* subscribers, Murray's November 2, 2005, account of the event is here: http://online.wsj.com/article/SB113088641320885637.html

INTERLUDE: SUPERIOR PEOPLE 4.

Stan: I think the depiction of the Red and Blue states is a news-people thing. It's a shorthand way for them to tell a story and it doesn't do justice to anyone on either side. We're just as varied here as they are on the East Coast or the West Coast.

Pat: But, frankly, I don't think we pay all that much attention to how the national media looks at us. Around here, in the great American desert, what's going on elsewhere tends not to impact on us all that greatly – or we on it. What we do focus on is what's in front of us for the day. I'd say we listen a lot more closely to our local radio station.

Rich: That's true. When you're raised on a farm, the biggest thing that happens is the weather. You hear that and you hear the biggest news of the day.

Pat: And for us, the commodity report is the stock market news. Because if the farmers aren't happy, no one is. As a grocery store owner, my feast or famine goes right along with those reports.

Stan: Still, as far as the outside world is concerned, I'd say probably ninety percent of us out here get our information from the evening news. I don't read the newspaper from cover to cover, like my dad did, or even our local paper – forgive me, Bill.

Rich: (laughs) You're the only one that doesn't, Stan.

Stan: But, at the same time, I have a terrible time trying to get accurate news out of the TV set. He news media is more slanted today than ever. In fact, lately I've been watching BBC news, because it seems they're more fair than any of the other newscasters, including Fox. Fox gets way out one way, and the rest of 'em get way out the other way, and you really can't believe anything. But there on BBC, they were talking about casualties in Iraq, and they went on to say that almost all of them had occurred in just three provinces, and the bulk of Iraq was peaceful and calm. That's a vital piece of information, and I hadn't heard it on a news program anywhere else. The rest of them just talk all the time about a civil war coming...Edward R. Murrow would never broadcast the way they do now.

Bill: He didn't embellish it.

Stan: Or talk down on one part of our country and up on another. You see reports on the Midwest, and it's the typical Eastern attitude. That this is a hotbed of ignorance and backwardness. A lot of people come out here from the East and are surprised to find it's a pretty nice place. The people are friendly, and they're not so dumb, after all.

Bill: One time Dan Rather's news people came to Superior to interview me about a newsletter we produce for rural single people. Of course I'm wearing a nice blue shirt and necktie for the interview. But they find a dirty pair of coveralls, covered with ink, and they tell me to dress in those. I say, 'Those are there to wash the press with, I certainly wouldn't wear them to meet someone.' But I did what they wanted, and they interviewed me in those filthy coveralls. Not that

I'm complaining, they made us lots of money. You couldn't buy that kind of advertising.

But then they go out to Lakeside, Nebraska, to talk to a rancher for the story, and like a lot of ranchers he's got a dog that rides in the pickup with him. Well, he has an old, greasy coat on the floor of the pickup for the dog, and they make *him* put the old coat on. No clue – they just had these preconceived ideas of how we were going to look, because she came to the Midwest to interview these farm folks.

Stan: It's true, there's really just not all that much interest in getting to know about people out here.

Rich: No – they've got all the wisdom back there. In the winter, when they go to Colorado to ski, they like to fly to avoid snow storms on the interstate, and in the summertime the roads are clear, but it's 490 miles across, which is the equivalent of three or four eastern states, and it's hot and boring. And that's pretty much what they think about Nebraska.

10

MAIN STREET MEDIA.

Behold. The label on a can of worms:

IMPORTANT NOTICE 911 CALLS

Statements by Jack Krier concerning dispatching, supported by Alan Shelton's comments, and printed in the March 16th edition of the *Smith County Pioneer* are ABSOLUTELY FALSE!

The sheriff's department will continue to dispatch all emergency 911 calls. Jack Krier's statement that we will not, is a total fabrication. Furthermore, I would advise all readers of the Smith County Pioneer that they should not believe any statements by Jack Krier regarding the Smith County Sheriff's Department.

Anything important about this department, which is printed in the Smith County Pioneer, should be checked out by calling us...and talking to Sheriff Murphy or Under Sheriff Tonya White.

I cannot control unethical and irresponsible reporters like Jack Krier, therefore, I ask you to please call us for the TRUTH.

Sheriff E.L. Murphy
Smith County Sheriff's Department

That ad ran in a Kansas auction tabloid, and it worked at least once: I called Sheriff E.L. Murphy for the TRUTH, but unfortunately, he wasn't there and my call was never RETURNED. But I eventually did get to talk to Tonya White, the Under-Sheriff, who discussed in broad and careful terms that particular tip of the Smith County iceberg that dealt with the local paper and Sheriff Ellsworth L. Murphy's feeling it had been inattentive to the facts.

After a few more calls and a couple of trips to Smith Center, the rest of the can was open, and what a mess it was:

- You had your rumors of a drug-dealing family—"I think all of us knew they were involved," a woman at the local paper said—and a police chief some claimed was far too sympathetic to the aforementioned family, maybe because coincidentally they were her brothers.

- Kansas has so many layers of government that the whole bureaucracy smells like ripe *Epoisses de Bourgogne*, so not only is there a Smith Center police department, there's also the Smith County sheriff's department, run, at the time, by a very crusty county sheriff so suspicious of the police chief's plots—not to help her brothers, but to scheme against the sheriff—that he did a little unofficial electronic surveillance, got caught and got the boot.

- As his successor, you had a 23-year-old hometown boy, mentored by his 50-year-old deputy, both of whom alleged death threats because of the presence of an overwhelming drug problem. Their solution was to resign and flee the state.

- That brought the former sheriff back to power, irritating the city-county attorney shared by Smith County and Smith Center, who says he just can't work with the sheriff, and who also says, approximately, "Drug problem? What drug problem?"

- The sheriff denies the claim that he won't respond to 911 calls and the attorney denies saying that he just can't work with the sheriff.

- The county splits into two factions. People tell me they're afraid to leave their houses. A man tells me he thinks he's being poisoned.

- A recall effort is mounted.

- The recall is successful. Murphy sues the county for emotional damages and withheld wages.

It's all right here in black and white in the *Smith County Pioneer*, along with many other equally rich stories of scandal, intrigue, property tax hikes and interesting neighbors.[48] There are only 1800

---

48 Including the Englishman from the Coldstream Guards who used to stand unsmiling in front of Buck House under a bearskin, but who moved to Smith County with his wife

stories in this not-so-naked city, but that's more than enough for the pages of the *Pioneer*.

The odd assortment of local residents and the dark peculiarities of Smith Center's headaches aside, the local press plays a different role out here than it does back there. In places like New York and Boston, only Amish nightshift security guards actually need a newspaper to get the news of the day. Imagine not knowing about 9/11 until the morning of 9/12. In fact, there's so much news so much of the time that in big cities, the role of a newspaper has changed. Where once, newspapers actually served up a daily menu of events from next door and around the world, now, because TV and the Internet make that news available instantly, blue state newspapers largely exist to create what marketing types might call a "community of shared assumptions"—not only an attractive cohort for advertisers, but also, and especially, a tool for helping people find a way to validate their (usually liberal) hopes, dreams and instincts: Iraq is Vietnam, Republicans hate the poor, Christian conservatives are intolerant, people in Kansas are stupid, the Midwest is nothing but empty desolation and all that. Big city papers present this epic narrative in aloof, authoritative ways that give comfort to their readers by letting them know that the pessimism they feel about their world is entirely justified, especially if there's a Republican in charge.

If mainstream media is distant from those to whom it appeals, main street media was walking down the sidewalk in Smith Center, straight toward me, just back from taking snaps at the local track meet. Jack Krier, who died in 2017, was the extremely plain-spoken owner of the *Pioneer* and 15 other small-town weekly papers in Nebraska

---

and son on an "entrepreneurial visa" under the terms of which he must either support himself or leave. According to the local paper, he's getting by making lawn jockeys ("Coleman's Concrete Creations") who will stand unsmiling in front of your very own house.

and Kansas. Krier was a familiar face in all of those towns, where local residents, working as reporters, stringers and editors, turned out the weekly chronicle of church suppers, Scout troop fund raisers, fairs and farm auctions, obituaries and marriages, all the business of the local cops and kooks. If you want to see a paper of record, forget *The New York Times*. You need *The Belleville* [Kansas] *Telescope* or the *Red Cloud* [Nebraska] *Chief*. The only assumption a small town weekly must validate is that what the world needs is a cheaper can of peaches — and it just so happens they're on sale at the local IGA.

"I was once at a [newspaper] meeting and a man said, 'Our job is to lead so change can occur,'" *Southwest Times* owner Earl Watt told me. "That is completely wrong. Our job is to reflect our community. We do that. We keep opinion off the front page but our editorials tend to be conservative, just like our community," which, ironically, in his case is Liberal, Kansas. "We don't think people like being preached to by their paper." The rule of thumb, according to Watt: Big city papers try to create change by attempting to lead opinion. Smaller newspapers simply offer the facts and by so doing create a possibility for change "when people feel it's necessary." Watt created his own "possibility for change" when he broke away from the distant owners of his hometown paper and launched a locally-owned competing paper, which eventually became so successful it bought out his old employer.

For an outsider used to seeing every issue through the conservative-liberal prism it's hard to make the adjustment. For example, in Smith Center, a local party official told me he blamed some of the town's problems on his political opponents, but when I asked Krier if the usual liberal-conservative split played a role in the sheriff controversy, he looked at me pitifully and said, "no, I don't think so." Weekly newspaper editors here have almost no professional interest in the big national debates. They know that if people want to know what Barack Obama or Nancy Pelosi — just saying — is up to, they'll turn on a radio, a laptop or their mobile phone and find out. A weekly newspaper's job is not to cover international, national, or, in most cases, even regional news. It's to cover what happens in front of them. Every small-town weekly relies solely on its embeds for its stories.

About ten years ago, when two rural school districts were debating a consolidation, I found myself the recipient of a very intelligent, perceptive commentary by a local newspaper editor whose views on the merger were, I felt, more than apt.

"So will you run this in the paper?" I asked.

"No," he said. And then said why: *The New York Times* can alienate half the nation if the guy who runs it wants to. Maybe he can afford to see the value of his company cut in two in the space of a few years, as has been the case at the *Times*. He'll still be able to pay himself a million dollars a year and lard on another half-mill as a "bonus." Nonetheless, even as readers dwindle and ad sales go flatline, the consequences of condescending to millions of people are seen to a typical *Times* employee as something distant and highly unlikely. "But if I do something like that, it's serious."

The editor of a newspaper with a circulation of less than 5,000 in a shrinking market is in the same boat as Pinch Sulzberger, but it's a much smaller boat in a much rougher sea. As a

First National Bank, Smith Center.

result, weekly newspaper editors are usually very careful practitioners of old-fashioned, non-partisan journalism. They know that it's hard enough to keep people happy by just reporting facts and events. Picking sides in a local dust-up is just suicidal. Krier told me he never shies away from local controversies. Maybe so, but the *Smith County Pioneer* got away with it in the Murphy case simply because Murphy's unpopularity was obviously widespread. When I asked him if Sheriff Murphy's ad had hurt him, Krier said, "No. It helps me. In some other towns [in which the auction tabloid also circulates], people may say, 'What's he up to?' But here, no. I think it helps us."

Tonya White told me I was the only caller she knew of who had responded to the ad. Besides, the things that got people riled up at Krier had more to do with his style than his substance. Attitudinally, he was a local Trump. "He'll just about say anything," my cousin Gloria, who edited the *Jewell County Record*, one county to the right of Smith Center, had told me. "Did you know he actually made a *blonde joke* in that paper of his?" She shook her blonde head in disbelief.

Krier was a conservative—"the other side of Attila the Hun," is how Linda Mowery-Denning, the liberal editor of the Ellsworth, Kansas, *Independent-Reporter* described him—as are most of his readers, and his entire career has been spent in small-town newspapers. Small towns are conservative places with a big appetite for local news, and in towns with populations barely reaching four figures, local news is so personal it often reads like blind-sourced gossip, except you know all the possible sources.

Every now and then, somebody will move into a small town and either start or take over a local weekly and run it with the lights on, clearly illuminating his own ideological obsession. If you're a conservative Republican, nobody notices. If you're something else, as many weekly newspaper editors certainly are, it's better of you keep it to yourself. A leftwing firebrand married to an abortion doctor, for example, didn't, and ran the venerable *Frankfort Index* into the ground before moving on to tiny Nortonville to do a pamphlet-and-blog publication called "Fightin' Cock Flyer" in which he likened the town's mayor to a crook who channeled messages from Hitler's bunker and so on.

The Frankfort example is a rare one. Certainly there are liberals in Kansas and Nebraska running weekly newspapers. Either through professional diligence or because local issues don't really conform to those broad classifications, the national politics of a weekly newspaper editor just don't matter. As conservative as Jack Krier was, he gladly gave state Sen. Janis Lee, at the time a local liberal Democrat, a half-page in his paper to expound, unedited, on whatever she felt she needed to do to convince her constituents that she's a) not a Democrat and b) not liberal, although she was clearly both.

Newspaper editors out here will expound at length on the difference between a daily paper, with the mayfly-like lifespan of each issue, and a weekly paper, which has a much longer life cycle. "Weekly papers get read more carefully," the *Superior Express*'s Bill Blauvelt told me. "You don't feel like you have to throw them out the next day the way you do when you get a new paper every day." Advertisers appreciate the traction they get from a weekly, but they're also drawn to the flexibility a daily offers. From an editor's point of view, it's hard to separate sensibility from sense: Although the amount of local news carried in the *Concordia Blade-Empire* would just about fill a typical weekly, that's not a likely turn of events. "I've never really given any serious thought to going weekly," Brad Lowell, a second-generation owner of the paper, told me. "Oh, there have been tough days, but I never really seriously thought about it." His main motivation for remaining a daily, even as larger regional dailies close in on him? "I think it gives a town a kind of importance to have a daily paper."

But as Kansas and Nebraska papers get larger, they tend to become more like big-city papers elsewhere in blue-state America—*The New York Times*, the *Washington Post*, the *LA Times* and similar newspapers—where most journalists at small, regional dailies find a sense of what it must mean to be successful in their profession. This has interesting consequences. For example, the first thing Lowell does every morning is read *The New York Times* and the *Washington Post* websites. Then the *Blade Empire* is assembled for afternoon publication. While its local sports coverage is excellent and its local stories are always well-written, its front page is heavily reliant on AP content that reflects what the AP always reflects—blue-state values with a tin ear for the interests of red state readers. The *Blade Empire* has a thin staff; front-page stories with a local slant are relatively rare. By reading papers with circulation difficulties in Washington and New York, is Lowell's idea of what a newspaper is supposed to be being influenced? I asked him. "Yes," he said. "The first paper I read every morning is *The Washington Post*."

The bigger these papers are, the less adept they become at understanding the point of view of most of their readers, let alone meeting the real needs of those readers, most of which involve a celebration of the place they live and the people they live next to. In Kansas, for example, the Harris newspaper chain operated regional dailies in Hays, Salina, Garden City, Hutchinson and some of the state's other secondary market centers, until it was bought by a huge (more than 650 markets) national newspaper conglomerate, GateHouse Media, in November 2016, Like the *Wichita Eagle*, the *Lawrence Journal-*

World and the *Kansas City Star*, the state's larger papers reflected the sort of view that voters in Manhattan or San Francisco, where the stereotypes of Midwesterners are so deeply embedded in the journalistic culture, would find very comfortable.

When I attended a special session of the state legislature in 2005, I often heard journalists join Democrats in routinely calling conservatives obscene names and I sadly must report the conservative legislators were far less imaginative in their language. One statehouse journalist did the whole elitist riff for me, telling me that the conservatives in the Kansas house were pitchfork-toting, overalls-wearing, clod-busting, sh*t-kicking, etc. He even did a little dance. "F-ing assholes," seemed to be the media's favored sobriquet.

At the same time, there are some very good reporters working in Kansas and Nebraska. Even those with the predictable media limp do their best and their biases are usually the predictable, unconscious ones. Their editors, however, are more premeditated.

For example, a local story that grew and grew until it shaped the state's budget: When a few students in Salina and Dodge City sued the state in an effort to squeeze hundreds of millions of dollars more from taxpayers—despite the fact that education was already the biggest ticket item on the state budget, and despite the fact that Kansas kids already routinely scored in the top ten in the nation—the *Salina Journal* dispatched Duane Schrag, a very accomplished journalist, to see how badly the children in whose name the lawsuit was filed were actually doing. He found they were doing great, playing sports, going off to college, getting scholarships, all that. He quoted parents saying their kids were doing fine, thanks, and that the only reason they were involved in the lawsuit was because the local school bureaucrats had asked them to play a victim's role. Then he discovered that the amount of money the state was being told by the court to pay was millions of dollars more than what was required. In a fit of honesty, the paper ran his stories—but education funding is the way government programs are camouflaged in Kansas, so the paper's then-editor, Tom Bell, a staunch advocate of more spending, ran an editorial suggesting that readers shouldn't be misled by what they had read in his paper.

There was very little Kansan about the *Salina Journal's* editorial pages. They usually featured a Toles cartoon—the *Washington Post* caricaturist who favors hospital-bed metaphors using amputee soldiers as fodder for his GOP-bashing—along with a daily dose of Doonesbury.[49] Until 2005, fiery conservative Ann Coulter made a weekly appearance—alongside equally fiery liberal Molly Ivens. But the Coulter column was dropped. Why? Her "cruelty" to "Cindy Shahan" [sic]. Coulter "crossed the line," the paper said, with her "vicious personal attacks" on Sheehan, the anti-war protester and Peace and Freedom Party politican. Editor Bell claimed he had been an eyewitness to one of Coulter's attacks himself. It happened when Matt Lauer read a couple of paragraphs from Coulter's current book aloud on the *Today* show.

On the front page of the *Journal* were huge editorializing headlines like the one reading "Solidarity" above a bunch of Mexican flag-waving demonstrators demanding benefits for illegal immigrants. Some of these "journalistic" techniques mystify many readers,

---

49 One time-honored amusement of many editorial-page editors out here: Manipulation of the letters column. Who would have thought that in Kansas the only people writing letters day after day to the editor of what is arguably the best newspaper in the state, the Topeka *Capital-Journal*, are liberals angry at conservatives? A random grab from August 31, 2005. Four letters that day from the readers in that Republican-voting city.
1. A warning against gay-bashing in schools: "I know that harassment of perceived gay students is tolerated by the district and little is done to correct the problem."
2. A reader from Massachusetts defending Cindy Sheehan.
3. A confusing diatribe against "radical-right Republicans."
4. A complaint from a reader that his 17-year-old had been approached by a US military recruiter while at the same time Pat Robertson was threatening Hugo Chavez.

while others, like the headline concerning a scandal above a photo of Sam Brownback—who wasn't mentioned in the article and had nothing to do with the story—are just bizarre.

Tom Bell, like his colleagues on other Harris papers, wrote with the shrill artlessness of those who fear they are not being read at all. One weekly newspaper editor—"not my name; I know those people"—told me he calls the *Salina Journal*'s editorials "tombells—they're like dumbbells, but dumber." By 2005, the paper's numbers were slowly sinking, even while Salina's population was growing. By 2016, Bell had run unsuccessfully (as a *conservative* Republican, no less) in a legislative election and gone on to become a PR man for a local health group.

To boost circ figures, the *Salina Journal* had tried to do what the *Wichita Eagle* and *Kansas City Star* had tried to do before: Widen its circulation area to take in small towns a hundred miles from Salina. The result: Well-designed newspapers that might as well be from Mars delivering ads to readers too far away to care. "I avoid it," a laconic cousin told me.

Joe Capolino, an editor-reporter for the tiny *Erie Record*, in Neosho County, can't avoid it. His town of around 1200 is sandwiched between two larger papers, in Chanute and Parsons. "Our competition is friendly but real. We cover local people, local stories, local stuff better. They aren't really able to compete on that." While Salina's population slowly inches up, Erie's keeps getting itself buried. "Our main problem is attrition by death."

Krier had agreed when I discussed it with him: "They [the larger papers] really can't compete with us. We're not like the big dailies around here, like the one in Hays [the *Hays Daily News*]. People look to us for one thing: Good coverage of local news, which they can't get anyplace else." Local news is the one commodity a small town newspaper has locked up: State, regional, national and international news are all over the internet and cable news. Buying a day-old version of it published in a town 50 or 100 miles away makes no sense. In fact, for a growing number of people, it makes no sense to buy the local daily if you live in a town big enough to have alternative news sources that provide more immediate reporting. Papers like the *Salina Journal,* Krier said at the time, are "dropping in circulation, dropping in advertising."

And readers don't seem to want what they print. Even the editors of small town dailies, like Allen County's Iola *Register,* have to remind themselves to keep their eye on the local ball games. "For so many readers we are their only paper," Susan Lynn, the *Register's* editor, told me. "I subscribe to the *LA Times* and *Washington Post* wire service, and I can hardly use it. My readers want to know what's happening in Allen County, so even though I personally like reading those, I'll probably drop them as soon as the contract is up. I never use them."

The most common reason given for buying papers like the *Journal* was the sports coverage. "But you get that better on the 'net," said a local teenager when he overheard an adult giving me his rationale for having bought a copy of the *Kansas City Star.* During the last decade, a great deal of effort and money has been spent wiring Kansas and Nebraska.

Everywhere I went, whether it was to small towns like Smith Center or to larger communities, like Concordia, where Brad Lowell, the editor of the *Blade-Empire* proudly describes himself as a "tax and spend liberal"—and a Republican, of course—the phrase "doesn't connect with readers" was the one used to apply to the larger Kansas dailies. "They'll do a story here and then nothing for ten days or two weeks," said Lowell. "It's just to show they've been here. That doesn't have much effect on us." The irrelevance of the liberal dailies is a judgment not limited to small town editors, either. And under GateHouse's vaguely center-left ownership (many of the company's papers carried the obligatory August 16, 2018, anti-Trump "fake news" editorial), that hasn't changed.

"There is no statewide paper," said Dale Goter, a former Harris paper editor and reporter, then the public affairs editor at KPTS, Wichita's PBS outlet, and today a city lobbyist. "The *Star* and the *Eagle* both competed for that, then withdrew. There isn't an issue here where the press has changed *anybody's* mind. Look at the immigration issue. The people know how they feel about this."

But that doesn't stop some editors from trying – or even from persuading themselves that what they write makes a difference. Take the Ellsworth *Reporter-Independent's* Linda Mowery-Denning. Like most newspaper editors in Kansas, she had opposed to the Kansas marriage amendment forbidding same-sex marriages. In 2004 she ran a determined editorial campaign against the measure, and was quoted as describing its supporters as "hatemongers." After the measure passed with 69.9 percent of the vote and became law, Mowery-Denning, with a stiff upper lip, proclaimed "We made a difference. It carried, but by not quite as much as it did in other counties." The "difference" was less than one percent.

Longtime Kansas journalist the late (2010) David Awbrey, who was the editorial page editor of the Wichita *Eagle* for a time, told me in a 2004 interview that he thought it was such shrill defensiveness that was largely responsible for the massive irrelevancy of the media in the region. Although they may still see themselves as small-town boosters, Awbrey claimed that they've become fringe partisans and unimportant in the lives of their readers. That seemed to be borne out in the conversations I had at the time. Most people told me they sometimes buy the dailies from the bigger cities, but only if there's a front-page story about their smaller towns. "The *Salina Journal* doesn't have much to say to me," said Brenda Losh, a Concordia realtor. "It's not really for people like us in small towns."

"They're completely disconnected from their readers," Krier had said of the Harris papers. "There they are in Hays and Salina, [ignoring] a big conservative base. Salina's paper is bad and the one in Hays is worse. No wonder they only circulate 12,000 copies over all these counties. And they slant their news coverage—and that's one thing we can't do."

Is it harder to torque the news if the news is local and personal? Probably—but it's doubtful that it feels that way to those who feel slighted. If you're angry at the paper, the last thing you care about is their market penetration and all that. A single afternoon in a small town, in fact, will convince you that the only people who really care what the papers say out here are journalists from elsewhere. "Their editorial pages just don't matter," said Alan Cobb, a political activist and then-head of the state chapter of Americans for Prosperity, a taxpayers' watchdog group. "The only people they persuade are donors. So in that way, they matter. But they don't change many minds otherwise."

Under GateHouse Media's ownership, the paper has taken a more balanced tone, with fewer incendiary headlines and right-bashing editorials. To connect with small-town readers, GateHouse has tried to cast a wider net on the news and enriched its local reporting. Not long ago, for example, they employed Rick Holmes,[50] a veteran features writer who struggles mightily to suppress his leftward limp, to drive through all the small towns in GateHouse's empire and

---

50 His columns are compiled at rickholmes.net.

report engagingly on the idiosyncrasies that make life in Smallvilles so interesting.

B ut if the disconnect between the majority of Midwestern people — in fact, according to polls, the nation — and the media class can be illustrated by a single event, one that changed a number of institutional and cultural relationships, it must be the "Summer of Mercy" that stretched over 45 days in 1991, when thousands of pro-life demonstrators converged on Wichita where Dr George Tiller, a partial-birth-abortion mogul, had his clinic. A quarter-century has passed since then, but the wound is still fresh.

The split that opened that summer has since widened into an unbridgeable chasm. Until that summer, the Sedgwick County political landscape had been decidedly left of center. Dan Glickman, a local resident whose family had been involved in the Wichita-area business community for a couple of generations (scrap metal), had been serving as the Democratic representative to Congress since his election in 1976, and had become the Congress's go-to guy on issues involving general aviation—a big deal in a growing city of more than 300,000 that has at one time or another served as the home of Cessna, Beech-Raytheon, Stearman, Lear, Mooney and other aircraft manufacturers. Cessna, along with Boeing, is still a big local employer. The statehouse delegation at the time was comfortably liberal, reflecting the interests of Wichita's old-line elite, with a mixture of Democrats and liberal Republicans representing the state's largest city. By the time it was over, nearly 3000 protesters had been arrested, conservative sentiment had been galvanized, and the credibility of the press in red-state America had been severely undermined.

The pro-life protest against Tiller's operation and others led by Operation Rescue had targeted Wichita early. In fact, months before the first demonstrator showed up, the *Eagle* was running warnings, such as this one from May 1991, on its front page: "A national anti-abortion group whose blockades of abortion facilities has led to thousands of arrests around the country plans a week of protests at a Wichita clinic in July."

"It was a solid grass roots effort," recalled Goter. "It came right from the churches," where abortion had already been a topic of conversation for nearly two decades, thanks to the Roe decision. "Those people had really organized and were very serious about it. It was a religious belief."

"We knew it was coming," said Awbrey, at the time an assistant editorial page editor at the *Eagle*. "But as far as the newsroom was concerned, it was just not on the radar at all. I would go to meetings and realize that journalists knew nothing about religion and even less about people with religious beliefs." The prevailing mood, Awbrey said, was one of "mildly irritated indifference. I just gave up. The *Eagle* marginalized itself. They just didn't get it."

The storm broke on a Saturday in July. The city was filled with thousands of protesters, demonstrating, picketing, singing and going belly-to-belly with the slightly surprised Wichita police, who were trying to contain them in some areas, and move them out of others—including away from the entrance to an abortion clinic. When that failed, 50 were arrested.

The *Eagle*'s reporter was Susan Rife, at the time a young general features reporter assigned to cover the demonstrations by an uninterested weekend editor. "We all did weekends," she recalled later. "If you were on the rotation you went. Because it wasn't what I usually covered, I didn't give it much thought. I certainly don't remember anything like a mobilization of the newsroom or anything. In fact,

I think the only time we mobilized the newsroom was for the River festival—well, that and the state fair."

The paper ran her two-paragraph report in a local round-up buried deep in the next day's paper.

At least initially, the decision by the *Eagle*—and by most papers in Kansas—to ignore the story was a combination of animosity toward anti-abortion protesters and a result of indifference toward the issue and those peculiar people who were so inexplicably worked up about it. However inadvertently, the *Eagle* set the tone for much of the coverage that would follow. Some regional dailies also decided against mentioning the massive demonstrations—certainly among the biggest in the state's history—in their July coverage that year. "They missed it," said David Gittrich, at the time the executive director of Kansas for Life. To him and to others, the lack of coverage was a deliberate and by now familiar attempt to shape news by ignoring inconvenient narratives. "They missed it on purpose. And people saw that. Not just some people, but thousands and thousands."

By the time it was over, journalism in Kansas had changed forever as abortion had gone from being a topic nobody wanted to discuss to the topic everybody—at least everybody outside a newsroom—felt compelled to discuss. "Suddenly it became an issue mentioned in *every* political discussion," said Goter. "And it really became an overwhelming litmus test." For reporters and editors, however, it remained an unexplored territory. "Abortion was an issue no reporter wanted to cover," Goter said. "It meant you were talking to people who were different from the people you covered in government."

"Newsrooms everywhere are insulated secular places," explained Awbrey. "I remember Susan Rife telling me she had never met a pro-life person. Yet here were all these religious people. Nobody really understood them at all."

But Awbrey, it turned out, had a degree in religious studies from the University of Kansas. "Word got out that there was a guy in the building who had read the Bible. I was doing Bible study with reporters!" Awbrey joked. "I could have sold a lot of copies of *Mere Christianity*, that's for sure. Reporters don't know this stuff at all. Try asking a journalist the difference between an evangelical Christian and a Pentecostal Christian. Think they know?"

The polarizing effects of the abortion controversy are now familiar, but at the time, they caught many off-guard. Having been forced by events to think about something most people didn't like thinking about, the strong consensus among newspaper editors was that abortion—or at least the gruesome partial-birth abortions that had made Tiller rich and had made Wichita the fly-in, anything-goes abortion capital of the nation—wasn't something most people wanted to support. This pitted them against a smaller but equally determined group who wanted the opposite. When judges and not lawmakers make law, as had happened with abortion, compromise is impossible. "I kept waiting for a moderate response to galvanize," said Goiter dryly, "but none ever did."

Eventually, the *Eagle's* editorial page caught up with public sentiment a little and began moderating their stance. Awbrey took over as editorial page editor on September 15, 1991. "It was just as the end of the 'Summer of Mercy,' and we decided to try to be a little more open about things. We definitely got the message much sooner than the newsroom did."

Awbrey recalled inviting different leaders from the community into the paper's meetings. "We tried to make it a real community discussion. People started talking with each other. Once I saw a Catholic monk having a quiet discussion with a hardline feminist. I thought,

'They do have something to say to each other.' You could start seeing respect, and that really helped."

From a conservative point of view, however, that respect may not have gone very far—in time or in space. In fact, one of the more indelible effects of the "Summer of Mercy" coverage—or lack thereof—was that it simultaneously animated both conservative political sensibilities and conservative skepticism about the role of the regional press and linked the two together. Conservatives and liberals live in parallel but different worlds now and what happens in one is often shocking to those in the other. In 1994, for example, Dan Glickman was defeated by a political unknown named Todd Tiahrt, whose campaign had been organized in church basements and on sidewalks, not on TV or in the newspapers. Tiahrt's victory was as unexpected and unfathomable as Trump's would be in 2016. The Votes are counted, the press is completely mystified by the result, and then asks "why didn't we see it coming?" until the next election, when they are again blindsided.

What caused the Midwestern press to achieve such massive irrelevancy in the public life of the region and its communities even before the sea change brought on by social media? Awbrey, whose father, Stuart, had been an editor with the Harris chain for 46 years, thought it was a combination of the growing public fatigue with the lunacy of the leadership class in both parties and across the political spectrum and the shrill defensiveness of a huge cultural institution—the media—that is no longer taken seriously by most people. Trump was no surprise. Out here, the pervasive influence of the media ends the moment you leave the local newspaper's office.

The declining significance of the national press, so faithful in mirroring the views and concerns of blue-state voters, is everywhere in the Midwest. When we spoke, Awbrey had ticked off a roster of names of editors from across the state, from Winfield to Iola to Marion to Marysville to Emporia—all of them no doubt self-described as "moderates" but seen in their own communities as marginal, if sometimes interesting, liberals.

"It all descends from that progressive Republican tradition that has been so strong in Kansas, from White to Alf Landon to Dwight Eisenhower," Awbrey had said. "Then those guys died off—and the legacy is something you can see in the Harris chain, that moderate, main-street, banker-type Republicanism, the small-town community boosters, movers and shakers.

"I grew up with Harris papers, and it's sad because they are all so disconnected from their communities. Jim Bloom [at the time, editor of the "progressive" *Hutchinson News*] in Hutchinson is just a joke. He's so far left—and that community is just not that at all." Awbrey claimed that although they may still see themselves as small-town advocates, to their readers, they've become partisans and therefore viewed more warily.

"They've really broken faith with their communities," Awbrey had told me. "It's just sad. In my father's generation, the community leaders would just get together at the country club—you and the banker and five or six other guys—and you'd all make decisions for the town. You don't do that any more but these guys still think you do. They have no understanding of their own communities or the people in them." What they do understand is their own point of view—but that, said Awbrey, blinds them to what matters a great deal to others. "They don't understand religion, for example," he said.

Awbrey, when we spoke, had returned to the Midwest from New England, where he had been editing a Vermont daily in order to be near his wife's family. He had reluctantly and temporarily accepted a job advising Bob Corkins, then the Kansas superintendent of education so despised by the state's dailies, on matters medialike. As a man liberated from the newsroom, he felt community issues had taken on a new importance and a new perspective.

"[The editors of regional dailies] don't understand what's going on right outside their door," he said then. "For example, the state board of education recommended teaching abstinence before marriage. Well, now I've got a six-year-old daughter—so to me that's pretty *good!* I'd *like* that to be taught in the schools. But Jim Bloom at the *Hutchinson News* took on the people who favor that and called them 'prairie ayatollahs' for 'imposing their religious beliefs' on the community. Well, I know a lot of secular fathers who dearly don't want their daughters to come home pregnant—but I guess that's a conservative religious value.

"That's the kind of reaction that these guys create. The Harris people, the *Wichita Eagle* is the same way—the *Kansas City Star* is *hopeless.*[51] None of these people have made any effort to get to know their own communities. Instead, they read the AP and they all bought the Tom Frank line, that conservatives are so stupid they don't know their own interests, that those people are so ignorant, so fundamentally moronic that we don't have to pay any attention to them, except to ridicule them.

"Except the media keep losing. They're on the losing side of history and they don't understand why. So they just keep lashing out, calling people 'prairie ayatollahs' and things like that. Then they wonder why nobody pays attention them. They're used to having the only soapbox in town. But now, with the internet and the democ-

---

51 In 2006, the *Star* accepted an award from Planned Parenthood. Conservatives would have been outraged, but, as one blogger noted, the *Star* doesn't report on abortions, Tiller or political donations associated with either of these anyway, so it's difficult to know what the award is for — unless it's for stories not covered.

ratization of information, people see they aren't exactly oracular. Suddenly, the walls have come tumbling down and they've all been exposed."

So is the heyday of Kansas journalism, once so vaunted and important, now finished? "Kansas is divided," Awbrey had said, " but those editors do have a constituency. And besides, newspapers— they're mostly there for advertising. The editors can be as crazy as they want, and people can ignore them, but if you live in a small town and want to sell your tractor or you want people to come to your store to buy appliances, where else can you go? Some of the things, like Craigslist and the internet, the things that are killing big city papers like the *Star* and the *Eagle*, haven't yet come to smaller communities to steal away advertisers—but they will. Then I guess we'll see." Ultimately, the staunchest advocates of community values — the small-town weeklies — saw the threat to their readership posed by Facebook and Twitter diminished by the personal loyalty readers felt toward the local editors who cover local schools and sports professionally and with great attention to important parochial details.

As Awbrey had suggested, there's a sense in which social class plays a role in how the larger media outlets in the Midwest see their readers, listeners and viewers. For decades the liberal Republican establishment—the Kassebaums and their kith—has been far more comfortable with Democrats than with conservative Republicans, whom they detest, personally, viscerally. Most journalists feel a class affinity with so-called "moderates"—a self-comforting description that fools no one—and respond easily to the kneejerk hatred of conservatives. Not since the days of populist class warfare, in the 1890s, has there been such revulsion felt by the moneyed establishment toward the underclass usurpers. Most moderate Republicans in

Kansas and Nebraska, after all, would be liberal Democrats anyplace else. They no longer have ownership of the hearts and minds of Republican voters. But they do have their redoubts in places where votes can't disturb them: The courts, the bureaucracy, the big-city papers, such as those owned by McClatchy in places like Wichita and Kansas City, and those clear-channel advocates of cultural elitism, the public broadcasting outlets.

Kansas has not one but *two* NPR faucets: Radio Kansas and Kansas Public Radio, the result of the efforts of two educational institutions seeking licenses more or less simultaneously. Kansas Public Radio is affiliated with the University of Kansas and covers Lawrence and Kansas City. Radio Kansas, affiliated with Hutchinson Community College, gets what's left. Of the two, Radio Kansas seems to make an effort to be something that most Kansans wouldn't tune out with a smirk. Their announcer has a Tom Burdett flat twang; you kind of expect him to say, "We'll leave the light opera on for ya." Kansas Public Radio, meanwhile, uses a woman with a British accent, caricaturing their listeners' fondness for cheap cultural chintz. Even a KPR staffer admitted to me that she sounded "incredibly phony" for Kansas. "I find they are remarkably similar," Radio Kansas's Ken Baker told me. "Great minds think alike, I guess. But I do find there to be a great deal more dissimilarity between these two Kansas stations and stations in other states." Radio Kansas attracts about 75,000 listeners each week; Kansas Public Radio draws about 5,000 more.

Neither are very similar to Nebraska's NPR outlet, Nebraska Public Radio, which is partially funded directly by the state and where condescension is delivered undiluted and the target is invariably the stupid hicks who are expected to foot the bill for the insults heaped on them. Example: The night before Easter 2006, for example,

Nebraska's public broadcaster offered "music for Easter eve" including songs like "Chocolate Jesus" and other juvenile blasphemies. Easter morning, while Radio Kansas was playing a little Bach and at least trying not to offend, Nebraska went with NPR's "Morning Edition" where the only mention of religion was a segment inspired, apparently, by the *DaVinci Code* that made the historically baseless claim that in the early Christian church, women "were apostles, priests, deacons and bishops"—then added ominously, "But the Vatican's official view of church history presents women in a different light." Those sneaky, by-the-book Papists again. Next thing you know, the Vatican will be claiming Christ rose from the dead.

In blue states, news is why NPR exists, of course. But out here, even leaving aside the absurdity of spending millions of dollars to deliver a little Rachmaninoff to the fruited plain, when a good CD player costs less than $20, the sensibility of NPR's news operation, both at the state and national levels, is just more Hawaiian noises to those who not only know a scherzo from a largo but also know when they're being fed blue news. "We're aware of that. It seems to be evident. But our guess is we have less crossover between our news and classical than, say, a Massachusetts station. So we make sure our promotional messages are aired in both parts [news and classical] to make sure we get the word out. We can accept the assertion that only the two percent of the most educated people listen to public radio, but that's not our choice." Baker also felt that didn't really speak to political affiliation, "especially out here. It's probably fifty-fifty."

Not that it matters. Obviously, on national issues, NPR isn't winning the hearts of the fine minds of the Midwest. As it is, the *Salina Journal* or the *Hutchinson News* is as influential in Kansas as *The New York Times* is. After all, the conservative movement is slowly converting the state's establishment Republicans—the so-called "moderates" who represent the Kassebaum-class of political elitists—into former incumbents. If the liberal Democrat running unopposed in the Ellsworth-Salina area is the darling of the liberal papers in Ellsworth and Salina, his darlingness with voters will only last as long as he keeps his politics in harmony with the Republicans he represents, not the editors who represent him. In fact, former Sen. Nancy Kassebaum's son was ousted from his state legislative seat in 2004 by Shari Weber, a savvy, solid conservative who ran against his liberal record—and against Kassebaum's mom, who campaigned actively for him. Jack Krier explained it this way: "The influence of a newspaper in a big city or a small town is completely overblown. No matter what I say, 15 percent of the people will agree with me, and another 15 percent will disagree. The rest will just do whatever they want."

But what the big-city dailies in Kansas and Nebraska find they can do is exert a great deal of influence two ways: First, in creating a very clear storyline along which a complex issue, like state funding for education, can be told. That's why, when that particular issue dominated the media in the summer of 2005 the narrative line was "conservatives want to close schools," a snapshot that fits comfortably with most journalists' view of right-wing heartlessness. The rest of the story was whether or not conservatives would succeed in their mean-spirited ploy. The other way the influence of the press out here can be felt even more sharply is by simply not reporting news clearly. This classic strategy of the mainstream media is used often in rural states; it gives cover to some of the state's most leftwing, tax-crazy politicians by simply obscuring their political leanings and dissembling when it comes to reporting their votes in the faraway state capitals.

This is possible for a number of reasons, but there are two that are most characteristic of rural red states. First, small town papers don't have a state capital bureau that reports on the individual votes of individual legislators. With almost no reporting resources available, weekly editors take whatever is given to them by local politicians and generally ignore polemical state issues unless they have a direct bearing on their towns. Second, and perhaps more important, state government—where so much leftwing misery is hatched, usually in the guise of education funding—is just not very interesting to most people. It's the flyover stratum of political life. When it comes to politics, people are passionately engaged at the local level, where they see their opponents every day and unclench their jaws long enough to mutter a begrudging "hello." And they're deeply entrenched on one side or the other of the great national divide between right and left. On both levels, politics lends itself well to simplistic views.

State politics is more complicated, usually involving discussions of economics and studies and experts, and is therefore simply less interesting to most people. Regional daily newspapers and local TV stations are the only source of information about what happens at the state house. That leaves isolated "moderates" and Democrats relatively untouched: The weekly paper will be happy to run their photographs at the local elementary school (if it hasn't already been closed because of consolidation), or run whatever press release a local politician cares to donate. But doing real coverage and analysis of statehouse politics is beyond the reach of many weeklies. And it's really not what weekly papers are in business to do anyway. Their job is to chronicle and celebrate the triumph of life in a hard place. A weekly is the only place you can get your picture in the paper without having to rob a convenience store first.

In Kansas, the "moderate" Republicans have been instrumental in creating some of the most expensive state legislation in recent memory by working actively with the governor, when a Democrat is in office, and the legislature's Democratic minority to defeat conservative Republican proposals to keep spending for things like education under control and to restrict the judicial activism rampant in Kansas's state supreme court. In any other part of the country, they would fit nicely under the left wing of the national Democratic party.

Loyd told me on the house floor that even though he often votes with Democrats, he ran as a Republican because if he didn't, he said, "I'd lose." Steve Morris, the soft-spoken, gentlemanly and reliably "moderate" president of the Senate, made it quite clear to me that he preferred working with the Democrats to working with the House leadership and other members of his own party. "It's ideology," he told me. "You just can't work with them [the conservatives]." The senate, the court and, during Sebelius' reign, the governor were ranged against the conservative House, and they always won.

Liberal Republicans have cost Kansas taxpayers hundreds of millions of dollars yet very few Kansans know this because nobody tells them. When I asked Watt about this, he said that the voters in *his* area were represented by Tim Huelskamp, at the time a conservative state senator backed by the local paper. But he admitted that when it came to the outlying areas of Hugoton and Rolla, home to moderates Steve Morris and Bill Light, respectively, and where his paper is the dominant daily, "We could have done a better job" explaining their positions to local voters. Watt vowed to turn over a new leaf: "We'll start trying to explain to people there [in Hugoton and Rolla] what's been going on in Topeka." Light was re-elected without opposition in 2006 and served until 2011.

Meanwhile, the rest of the area's regional dailies painted conservatives in broad often brazen strokes and clichés—or worse. Religious people are "ayatollahs" and "right-wing religious kooks" and the like. Other than conservative email-list types, nobody monitors the press out here so playing with stereotypes is common, and not just along the Republican River, either. It's a tried-and-true journalistic practice: For years, Jews were driven crazy by the reflexive insistence by TV news producers to reach for a clip of Brooklyn Hassidim every time a story about Jews aired. When the national networks reported that a young man had murdered some people in southeastern Pennsylvania, the instant tag was "Murder in Amish Country", so viewers were treated to factoids about the Amish and their quaint folk ways even as they watched the bling-laden African-American kid who was arrested for the murders being taken from a squad car for processing. To large blue-state newspapers, the stereotypical "red state" is that place of empty dereliction. To talk about Kansas or Nebraska is to talk about civic death.

Maybe it's the distant, uninterrupted horizon—what blue-staters might see as the endless flatline of a dying middle America, but which people out here see as the natural limit of a normal man's ambition.

Superior's a spot on that horizon. As Nebraska market towns go, there's not very much strange about the place, except maybe its annual Lady Vestey Festival, commemorating a local girl who managed to marry an English lord rich enough to give the town a bona fide hospital. But when *The New York Times* wanted to do a story about small towns in America, they sent their man to Superior, because for the Midwest, they figured Superior is about average, red-state-wise—"old, white and relatively poor." If you could only drop that "poor" part, you'd be saying "West Palm Beach," where people are rich, old and white.

The *Times* loves this kind of exotic locale. It is very reassuring to blue-state readers, so the paper runs pieces like this as if they were annotating that famous *New Yorker* cover that shows a map of the US from a Manhattanite's perspective: The Hudson River, then… well, really nothing. Remember the screenwriter who reported to the *Times* that he had discovered by driving across Nebraska that there were acres and miles of yard between the houses? In 2005, the paper found a county in Texas that had 66 people in it! It was like a new planet; it was front-page news. When the *Times* reporter and his photographer showed up in the county seat, the population immediately grew by more than 10 percent, plus two smirks. The template was the same one a New York reporter, Timothy Egan, used in the story about Superior:

> In many ways, Nuckolls County is not unlike any other rectangle of open space in the American midsection. Over the last half-century, when the United States added 130 million people and the population grew by 86 percent, rural counties in 11 Great Plains states—those counties without a city of at least 2,500 people—lost more than a third of their people. The farm-based counties, and those away from interstate highways, lost the most….
>
> When Sylvia Crilly moved to Superior, she said she was surprised by the open secret of rural America.
>
> "As an urban person who lived within blocks of the East Oakland ghettos, I have been just shocked by

some of the poverty I have seen here," Ms. Crilly said. "Some of these people are just drowning."

She noted that 26 percent of children younger than 5 lived in poverty in her community. During the greatest economic boom in modern American history, the late 1990's, the income gap between city and rural workers opened wider than ever. People in rural counties of the Great Plains make 48 percent of what their metro-area counterparts make. That compares with 58 percent in 1990, according to one study...

For these communities to survive, they will have to loosen their dependence on farming, many economists say.

If not farms, then what? Factories? The state has been helping with grants for small-town industrial parks. But companies sniff and go elsewhere, to counties with mountain views or even better tax incentives.

"You can go to any county in Nebraska and you'll see the same thing—these empty industrial parks," said [an official] of the rural affairs center.

Personally, I was quite impressed with Ms. Crilly's ability to note that 26 percent of children younger than five lived in poverty in her community. When I asked her about the story, she said the positive details had been dropped from the piece. The reporter had simply told her that editors in New York had cut her quotes. Just something you keep track of if you're a former urban person, I guess.

But you get the picture: It's the turtle crossing the road story, the unpopulated plains story. Nebraska looks to the Times the way the newspaper industry looks to the rest of the country. Want to see decline? In 1900, there were 2726 newspapers in America; 100 years later, 1480—and the biggest ones are all slowly going broke, too.

In 2006, the Project for Excellence in Journalism (since renamed the "Pew Research Center's Journalism Project") began its annual report this way: "Scan the headlines of 2005 and one question seems inevitable: Will we recall this as the year when journalism in print began to die?"[52] Maybe, but such is the residual power of the press (especially in the eternal archives of the Internet) that in Superior a full year after the *Times* article appeared, the phone was still ringing with new businesses looking for a home. "Nobody knew about us until the *Times* printed our obituary," *Superior Express* editor Bill Blauvelt, an stute and independent newsman, told me, sitting in Evelyn's, a "fine dining" restaurant opened by a chef from Denver and his brother from San Francisco after reading the news in the *Times* that Superior was a goner (and now the restaurant is too). One day, the entire mainstream news industry may join them. When I set about finding a place to live and write while working on this book, I had tried to find a house in Superior big enough for me and my family. It was impossible. Everything had already been rented.

The real problems faced by Superior aren't those found by reporters from New York City. For example, Superior's a retirement community for many; the Hotel Leslie I once painted has been done up as a fancy elder-care residence because newer, more modern hotels have been built nearby. The town has tremendous stability because

---

52 Ten years later, the center's annual report started this way: "In 2015, the newspaper sector had perhaps the worst year since the recession and its immediate aftermath. Average weekday newspaper circulation, print and digital combined, fell another 7% in 2015, the greatest decline since 2010."

the median age is 45.7 years, some eight years older than the national average. And it's a farming town, which means that while in terms of buying power, Superior's less affluent than, say, a neighborhood in the Bay area, the cost of living is much lower—you can buy a two-bedroom house in Superior for much less than what a *Times* reporter spends on her new Prius—the crime rate is microscopic, there's a great hospital in town and the people who live there know they could move up to Grand Island or even all the way to Omaha and make more. But I guess maybe they feel that in all the important respects, you just can't get better than is Superior, so what's the point?

The town had changed a lot in the years I was away. When I was young, it was an electrified, motorized version of the 19th century. Now it's much more a part of the 21st, distant from other places in America geographically, but right next door culturally. We used to have to wait until the sun went down to get the only rock n' roll station audible on the Great Plains, the fabulous KOMA in Oklahoma City, where the location of every Legion-hall dance in ten states was read by the DJ. All you had to do was get to one to meet a pretty girl on a hot night. Now, with a simple internet connection, you can listen to hip-hop from New York City in stereo in Superior, if you really want to.

NBC News sent a crew to Concordia in 2005 to do a story about the irrational support of Republicans in the heartland: Exactly how endangered a species were Kansas Democrats? A producer went to the local newspaper to get some help ferreting out a local Democrat or two—surely a newspaper would know where to find a one, yes? Yes! Sure enough, a pleasant young Democrat working at the paper duly directed the network to some local blue voters who made jokes about meeting in dimly lit basements and exchanging secret handshakes. They knew it was a joke; NBC's correspondent didn't seem so sure. In 2004, Bush carried Concordia by 50 percentage points, 75 to 25 percent; 12 years later, Trump did almost exactly the same. That still leaves more than several hundred Democrats—enough to have safely delivered the county to Democrat Sebelius in 2006. Of the townsfolk NBC interviewed, other than the Democrats, another was a Democrat—"but I register Republican," he told me. "Doesn't make sense not to around here"—and the other was also a Republican "moderate"—pro-choice but also pro-Bush. "I'm a moderate but I would *never* have voted for Kerry," she said, laughing. NBC was unable to find a single conservative Republican in Concordia, Kansas. They missed the wheat, too.

Voting preferences have followed the nation's trend toward polarization. More and more Kansans have chosen one side or another — just as they did in 1854.

The day after NBC's 2005 broadcast, I called Kirk Lowell, the town's economic development director, to get his view on what national exposure on network news might mean to tiny Concordia, but he didn't know what I was talking about. Same thing at the local supermarket. Perplexed, I sent my daughters on a polling expedition up and down Concordia's business district asking if anyone had seen their town's star turn on NBC's Nightly News. Not a soul—except for a teenager they found at Creations, a local hair salon. "Remember, mom?" she said to her mother. "I told you it was on." The mother just shrugged. Nobody else the children talked to saw NBC's John Quinones remark acidly that "even the river's Republican." Yawn. These days, Quinones hosts a hidden-camera TV show.

The news never stops, as they say. Just outside Smith Center a week after E.L. Murphy's ad ran, a group of followers of the late Maharishi Mahesh Yogi broke ground on a $14 million, 480-acre commune, organic farm and "coherence creating center" where a little "Unified-Field based political science [sic]" would be taught. At a press conference, they announced to a bunch of reporters and a few alarmed residents, to become the US Peace Government's capital of the Global Country of World Peace, lending a little Vedic aura to the spacious plains. The president of the US Peace Government,[53] sometime Natural Law Party presidential candidate John Hagelin, an Ivy-League-trained, self-described "meditating physicist" who, perhaps not incidentally, favors decriminalizing drugs, showed up for the groundbreaking and so did the Global Country of World Peace's governmental relations guy. The Maharishi's followers—who have included the Beatles, Mike Love, Donovan and Mia Farrow but who are

John Hagelin

perhaps most famous for offering courses in levitation at the small college in Fairfield, Iowa, they took over—said they were just looking forward to living in the middle of the USA—they call it the *Brahm-asthan*—in quiet, rural splendor.

The then-mayor of Smith Center, Randy Archer, told one reporter [54] that he had finally overcome his earlier prejudices. "Rumors are it's a cult and they are going to make underground bunkers and build nuclear weapons," he said. "That's not what they are about." He also offered consoling words to the *Pioneer*'s readers: "Their ceremonial

---

53The group's literature explains that the US Peace Government isn't competing with the other, empty-headed US government. There's no need, really, since, "The US Peace Government will actually rule the country at the fundamental level of consciousness."
54 The often brilliant George Deipenbrock of the Lawrence *Journal World*, Tuesday April 4, 2006.

garb is unusual to us, but it is their 'dress-up' clothes....Just give them a chance."

Townspeople at first were not very concerned either. "They're just regular people," the clerk in the convenience store at the junction of 36 and 281 told me. "They come in around 8, 8:30 in the morning and sit right there." He pointed to a little cluster of plastic tables. "Some get up and go, and then others come in. They're very nice, quiet people. *Never* a problem. They say they're going to send their kids to the school, so that will mean more kids and money. Maybe we'll get a boost up to 4A. That would be good." When I asked if he thought they would take over the small community, the man had echoed the comforting words of Mayor Archer as carefully reported in the *Pioneer*: "They are like you and me."

"They're really very normal," the convenience store clerk agreed. "We really get along. I always let them park their limo out there by the pumps."

But soon, the Global Country of World Peace had put together a 1500-acre "campus" and started construction on ten buildings using imported labor and materials bought elsewhere. That brought the local community back down to earth. When the Maharishi died in 2008, work stopped. Today the campus is down to380 acres. Most of it is used to grow organic crops.

INTERLUDE: SUPERIOR PEOPLE 5.

Rich: You know, personally I hear the word 'progressive,' which is what some liberals call themselves, and I wonder, 'what do they think they're progressing toward?' If we're progressing so our children have less respect for marriage or their marriage vows, is that really progress?

Pat: The way the culture is today, you've got to pack as much of your value system as you can into your children by the sixth grade. After that, it's probably too late—you've gotta throw them in to swim with the sharks, and hope they're equipped to deal with it.

Rich: So much of it has to do with mothers no longer being in the home. Until the last couple of decades, she was always there to send the kids off to school, and she was there when they got home. On the farm, she was the one instilling values and responsibilities— from gathering the eggs to feeding the bucket calf to driving the tractor. I'm talking at the age of six or seven. You talk to a kid in grade school today, and maybe he'll know about a tractor—he could explain it to you and tell you what one was—but that's as far as it goes. I'm not trying to be sexist here, but if we could turn back the clock maybe thirty years in that regard, it would do a world of good.

Bill: Well, back then, both parents felt that way, that family came first. Early on, Grandfather worked a little while as a brakeman for the Rock Island Railroad. But then he meets Grandmother and marries her, and quits. He says the railroad is no life for a married man – he should be home with the kids.

Rich: That hits it on the head. He gave up his career for family. We have sold ourselves short lately in this country because so few people are willing to do that.

Pat: That's a bill of good that's been sold *to* us in this country. So many people are looking to have a million dollars in their lives. In this part of the world, you still meet a lot of people looking to have a million-dollar life, sure. But they realize you can't take a U-Haul to that cemetery. It's probably against some state law, anyway. (Laughs.)

Stan: The trouble is, you have a concentration of liberal people on both coasts, and they have a lot of influence. They control the media, they also control the colleges….

Rich: And Hollywood. Let's face it, sin sells, and they're very successful at glamorizing it. People with a more conservative viewpoint—the ones trying to hang on to what used to be the norm—they see that, but they don't have the means to compete. So they try to hone in on areas where they feel they can still have some control and some influence.

Val: That's very true. Even in sports we see that.

Pat: That's why you're seeing a lot of people around here turn to home schooling—because they don't like the values kids are picking up in our public schools. I'm a teacher by profession, and even I agree with that. The parents are concerned, legitimately so, with the bad social environment—the bullying, the vocabulary, the lack of respect, and honor for your elders. And, of course, the poor quality of instruction.

Rich: And what are we paying for that -- $8000 per student? More? I started out in a one-room school, and by every account the education in those days was superior at a tiny fraction of the cost.

Stan: Well, I suppose when it comes to morals, people on the coasts just think we're behind the times. (Laughs.) Heck, our kids live together before they get married, just like they do everywhere else.

Pat: But I do think that it's different. They have a pretty good sense of reality. To a certain extent the slower pace here is a counterbalance to all the ram-and-jam they see on MTV. The kids from here may go down to spring break...

Stan: To South Padre Island, Cancun...

Pat: But the difference is, our kids have to pay for their own tickets. (Laughter.)

Stan: That hits it right on the head.

11

COMPASSIONATE CONSERVATISM (THE EARLY YEARS).

There's a certain irony in the ubiquitousness of museums in little towns with a history that's barely longer than a lifespan. Practically every small town has a museum, including towns that barely existed to begin with and continue now only because there's a museum of some sort in one of the old buildings.

In fact, sometimes the museum grows precisely because the town is shrinking. When the last grandkid sells—or simply abandons—the house that once sheltered his mom or dad, he'll donate to the local museum several generations of Army uniforms and wedding dresses, along with an assortment of other household odds and ends, on the assumption the museum will care for it. Lacking antiquity and an abundance of fine art, the effect is less Louvre and a little more turn-of-the-century Sears catalogue. Most small-town museums contain an astonishing assortment of items: household goods, typewriters, ancient tractors and farm implements, antique baseball gloves and uniforms, musical instruments, bottle openers, artifacts of war.

In larger towns, the museum grows because the trustees think it can become what the marketing people call a "destination." That's what happened in Hastings, Nebraska, for example—much to my surprise, since I had always figured the museum was already a destination. This was especially true in July or August, when, on a 100-degree day, the museum was totally cool. I used to ride bikes with my city cousins across Hastings, get good and lathered, then go into the museum and catch a cold while we looked at the dinosaur bones and arrow heads—the stuff that constituted two of the three dots on what we imagined to be the timeline of Midwestern history:

The Natural History of Nebraska

._____._____.

Dinosaurs.   Indians.   Now.

Roy Chapman Andrews, the famous dinosaur hunter, became my hero for a summer or two, and when I'd get back to grandad's farm, I'd walk everywhere watching my shoes to make sure I didn't accidentally disturb the stegosaurus jawbones that I was sure were down there, if I could only find them. Andrews found huge monsters in nondescript pastures just like these. If he could do it, why not me? The closest I came were seashells from the days when Kansas was an ocean floor—hardly museum pieces, although they did decorate a shelf for me.

In its own way, the museum in Concordia is a destination itself. Housed in a mammoth neo-classical structure that was once the Carnegie Library, the museum—officially, "The Cloud County

Historical Society"—attracted the attention of a visiting friend from the East who pronounced it reminiscent of the New York Historical Society. Its contents, which include a small, portable jail cell, arrest the unsuspecting visitor at every turn.

The place certainly detained my family: My wife and children volunteered to help organize the museum's costume collection, which is as massive as that once found on MGM's back lot; and which, in sum, gives a complete picture of the sartorial tastes and habits of an America now recalled only in sepia photos. Here's a turn-of-the-century dentist's office, over there a dry grocery; to the left, the jail cell (complete with bunk bed and ball and chain), to the right, a delivery truck; and above, an old airplane.

Then there are the fascinating displays doubtless unlike any found in any other museum anywhere. In different ways, both speak to a quality common to rural Midwesterners little appreciated in other parts of the country -- particularly, of late, by urban Americans. In an age increasingly given to ostentatious, celebrity-driven displays of concern for the less fortunate – think Oprah, or any of several dozen rock star pop-empathizers, or the innumerable grandstanding politicians – people out here tend to be notable for their reserve; given how they usually vote, those who view the world through blue-tinted glasses readily take this as callous disregard for others. In fact, as the historical record shows, Midwesterners have always been among the most generous spirited of all Americans.

The museum's first display was devoted to Camp Concordia, a prisoner of war camp, located just over two miles northeast of town during the final two years of World War II. With a capacity of more than 5,000 (which is nearly the town's population now), it contained more than 300 buildings—including a bakery, a library, a performance area for the camp's symphony orchestra and a 177-bed hospital, all neatly organized up and down streets named after people like Davy Crockett and Sam Houston. There were more than a dozen POW camps in Nebraska, Kansas and Oklahoma, with dozens more "satellite" camps where smaller contingent of Italian and German prisoners were housed. Indianola had a POW camp; Alma had a satellite camp. There were thousands of prisoners scattered across the Midwest, and even more in the south and southwest.

My grandfather agreed with other locals who said the choice of such Midwestern sites was due, at least in part, to the intimidation factor: heading west on slow-moving trains, overawed Jerries would come to see that escape from, let alone victory over, such a vast and powerful country was impossible. "Very impressing," as ex-prisoner Franz Kramer wrote to a Concordia man after the war. But what was impressing the Germans as much as anything was that, after all the boxcars they'd ridden in Europe, even as prisoners, in prosperous, generous-spirited America, they got to ride in comfy passenger coaches.

To be sure, Camp Concordia had its Hogan's Heroes moments, like the time the camp truck carrying prisoners overturned on Sixth Street,

The camp newspaper's banner.

knocking out the guard and leaving his rifle in the middle of the street. A prisoner quickly grabbed the rifle then ran through the gathering crowd thrusting it at alarmed people and shouting "you take!" until he finally found a Concordian willing to guard him and his fellow prisoners until the American soldier came to. Meanwhile, the POW newspaper, *Neue Stacheldraht Nachrichten* (Barbed Wire News), had to be shut down after it was discovered to be "one of the cleverest pieces of Nazi propaganda fostered in a German prisoner of war camp in this country," according to an offended US military inspector. There was also at least one notable escape: a German in full uniform made it as far as Belleville, about 16 miles north, where he tried to buy breakfast but couldn't speak English very well and had trouble working out American money. The waitress was suspicious. The German was arrested while waiting for a train out of town by the police chief of Belleville. Fifty miles to the north, in York, Nebraska, a German POW was arrested in a bar, 375 miles from the camp at Fort Robinson, when it was discovered he had problems ordering a burger in English.[55]

And of course, among the prisoners there were some unregenerate fanatics. At the Concordia camp, some anti-Nazi prisoners met mysterious deaths—always claimed to be acts of suicide by the Germans. Among the items seized from the barracks was a giant map of the USA, drawn by a prisoner with plans, showing all the major American cities and the railways that connect them. You can see it at the museum.

But mainly what remains in memory, both for most surviving prisoners and elderly townspeople, is a surprisingly large reside of good feeling. Captured in North Africa or France, the POWs found themselves in the equivalent of a country club, with frequent concerts, plays, movies and a casino, rathskellers, bars; and even the "University of Camp Concordia" offering hundreds of courses taught by inmate professors and so widely esteemed that they were recognized for credit by the University of Kansas and, after the war, by several

---

55 There's a very charming video of the waitress involved in this arresting story at http://www.livinghistoryfarm.org/farminginthe40s/money_04.html

German universities. Germans took up painting with a passion – several examples are on display in the museum—while Rommel's military band, captured en masse in North Africa and shipped to Concordia, provided musical interludes.[56]

The town's residents, for their part, were proud to be playing a part in a war that was in many ways far removed from this part of the world. Moreover, when the camp opened in July 1943, many suddenly found themselves mixing with people they'd heretofore known only from geography texts and newsreels. Some worked at the camp itself, and innumerable others brushed against the Germans who were used as free labor on local farms. Accompanied by armed guards, these were technically forbidden to mix with the civilians, but the rule was widely disregarded. "The first day, my mother insisted they were to come in an have lunch with the family," recalls one local man, a young boy at the time, "and they did every day after that. They were very intelligent and very cultured – one guy played the violin."

Indeed, as the letters from former prisoners on display at the museum reveal, the Germans found their treatment at the hands of the locals not just amazingly decent, but enlightening; for many saw it as representing the ideals of America itself.

"My rethinking [of Nazi ideology] started already after my first contact with the Americans at the beginning of my captivity," as one ex-

A camp guard tower

---

prisoner, Reinhard Mohn, recalled to the Topeka *Capital-Journal* in 1994. Returning to Germany from Camp Concordia, Mohn soon took over the family business—Bertelsmann, now one of the world's largest media companies and the publisher of this book. The band's wooden chairs are still in use at the Brown Grand.

The camp closed in 1945 and was quickly dismantled. At the museum, however, the appearance of old German ex-POWs—or their curious family members—is a common occurrence. Indeed, some former prisoners returned to the area after the war and settled along the Republican River.

B ut it is the other unusual exhibit at the museum which more fully conveys the quiet generosity long so common to this region: the exhibit devoted to the "orphan trains" that between 1853 and 1930 brought more than 200,000 children from the crowded, filthy alleys of New York, where at any given moment as many as 30,000 homeless children roamed the street, to new homes in spacious places like rural Kansas and Nebraska.

As migrations go, the system of rounding up kids—some genuine orphans, some juvenile delinquents, many just abandoned —and placing them in the homes of strangers strikes the contemporary sensibility as more than a little shocking. "It was certainly not a politically correct way to treat a social problem," as Susan Sutton, who serves as the president of the National Orphan Train Complex in Concordia, told me. And, to be sure, it could never be undertaken today – not with the maze of regulations governing adoption and child welfare, not to mention the racial politics.

But here's the thing: it worked. Not always, of course, but usually, and usually better than anything tried since.

It was the vision of a New York clergyman, Charles Loring Brace,[57] who organized the New York Children's Aid Society in St. Mark's Place and spent the rest of his life exporting children from Manhattan to small towns everywhere—and especially the Midwest—and encouraging other organizations to do the same. The result was a network of orphanages and agencies that fed children into the embrace of Children's Aid and, for Catholic children, the similarly-intentioned Foundling Hospital, created by the Sisters of Charity out of fear that Catholic infants may fall into the hands of Protestant zealots.

The placement of Children's Aid kids was left to enterprise and chance, with the assumption that there was a boundless reservoir of decency in the middle of the country: Ads would appear in Midwestern newspapers announcing the arrival of "asylum children!" who would be put on display for a day so locals could meet and choose the children they wished to adopt. "The sight of the little company of the children of misfortune always touched the hearts of a population naturally generous," wrote Brace. After the children were placed, agents from the Society would periodically revisit them to check on their progress.

The results were staggering. Though occasionally a match went badly—some of the children placed were treated as free labor and given little affection or education—according to the Society's carefully kept records, nearly nine of every ten placements were deemed successful. Written off as the dregs of society, many already in trouble with the law, the children found safe, comfortable homes far from the perilous and brief lives they would have led on the streets

---

57 Brace later wrote *The Dangerous Classes of New York and Twenty Years Work Among Them*, a good Midwestern book title if ever there was one. For historical details, I consulted *The Orphan Trains: Placing Out in America*, by Marilyn Irvin Holt (Nebraska), and *The Story of the Orphan Trains*, by Michael Patrick et al. (Donning Company).

of New York. "Many of them grew up," as Annette Riley Fry reported in *American Heritage*,[58] "to be pillars of their communities – farmers and farmers' wives, doctors and lawyers, preachers and teachers, a couple of governors and a couple of congressmen, mayors and judges – in short, solid citizens by the score."

"What I would have been if I had stayed in New York, God only knows," wrote one grateful fifteen year old in a letter found in the Society's files. "I had not gone far in vice when you rescued me, it is true, but I was rapidly sinking into that terrible pit of darkness."

"I will always be grateful for what I was given," Anna Harrison told me. As a young girl, she had ridden an orphan train West and to a new life in Nebraska. "I can't imagine what would have happened to me."

I was talking to Tina Long, at the time, the communications director of the Wichita-based Kansas Child Services League, about the orphan trains, venturing that such a thing must seem pretty far out to people like her in the adoption business. "Actually," she said, "there are more similarities than differences. They were going out and trying to find homes where people wanted kids, the same as we do now. It was very similar—other than the sometimes maddening bureaucratic process."

But, of course, the bureaucratic process is key. As far as many Midwesterners are concerned, in other places the government has largely mucked up this vital aspect of life, as it has mucked up so much else, resulting in child care systems that leave countless children consigned to poverty and neglect and all to often dead at the hands of those who escaped the notice of children's services bureaucrats. And for all the incessant talk of government acting "for the children," no one seems inclined to change any of that.

---

58 "The Children's Migration," December 1974.

Indeed, the one politician who even dared to suggest a meaningful alternative to the current system—former House Speaker Newt Gingrich, who speculated in 1994 that high quality orphanages might be a more humane approach for children languishing in the circumstances found in New York and Los Angeles—was widely denounced by "child care advocates" as a Neanderthal. "It seems like an awful experiment to do to children," as Miriam J. Cohen, a history professor at Vassar College in Poughkeepsie, N.Y., and a specialist in the history of welfare and reform, put it. "It's a radical experiment in something we haven't seen in a hundred years." She added dismissively, "What's new about it, is what I haven't seen." Gingrich quickly dropped the subject.

But of course, in places like Kansas few take it for granted that the best way to attack a social ill is with a massive government program. In New York or Los Angeles, this easy disregard for ambitious government plans is regularly caricatured as indifference, just more anti-government talk dismissed as the self-justifying nonsense of hard-hearted, Republican misanthropes. But to people out here it's just common sense, based on long historical experience and a confidence that individuals, not the government, come up with solutions that are more humane, not less.

"Based on our experience of working with foster care and those who need homes, you find a lot of people who are supportive," said Long, "and a lot of support for the families themselves within their communities." Most of the kids they place are African-American children from Wichita and Kansas City; most of the new parents are white folks from smaller communities. "We work with 40 newspapers and TV stations across the state who donate air time or space to show pictures of kids who need homes. We could never pay for that."

Still, the media-bred image of red state callousness is so pervasive these days that even those who should know better can get caught short by the far more nuanced realities. I was standing in a passageway in the Kansas House of Representatives one afternoon when a cute little African-American boy scooted past, clearly making a break from his father—who, it turned out to my surprise, was Tim Huelskamp, at the time a very conservative state senator from Fowler who went on to win a congressional seat and from there to the Heartland Institute, where he serves as president. (He was replaced in Congress in 2017 by Roger Marshall.)

In fact, Huelskamp's son is one of fivea dopted black children in Fowler, a town of only five hundred. Every African-American in the community—all five of them—has been adopted into not just a family, but by "the entire community," said Denise Kuhns, editor of *The Meade County News*. "In fact," she added, "they're not the only African-Americans in Fowler, but in the whole county, I think." She was unaware of any incident that would make the children feel unwelcome. "You know, kids are colorblind," she said, "and we should be too."

Three of the kids—aged 10, 9 and 4—are Huelskamp's. "It's really just us and another family," he told me. Huelskamp had been a primary sponsor of the Kansas Marriage Amendment, the bill that eventually led to the state's ban on same-sex marriages. He was the kind of legislator who was normally happy to talk to journalists. But he was a bit reluctant to discuss this. "We don't make a big thing of it," he explained. "It's just something we do that's consistent with our religious faith and our belief in the sanctity and value of every life." Huelskamp, a Roman Catholic, admitted that some people were surprised. "But I don't know why they should be. We're just like most people. We love our kids."

In New York or Washington, DC, placing African-American children with white families can be politically problematic. Stories about white families being denied the right to adopt African-American kids in need of homes are commonplace. The fear is that black children raised by white parents won't learn how to deal with racists. As it happens, on the day I'm writing this sentence, the *The Philadelphia Inquirer* is reporting just such an instance:

> Though white people might view interracial adoption as evidence of societal progress, experts say, for many black people it is a painful harkening back to a time when their ancestors were treated as property - and proof that the child-welfare system discourages African American adopters.
>
> "The race issue gets played out right through adoption," said Joseph Crumbley, a Jenkintown family therapist who studies the issue...
>
> Some social workers and educators question whether white families can learn, much less teach, black children the survival skills that African American parents already know.
>
> Last month, a judge denied a white Chester County couple's bid to adopt the black foster child who had lived with them for nearly two years. U.S. District Judge James T. Giles ruled that Randall and Susan Borelly of Uwchlan Township failed to prove that county officials racially discriminated by refusing to let them adopt Kevin, almost 4. [59]

---

59 "For Adoptees, Racial Divide Still Wide," Jeff Gammage, May 8, 2006.

"Not in Kansas," said Sanda Dixon, vice-president of social services at the Kansas Child Services League. "We have a multi-ethnic placement act that says you can't deny permanency because of race."

As Long observed, "If you're looking for a loving home [for a child] in Kansas, race doesn't play a role." A good thing, too, since, as Long noted, "In Kansas, most people who want to adopt are white. We just have a lot of white people here."

They're also people with a long history of racial tolerance, from the determination of Free Staters in the 1850s, through the arrival of the black "exodusters" in the 1870s who came to build successful, all-black towns, like Nicodemus, after Southern Democrats began rolling back some of the post-war progress African-Americans had made, to the Brown vs Board of Education case in the 1950s, when Republicans took control of the Topeka school board and sent the case to the US Supreme Court in order to get rid of "separate but equal" segregation that had been imposed on Kansas's largest towns; there had never been segregation in any of the medium- or small-sized communities in the state. "I'm proud to be a Republican and I'm a Republican on principle," said Cheryl Brown Henderson, the sister of Linda Brown, the little girl at the center of the case. Brown Henderson is also the president of the Brown Foundation and the family's spokesperson. "This wasn't Alabama here," she told me. "We weren't marching through lines of National Guardsmen. We in Kansas didn't want that law at all." Kansas isn't Boston, where race riots marked integration and bussing, and there are no Rodney Kings in Topeka. "We were never under threat here [because of race]," she said. A sometime candidate, Brown Henderson ran for the state legislature in 2004 but was defeated by a Topeka Democrat with union backing. Is her sister a Republican? "She was the last time I ran. I know, because she voted for me."

Lori Kemling, a 30-year-old part-time physical therapist who lived across the street from me in Concordia, has the kind of family that would look familiar to young professionals in New York or Boston: she and her husband, Brian, a local banker, are the parents of two adopted southern Indian children and they're expecting their third—a baby from China.

But reasons for her choice would surely be ridiculed by many readers of newspapers like the *New York Times* or *The Boston Globe*. Describing herself as a more or less typical Kansas conservative Republican, raised on a farm and educated at a good college, Kemling sat at her kitchen table chatting with me and watching her daughter play. "We are led by our faith," she said. "In fact, I don't know how you could explain this any other way. How would I explain this to them?" She nodded toward 4-year-old Sreya who had just discovered how to make a catapult out of a plastic spoon, a child-sized miracle if ever there was one. "That's what we tell them all the time, that God brought you to us, because, really, literally, He did."

Alien as this sounds to many contemporary ears, it is entirely in keeping with local tradition. The Children's Aid Society, too, was fundamentally a religious mission, and its legacy continues to loom large on the plains. Indeed, in Concordia, an old railway station was converted into an orphan train museum, housing files of photos and documents, detailing the experiences of children who once lined up at such stations to find new parents and new lives.

One such account, found in one the Society's annual reports, speaks eloquently to this region's long history of acceptance and toleration. It is about a four-year old named Willie, found on the streets of New York and initially adjudged to be "almost beyond hope." He was carried from the station by a German immigrant farm couple, angry and screaming, and when a Society agent returned to check on him a few months later, the farmer approached him in disgust. But it was not for the reason he thought, but because he feared the agent wanted to take the boy back. "I haven't come to take him away," the agent explained. "But how in the world do you manage him?"

The agent recorded the response of the farmer's wife, accent and all: "Oh, dot's easy. You see, we all luff him."

"There is an abundance of love and shelter and pity out here that will never be exhausted," the agent wrote his superiors back in New York. "Send out the little ones in yet larger numbers. The work is a success."

12

LEARNING, THE HARD WAY.

The Journal knows a good joke on a Salina man. This man ordered a book from London, England. The book was one that cannot be procured in this country. It came all right, but most of it is printed in Latin, and it has been 20 years since the Salina man looked into a Latin book. He is going to have his children read it to him at nights.

—*The Salina Journal*, October 4, 1905

A century later, the joke's on Salina—and almost every other community in America, where "Latin" describes a musical style, not a classical language. As every attentive parent knows, public education is both in collapse and denial. Not long ago, *The Chronicle of Higher Education* published a survey[60] showing how well American college grads were doing. The results were of course depressing: In

60 Mark Bauerlein, "The Long Disengagement," *The Chronicle of Higher Education*, Volume 52, Issue 18, Page B6.

history, civics, geography and literature, results are declining. This is consistent with other studies, including the National Assessment of Educational Progress "report card" that shows that even though Kansas students edge out New York kids, about two-thirds of Kansas 8th-graders consistently lack proficiency in math and reading—despite sharply escalating expenditure per student. In fact, almost all studies show no correlation at all between expenditure and outcomes.

Yet the pressure is greater now than ever to increase spending on "education" even further—especially since state courts in Kansas and elsewhere have insinuated themselves into the business of setting consistent funding levels for public schools, traditionally the role of the legislative branch.

For Midwesterners—as for most Americans—already there is no more expensive, invasive, powerful or arrogant example of governmental overreach than its control over local schools as they have grown to provide a welter of social programs and services, may of which have nothing at all to do with education. And what has all the additional spending on education bought Kansans? Not much. A hundred years ago, when Kansas had 9106 schools, most of which were little wooden sheds scattered across an empty landscape, many rural Kansans could in fact read the *Georgics* in the original. Even if a mastery of Latin isn't the best way to measure scholastic excellence, in the eyes of a lot of sensible people out here, it definitely beats all hell out of mastering the stuff handed out in diluted, politically correct, culturally torqued courses that are increasingly the norm today.

Many parents may resent this morphing of the little red schoolhouse into the big nameless bureaucracy in charge of social engineering, but, as cynical politicians know, the last thing parents want to do is get involved in education. Perhaps as a result in Kansas today public schools chew through two-thirds of every taxpayer dollar, leaving pocket change for everything else, from highways to troopers to courts to jails to old folks. And the same is true in most Midwestern states.

You can see the difficulty of trying to maintain expensive, unwieldy institutions in the ongoing consolidation of small school districts into larger ones—such as recently happened in Cuba, pop. 231, down a mere 10 people in the 1990s.

Historically, the school in Cuba was typical of that in many in the rural reaches of Kansas and Nebraska. Small and locally-run, housed in a modest facility, it was the single most important totem of civic life, scene of generations of proms, football and basketball games, wrestling tourneys, golf triumphs and homecomings. But no more. The school in Cuba has been consolidated with the school in Belleville, the seat of Republic County. So now every morning Cuba's children board buses and ride off to a cluster of buildings which belong to the local school district, one of the largest employers in the area, as school districts often are elsewhere in the rural parts of red states.

The decisions to close the Cuba school came a couple of years ago when the school board of Cuba met in the basement of the town hall with that of Belleville, the discussion wasn't about whether Cuba wanted to lose its school— thanks to school administrators that was a *fait accompli* – it was only about how soon it could be made to happen. Since everybody knew that without a school, you might as well just go ahead and move to Belleville, essentially Cuba was negotiating the terms of its own municipal death. It was painful to watch.

At one point in the strained discussion, a disheartened Cuba school board member turned to the guy next to him and asked, "Do we have any alternatives?"

The other guy could only shrug.

He looked up at the school superintendent standing next to him. "Well, what about charter schools? Can we get money for that?"

"You'd be the first," said the superintendent. "I wouldn't go there." That effectively put an end to that line of inquiry, and everybody turned again to Cuba's civic demise.

Tipton school and grounds.

Of course, there were (and are) alternatives. For example, in tiny Tipton, Kansas, a town about the size of Cuba and less than 100 miles away, consolidation became an issue in 2003, but unlike Cuba, Tipton simply said, "No." Led by Fred Smith, a retired Chicago cop who had moved to the town where his grandmother had lived, Tipton's residents needed only 41 days to build a perfectly-sized, modern school for the community's kids—for less than $60,000. Then they sold the old public school to a private company that specializes in educating kids with special needs, and at the same time set up an endowment to help support the local Catholic high school—with 30-odd students, the smallest high school in Kansas. In Lindsborg, Smoky Valley High School launched a virtual charter school to work with area home-schoolers and other farflung students. Kids in grades 7 through 12 are equipped with a Mac laptop loaded with the state curriculum and provided access to teacher/tutors whenever one is required. As a consequence, Smoky Valley has students all over

Kansas and the US—and even in Europe. For those willing to create alternatives, alternatives exist.

The trouble is, many Kansans don't want "alternatives." Thirty-odd years after the non-stop inflation of what constitutes a public school, parents in even the smallest town now expect to get the kind of school only a big government—and especially a big government in a big city—can provide, one with a big, expensive sports program that generates lots of college scholarships, along with a menu of other stuff that has nothing to do with reading and writing. As one mother in Mankato, Kansas, told me, "If there aren't extras [free food, sports, programs for "at risk" students, social work, counseling, proms and the like], then they can just close the school as far as I'm concerned. Those things are what school's about."

After four decades of providing a growing list of goods and services through the schools, it's no wonder that, at this point, the consolidation of small schools is standard state policy. Sold to parents as a cost-cutting measure, smaller schools are pushed to join larger ones, who in turn join even larger ones. The same thing that Cuba went through is happening in rural areas all over America. Indeed, in Kansas, there are rumors that soon there will only be one "unified" school in the biggest town in each county—and those will eventually be replaced by a scattering of big regional institutions. In 2004, I asked Larry Lycell, then Belleville's superintendent, what the long-term prognosis was for the local school. "If Concordia [20 miles to the south] builds a big school north of town, then we could eventually see our school close and consolidate with theirs," he said. There's even talk of putting up dormitories to house 10-year-olds who'd have to travel for hours to get to school.

The other theory behind all this is, of course, the obvious one: As experts will tell you at length, economies of scale and all the rest mean that larger schools must be better for kids, especially poor ones. And in the Midwest, as everywhere else in modern America, "better for kids" is a magic incantation. At a special legislative session held in Topeka in 2005 to implement a court-ordered increase in funding for schools, I clocked the phrase "for the children" seventeen times over one 20-minute span. And in fact, the argument for consolidation is pretty compelling: What could be better—you save children *and* save money. Sadly, the facts don't support this. For example, a 2003 Louisiana report summarizing the research into consolidation pointed out what every small-town educator already knows: *Small is better*; small schools are much better at narrowing the gap between rich kids and poor kids, ahile large schools are unruly, unproductive, wasteful; large schools often end up spending more money on non-essential services and program unrelated to education; and the myth of economy of scale is just that—a myth.[61]

Common sense (not to mention all those pesky studies) would suggest that what's "better for kids" is a system that creates more

---

61 Louisiana's education department studied all the available research relating to school size and performance, and they were unable to find a single instance of performance improving as school size increased. Their conclusion: If you send a kid from a small school to a larger school, he'll get a worse education every time. "Small School Districts and Economies of Scale," Louisiana Department of Education, May 2003.

But of course with so much at stake there is an ongoing effort to use statistics and studies to buttress one view or another of the government's role in children's education. Like everything else in 21st century America, education is just another political tool and both the Bush administration with its No Child Left Behind farce and the liberal political establishment, with its reliance on "education" as a way of growing government have a great deal at stake, so it's unsurprising that so many assessments are configured to reveal desired outcomes and that Trump's education secretary is under constant fire.

The release of one recent NEAP study, for example, was given the predictable head-line in the July 15, 2006, *New York Times*, which opposes school choice: "Public Schools Perform Near Private Ones in Study." The Times report said, "Children in public schools generally performed as well or better in reading and mathematics than comparable children in private schools."

The *actual study* said, "In grades 4 and 8 for both reading and mathematics, students in private schools achieved at higher levels than students in public schools."

The only similar outcomes in the study were for poor public school kids and poor private school kids. Sadly, because school choice does not exist for most poor parents, there aren't very many poor private school kids.

smaller schools, not fewer larger ones. But, of course, there is a larger agenda at play here, one dictated by those with a view of government very different from the one that has long held sway in Kansas. For while the value of the educational "reforms" may be in doubt, there is no question what the new education policy *does* achieve: vastly expanded government power and influence over the most important of all relationships, that between a parent and a child. The growth of public schools not as educational institutions but as government services centers only creates more dependency on government to save parents from having to get involved, even marginally, in the education of their children.

Many Midwesterners have learned, to the dismay of some, that as long as a reform ostensibly benefits children, you can grow government as high as an elephant's eye; and, indeed, since the bureaucracy's notion of benefiting children is so elastic it can be made to include keeping kids in school longer, starting younger, that even values rooted in generations of belief and practice can be readily undermined. The village it takes to raise children in Kansas is as big as the whole state.

If you want to find one of the richest people in almost any middlin'-sized town in Kansas, just stop by the local school superintendent's office, a tiny blue island in the big red sea. There you'll find a vastly overpaid functionary slicing and dicing policy for gullible, busy parents populating a school board that is usually convinced that the superintendent, as the resident expert, probably knows what's best. "They are the wall against reform, the six-figure-salary fat cats," said former Kansas State Board of Education member Connie Morris.

When I asked Larry Lycell, the then-superintendent of Belleville's schools, how many conservative superintendents he could think of, he said, "two"—and he was not one. Overwhelmingly, school administrators are liberals, typical of educrats everywhere in the US, and consequently they generally enjoy the support of the state's daily press. School administrators are very adept at spending money on themselves and on the administrative layer of public schools.

In 2005-2006, the administrative costs of the 300 school districts in Kansas, according to the Kansas Association of School Boards, will gobble up more than $300 million, more than any other category of non-instructional service—and more than twice as much as is spent on libraries, technology and testing combined; more than the state spends for "student support," including social workers, truancy police and public health types; more than the cost of operating, maintaining, heating and insuring the state's school buildings; more than is spent for all the food served to Kansas students; more than Kansas spends for all the buses on which the state's kids ride to school. Some of this administrative windfall pays the salaries of school principals and other essential personnel, but almost half goes to pay the local superintendent and his small bureaucracy.

In tiny Republic County, where barely more than 800 students attend the public schools, more than $550,000 is paid to administrators. The hardest working of these—the school principals—usually get the least. Teachers aren't even on that list. Further to the south, near Wichita, there's a district with three people—the superintendent, the assistant superintendent and the "business manager"— who together pull down a quarter-million a year, all for running a district with around 150 kids. The performance of that district is routinely overshadowed by a local Christian school where students easily outscore kids from the nearby public schools in standardized tests—and where administrators make a tiny fraction of the salaries paid to the public school officials. The superintendent of Catholic schools in the diocese where Cuba is located looks after the needs of thousands of students in large schools and small where scores are always higher than those seen in public schools—and does it all for less than $70,000 a year. As is invariably the case, student performance in smaller towns like Concordia and Lindsborg, where superintendents are paid more modestly, is generally better than in places like Salina and Wichita, where school administrators are paid much more.

In 2005, the average salary for the average Kansas super in an average town the size of Salina or Dodge City was $150,000. The average benefit package:

- $600 a month car allowance.

- $50 a month for cell phone.

- $260 a month for health insurance.

- $1,900 a year for disability insurance.

- $5,100 a year for life insurance premiums.

- $15,000 a year for the Kansas Public Employees Retirement Fund.

- $15 a year for a medical exam required by the contract.

- An undetermined amount for membership dues to professional organizations, to be approved individually by the board.

- One-time moving expenses not to exceed $10,000.[62]

---

62 All this legwork courtesy of Michael Strand who reported it for *The Salina Journal*, Feb. 11, 2004. I bet that cell phone allowance has gone up by now. Strand also notes

As it happens, my cousin, Dale Boyles, was for many years a school superintendent in north central Kansas, buying blackboards and hiring teachers for more than thirty years until the early 1990s. When I was young, I remember standing with my grandfather while he talked to Dale. When he was done, we headed back down the street. Grandad said, "Your cousin is a great man, Dee," and I believe he still is. In his day, he was an underpaid man in a poor district, working more or less the way local government workers do elsewhere in the Midwest: Doing as much as possible for as little as possible because nobody else felt like doing it. He had started teaching in one-room schools even before he had graduated from one himself. Eventually, he became a supervisor in towns like Downs and Cuba. His schools flourished, even though Dale was so tight with the taxpayers' money that he personally drove the school bus on its daily rounds to save paying a driver.

I told him I was having a hard time trying find a relationship between the amount of money paid to school superintendents and the amount of work they did or how well they did it. I had a page full of notes and figures with me. It seemed that in the last ten years, superintendent's salaries had ballooned. Example: The superintendent who told that school board in Cuba there were no alternatives was paid $103,000 a year—the salary paid to the governor of the state of Kansas—to look after two schools with a combined enrollment of under 250.

"If you're looking for a correlation between pay and performance, you won't find one," he told me, quite correctly. "They get paid whatever they can convince people to pay them."

---

that the average pay for the 15 largest school district supes in Kansas is $150,000, not including all those perks.

To do what, exactly? Well, said Dale, to implement education regulations imposed by other educational bureaucrats. To set goals. To create procedures and processes you couldn't possibly understand without an advanced degree in educational process making—basket-weaving without baskets. According to cousin Dale, "It's mostly PR"—convincing the locals that they've got a great school and traveling to Lincoln or Topeka to convince the state to give them even more money.[63]

And when that doesn't work, doing what seemed to be working so well: Sue the taxpayers to get even more money.

That's what the school superintendent in Salina did, setting off a chain-reaction of judicial excess in a case called Montoy vs. Kansas that will burden the state's taxpayers for a generation—without doing a thing to improve the education of Kansas kids.

The political implications of the Montoy case form the basis for a subsequent chapter in this book, but a summary might be useful.

The lead plaintiff in the case was Ryan Montoy, the son of a Salina administrator who admitted to reporters that his problem wasn't with academics; he just wanted better athletic facilities for his school because one of his kids, Ryan, was a member of his school's football team, was a good athlete. Montoy had been called by his boss, Gary Norris, then-superintendent (salary: $131K, plus perks) of the Salina school district, and president of something called "Schools For Fair Funding," a group of 14 cranky, mid-sized, litigious school districts in Kansas run by administrators who wanted more money.

Norris was looking for some plaintiffs of an ethnic persuasion, and Montoy—well, that was Hispanic enough to work. Besides, the

---

63 One favorite tactic, according to Dale: Across-the-board pay raises. If a superintendent offers, say, a 10 percent pay raise across the board, that means $3000 or so for every teacher—"everybody likes that"—but it also means another ten grand for the superintendent, who's already making three teachers' salaries.

guy worked for him. So Montoy said yes boss, and so did a bunch of other people Norris rounded up, some of whom were completely befuddled by the whole thing. He and the others sued, claiming the state didn't do enough to support "at risk" students—a formulation used to determine who gets cheap meals in the school cafeteria. If you're a family of four with an income of around $36,000 a year— above the average income in the state—your kids are victims and "at risk." The Kansas state supreme court made Montoy law in June 2005.

"This is wonderful news for kids in Kansas," announced Norris, who has what must be an appropriate academic background for a school superintendent—he's a former school chorus leader with a PhD in "education leadership." His other notable achievement in Salina: he helped implement a local sales tax to fund schools before leaving Kansas for Florida. On his way out of town, he told a reporter from the Pittsburg *Morning Sun*,[64] "We now get the chance to prove in court that the school finance system in Kansas is broken. The end result should be a more adequately funded system that is more fairly distributed to Kansas school districts. Eventually, kids will win."

Especially once they adjust to the new artificial turf (cost: $537,000)[65] Salina installed after the decision. Rah!

Obviously, the massive governmental failure that is public education is accompanied by a shift in how today's administrators define an "education. At the beginning of the last century, it was widely understood that the purpose of an education was to sharpen the mind and stimulate intellectual and spiritual health. Back then, for instance, the kids in Kansas's Wyandotte County were

---

64 Norris quotes: Olive Sullivan, "USD 250 leaders closely following education funding lawsuit," *The* (Pittsburg, Kansas) *Morning Sun*, Jan. 28, 2003.
65 *The Salina Journal*, August 25, 2005.

expected to achieve marks at 80 percent or better in science, arithmetic, reading, writing by the time they left high school —along with all that Latin stuff.

By 2005, nearly three-quarters of the 11th-grade students in Wyandotte County schools could not read well enough to meet the state's minimum level of proficiency. As a rule, when this happens, "reforms" are made to create a better outcome, but even that can't mask persistent failure. In fact, the most consistent outcome of "education reform" is more education reform. Often, the only way to disguise the fact that public education has failed in Kansas, as elsewhere, is to stretch the concept of education to include the distribution of social welfare services.

This is something many school systems in Kansas have sought to do with vigor. While, for example, the Wichita schools lagged behind both the Kansas average and the national average ACT scores in 2005, they did rather well caring for the physical and emotional needs of children that were once the province of parents. The schools coordinated "psycho-social groups," conducted various outreach programs and fed children breakfast and lunch on school days; nearly a third of the state's 440,000 students ate at little or no charge. Some children left school on Fridays having been given enough food to last them through the weekend.

"Pardon my French," as one Wichita teacher disgustedly summed it up to me in plain English, "but we can't teach them because we're too busy raising them."

Many of the social programs operated without the kinds of controls and accountability that govern conventional government services. Wichita's backpack program is an example. As Lena Lank, a program director at Communities In Schools of Wichita/Sedgwick Co., Inc., told me, her program "can't really follow-up" on making sure the help is getting to the right people or that the food they distribute for kids ends up feeding people. "We just can't do that."

Her program provides food to "chronically hungry kids"—identified as such not by medical staff but by teachers who are asked to help implement the plan. First introduced into primary schools, the program soon expanded to include middle school students, and joined a raft of other welfare programs administered through schools.

No one doubts that social programs like these may be very valuable services. The question is whether this is something one can reasonably call "education"—or whether it's a faith-based initiative for those who have faith in government.

But by now it's clear that no matter how many dollars the educrats extract from government, shuttling off to Lincoln or Topeka to convince the state to give them even more money, it can never be "enough."

Using education as a way of growing government isn't peculiar to Kansas, of course. In Oklahoma the push recently has been for school from the cradle onward; a result, of all things, of Governor Brad Henry's trip to France, of all places, late in 2004. Of all the cool French things Gov. Henry, a Democrat, might have found to bring home to Oklahoma—an Eiffel Tower-sized oil rig for Tulsa, maybe, or a topless beach to amuse the fisherfolk of Grand Lake— what he found most appealing is the way the government of the Fifth Republic sees to the "education" of French toddlers. (While it's hard to imagine instruction for a two-year-old going beyond real training in the use of WCs, in France it's not unusual for even the littlest students to be in state care for ten hours a day). Among other things, the governor saw free day care as a sure-fire vote-getter.

Of course, the French educational system is entirely consistent with the way the French view government as the ultimate provider of goods and services, from good TV shows to fat pensions, to efficient planes and trains – all at a cost of a mere 70 percent of combined earnings in taxes.

The American—and, even more so, the Midwestern—tradition is very different, grounded in the belief that government's role is to establish laws and enforce them so we don't kill each other while trying to make a buck—and then get out of the way. Our assumption is that personal responsibility is the preferred means of insuring our own welfare.

Alas, thanks to lawyers, judges and their politician allies, education in America, and even out here, is becoming more and more French by the minute; and so, in subtle ways, are other aspects of Midwestern life. Every minute of every day, Midwestern schools become bigger, more expensive, more intrusive and less effective, less able to teach basic skills. Big-government advocates know that if red states are to turn blue, the dye must be cast in the Midwest's schoolyards. It's the one area of government expansion that people will embrace uncritically, regardless of their political inclinations. No matter how low outcomes are, the solution is always going to be money.

It must be exhausting to challenge what has become the prevailing educational orthodoxy, that money is the solution to what ails education, because when political and community leaders object to over-funding education, the press portrays them as hateful and worse. When the Kansas branch of Americans for Prosperity took a bus tour of the state in 2005 to stir interest in a tax-limiting statute, they were met at most of their stops by angry school administrators and board members, the people most responsible for bloating the state's education budget to the point where nobody's certain exactly how they can spend it all. The Kansas Association of School Boards is militantly liberal, demanding ever more money for administrators and the districts they administrate. And school administrators themselves often lead the charge for bigger checks.

At one stop in western Kansas, tour organizer Alan Cobb recognized the superintendent from Ashland who had taken time off from his job to drive over to spend some time screaming at the top of his lungs trying to interrupt the visiting speakers. At other stops, such as the one in Salina, a couple of protesters told me they'd been contacted by the League of Women Voters and asked to go along to wave a sign or two. Everywhere the bus went, Cobb told me, school administrators or their staff members showed up to try to shout down the anti-tax speakers. Their behavior, he said, was "just rude. They were the ones who yelled the loudest."

Someone else trying to slow down the runaway expansion of "education" is a former ice-cream exec-turned-seminar-leader from Iowa, Jamie Vollmer, who visits some 80 districts a year to give pep talks to school administrators. Vollmer hands out posters with a long, long list of all the social engineering and government services that have been added to what schools are supposed to do in addition to teaching the basics. The list is presented as a time-line and starts with teaching "health" in 1900 and goes on through the decades to include teaching "peace"; drug education; "character education," whatever that is; women's studies; "inclusion" and, inevitably, "death education." Teaching reading, writing and arithmetic to kids is what parents like to think their school is doing, but there's no time for that kind of education in a modern public school. Vollmer sees a near-complete disconnect between the community's perception of "school" and what the thing actually is and does. "Parents just don't know," he said.

An enormous part of the problem is the accretive nature of the educational bureaucracy itself. Bob L. Corkins, who served briefly as state education commissioner, seemed to share some of the concerns of those who think public education in places like Kansas needs a serious rethink. When I asked him about the crazy compulsion to consolidate, for example, he told me that he felt the state "should try to help small rural communities and try to give them choices and alternatives." Corkins was an outsider to the state's education establishment, something he had in common with many parents who may have wisely suspected that after decades of same-old approaches to solving the growing problems of public education, an outsider was what was needed. So naturally, Corkins was reviled by the state's liberal politicians and press. Even before Corkins had a chance to start work, Kansas liberals were furious because a school administrator hadn't been named to the post. When Corkins suggested vouchers and school choice might merit consideration, they went ballistic. Not surprisingly, Corkins is now gone, along with a couple of the conservatives on the Kansas State Board of Education, all targets in the 2006 elections.

Consolidation will continue no matter who's in office, of course, but for those who are serious about innovation in education, especially in smaller, rural districts, some Republican state legislators seem willing to pitch in to help. "I think there are a number of us open to finding new solutions," said former state Rep. Kathe Decker who chaired the legislature's education committee in 2005. "If they [rural district school boards] come to us and say we want to do something new and present some different ideas, the legislature would embrace that," she told me at the time. "You do what you can, whatever it takes, to save your school."

Decker's replacement was Clay Aurand, the former majority leader in the Kansas house and a farmer who represented Formoso, Mankato and Burr Oak. "I'm surprised more [parents] haven't come forward to ask for help," he told me. "With consolidation and these other problems, we have some ideas that can help. But they have to ask. I wish they would."

Indeed, ironically, these days in Kansas (as in Nebraska and elsewhere in America), the greatest obstacle to restoring common sense to public education may be parents themselves. Parents everywhere need help. As more than one told me, it's hard not to be seduced by the array of government services there for the taking, many of them through the schools, even if it also means the schools ultimately will shortchange the children. Kansans watch Oprah and the View out here as avidly as any other Americans, and taxes always go up, so who can blame them if they're increasingly open to the notion that social welfare *should* be as much, maybe more, of the school's responsibility as teaching kids how to read and write? It may be a notion that would have struck their forebears as a joke, but today it's no laughing matter.

13

JUDGING POLITICS.

You'd think that if a runaway judiciary could be stopped anywhere, it would be in Kansas, where common sense and rock-hard pragmatic populism are export crops.

But all those "moderates" have spent most of the 20th century building a fortress judiciary, one designed to stand up to decades of protest, ridicule and resentment. Small wonder Kansans have been as unsuccessful restraining their judiciary as everyone else. And now they're going to pay for it: Like the taxpayers in 45 of the 50 states, Kansans are being forced to pay a tax imposed on them by judges deciding exactly how much money taxpayers should spend on schools.

In Kansas, as elsewhere, these decrees are usually a consequence of a ruling in an "equity" lawsuit. There are dozens of these lawsuits going on at any given time in almost every state. Many of them involve hundreds of millions—even billions—of dollars. For lawyers, education is the new tobacco, and business is smoking. For bureaucrats, it's a genius way to sneak big government into communities suspicious of it.

As a rule, educational equity lawsuits involve relatively small cohorts of plaintiffs with specific gripes—in Kansas, for example, a small group of parents and the school administrators those mid-sized school districts in Salina and Dodge complained that small, rural districts got more per pupil than they did. They also complained that big schools in affluent neighborhoods were able to augment state funds with local levies. In *Montoy v. Kansas*, they said they wanted more money for some of their Spanish-speaking, disadvantaged and other "at-risk" students. The basis for the complaint: A lawyerly passage in the constitution that said the "legislature shall make suitable provision for finance of the educational interests of the state." In Kansas, the word "suitable" has cost state taxpayers hundreds of millions of dollars.

Of course, that's probably what most Kansans thought they were doing already. Not much was the matter with education in Kansas. The 2005 session of the legislature saw a $142 million increase in educational spending, a boost to make up for not voting increases for several years. Funding throughout Kansas was rising faster than school enrollment and even without the increase, the state spent more than its neighbors on schools—two-thirds of the state budget, in fact—and already distributed that money more equitably than most other states did. Every year, nearly ten grand is spent on every student in the state—up from just under $7000 a mere five years ago. Kansas pays its teachers fairly; they make more than most citizens in this low cost-of-living state. The state produces graduates whose performance is in the top ten nationally, something that has been constant for the last few generations—although in 2005, when spending reached an all-time high, achievement in some areas began a slow decline.

As the *Wall Street Journal* noted that year, "the link between school spending and educational achievement is close to nonexistent." Nonetheless, in *Montoy*, the court found that the word "suitable" translates in money-talk to exactly $143 million *more* than the $143 million the legislature had just approved. In 2007, that figure, experts said, would begin to swell, until it reached nearly a billion dollars and start costing the state jobs and a loss in productivity.

Call that crazy optimism. By 2017, the budget was bloated to Zeppelin-like dimensions and stood at more than $4 billion. What did it buy? No noticeable improvement in educational performance. Instead, taxpayers bought: At-Risk 4-year-old program, At-Risk K-12, Adult Education, Adult Supplemental Education, Bilingual Education, Virtual Education (beginning 2008-09), Capital Outlay, Driver Training, Extraordinary School Program, Food Service, Professional Development, Parent Education Program, Summer School, Special Education, Vocational Education, Area Vocational School, Special Liability Expense, School Retirement, KPERS Special Retirement Contribution, Contingency Reserve, Textbook and Student Material Revolving, Bond and Interest #1, Bond and Interest #2, No-Fund Warrant, Special Assessment, Temporary Note, Cooperative Special Education, and Gifts and Grants.

According to the Kansas Policy Institute, "The new school funding record of $6.084 billion doesn't include new funding approved by the Legislature. An additional $293 million in state aid is scheduled to be added over the current and next school year, but total aid will likely increase even more. The additional state aid allows school districts to increase local property taxes to expand their Local Option Budgets, and that will cause an increase in state equalization aid. KPERS pension payments will also need to be increased based on the amount of new state and local aid spent on employee pay increases and new hires.

"But even that is not enough to satisfy the Kansas Supreme Court and the education lobby. The court appears to demand at least $600 million more in addition to the $293 million already added for the 2019 school year and the school lawyers say they are entitled to about $1.4 billion more. Should the Legislature choose to meet just the minimum demand, either state school property taxes would double, the state sales tax would soar to the highest rate in the nation or there would need to be a 20 percent income tax surcharge. Alternatively, General Fund spending on everything else would need to be reduced by about 19 percent to meet the minimum demand."

Brownback's attempt to cut taxes in that face of that huge money-grab was doomed to fail. In fact, the conspiracy to inflate the state's education budget had started in 2004, when the court found a $850 million figure by accepting as evidence a discredited 2001 study by Augenblick & Myers, one of a handful of education experts retained by states to help them think about how much should be spent on reading, writing, arithmetic and condom-use for middle-schoolers. They think big.

Consultants like A&M are notorious for their methodology—findings are often heavily influenced by simply going to school administrators and asking, "How much money do you need"—roughly akin to asking a meth-head, "How much crank would you like" The huge sums these experts recommend are laughed off by the legislators who ask for them: When they got to the bottom line on the A&M study, for example, the Kansas legislature didn't even bother saying, "Forget it!" before tossing it aside.

But it's dangerous to leave studies like the one commissioned for Kansas lying around. They're loaded guns in the hands of lawyers—in Kansas, it was a politicized sexual harassment/workers' rights litigator named Alan Rupe—who grab them and bring them to court along with bales of even more data harvested from the massive, ugly, ill-conceived love child created by George W. Bush and Ted Kennedy: The hideous "No Child Left Behind" education plan, with its stacks of test-scores, charts, graphs and other fodder for brief-filers.

The judge in the *Montoy* case was Terry Bullock, a colorful, some say eccentric judicial character, who drew on decisions by other activist judges in crafting his own and who used the A&M study as evidence because there was none otherwise. In his decision, Bullock admitted that "ordinarily it is not the Court's role to direct the Legislature on how to levy taxes or on how to spend the funds it does collect, this case is the exception…[the legislature] has no choice when it comes to funding education. Under the Constitution, it simply must do it and do it adequately." He ordered the legislature to allocate the additional $143 million or he would close the state's schools. He also took local funding control away from the school districts so parents in wealthier areas, where taxes are higher, wouldn't be able to augment state money, thus requiring state levels to be increased everywhere—that was the "equity" part of the deal. Then he retired and opened a mediation business.

But of course the real nature of Bullock's interest had never been education. It was, he brazenly pointed out, taxation: "As a result of the significant tax cuts passed by the Kansas Legislature during the past ten years, the state has forfeited nearly $7 billion in funds which it would have otherwise had in the treasury. The depletion for 2005 alone is $918 million!"

Forfeited? Depletion? Exclamation point? Funding schools is one thing. Writing tax policy is another. Neither of them is typically a judge's job. By making it his, Bullock worried more than just Kansans. Concerns rippled across the country. In Washington, DC, attorney Megan Brown, a former counsel to the US Attroney General, commenting on *Montoy*, said, "If more states follow this path…reducing deference to legislatures in administering school systems, the jurisprudential and practical effect may be to substantially erode the functional and structural separation of power between branches of state government…."[66] Bullock essentially took the power of taxation away from the elected legislature and its unpleasant array of conservatives and put it safely in the hands of lawyers, "experts" and liberal judges like himself.

Foolishly, the legislature failed to take Bullock's odd decision seriously, assuming the state's Supreme Court would do what other courts around the country had done and declare the funding of public education a political matter. The legislature treated the Bullock decision the same way they treated the Augenblick & Myers study: They ignored it and assumed the state's supreme court would throw the decision out. Of course, it didn't.

The court—and especially Donald Allegrucci, whose wife had been the governor's chief of staff and whose stepson Gov. Sebelius had appointed state tourism director—was not very subtle in hiding its disregard for the legislature, and especially for the conservatives who led the House. The justices were said to be angry that legislators had not been increasing its spending on education and they hammered the state's attorney, Kenneth Weltz. At one point, when it was pointed out that the legislature had just approved $143 million

---

66 *State Court Docket Watch*, August 2004.

more for education in the 1005 regular session, Allegrucci snorted, "That's not saying much."[67]

In the end, of course, the court not only upheld *Montoy*, it went further: In addition to telling the legislature to spend the money, they also told them how *much* to spend—another $143 million they thought was a good start, with hundreds of millions more to come. If the legislature failed to come up with the money, the court said, the schools would be closed.

The court was now in a pitched battle with the conservative Republicans in the house. The court didn't like those tax cuts Bullock had yelled about either, so either the tax cuts would be rolled back and more the money spent, or all the schools in Kansas would be closed—a thought that the court thought might get the attention of most parents. Politicians from both parties, along with a majority of Kansans, agreed with the common-sense observation that the court overstepped itself and some legal experts thought the same thing. In making its decision, attorney general Phill Kline told me, the court "clearly demonstrated the creative evasion of constitutional principles."

Reading the polls wasn't difficult for Gov. Sebelius. She did a Clinton-class waffle: "While I share the displeasure of many Kansans at the court decision, especially ordering the Legislature for a specific amount of money and weakening our local control over schools, I believe that investing in our children and their education is the best way to guarantee future prosperity for our state."[68]

But thinking the court was wrong was one thing. Exploiting the court's wrongness was something else. Lots of people were much more interested in milking Kansas taxpayers than the subtleties of

---

67 *Topeka Capital-Journal*, May 12, 2005.
68 June 22, 2005

Marbury v Madison, so the governor, joined by liberal Republicans and Democrats, all quickly lined up behind the court, while the House—dominated by conservative Republicans under then-speaker Doug Mays of Topeka—dug in for a fight they thought they might not win, but at least had to wage. The press waded in with its narrative: Mean-spirited Republican conservatives were trying to close Kansas schools! and wasting everybody's time in order to avoid spending a little money on the children! To this narrative would all details conform in the weeks to come.

If the legislature, to its own harm, had ignored the Augenblick & Myers study and the Bullock decision, Gov. Sebelius and her allies were happy to ignore the significance of this nutty judicial power grab by what amounted to a group of the governor's friends and political allies. She moved quickly to lend support the media narrative and make it clear just who the bad guys were: "The Legislature's inability to fulfill its obligation to Kansas students has finally come home to roost," she said in a prepared statement when the verdict came in. "Still, I am relieved that the Legislature, after six years of wrangling, has been given another opportunity to find a real solution for funding our schools. We need to act in the best interests of Kansas children and their parents, above all else, and we cannot afford more legislative irresponsibility."

Releasing this statement, on June 3, 2005, was as close as the governor ever got to providing public leadership on the potentially volatile issue. She simply went mum, retreating behind closed door and began working on strategy with Democrats and liberal Republicans to defeat the House leadership. The court had done its part and now Kansas' ruling elite would do theirs, with the apparent support of state taxpayers who ignored their chance to make a fundamental change in the situation by unseating the four state supreme court justices most frequently supportive of funding increases — Lawton Nuss, Marla J. Luckert, Carol Beier and Dan Bile. When voters were asked if they should unseat or retain the four, voters selected "retain" and so they all continue to warm the state bench and drain the state treasury.

The budget Gov. Sebelius had presented in 2004 had asked for an additional $310 million spread over three years for education—but with an income tax and sales tax increase to pay for it. The legislature looked at the performance of Kansas students, saw they were among the best in the nation and voted the tax increases down.

In January, the state's Supreme Court had made its decision to set funding (and therefore tax) levels for education, and given the state until April to do the work. The legislature paid as much attention to this as a Supreme Court justice would to a parking ticket issued by a legislator. As for Gov. Sebelius, she simply went mum, since her work had been done for her. Her 2005 budget asked for more money for state bureaucrats and more money for welfare—to be paid for by drawing down the state's reserves—but not a cent more for the public schools.

In January, when the court had fallen in line and backed Bullock, Gov. Sebelius staked out her strategy: "I think it's important for the majority party who runs the House and Senate to have a plan that they think meet's the Supreme Court challenge, and then we can talk about it," she told the AP.[69] "So I'm just saying to the leaders, 'Show me the meat, boys.'" Gov. Sebelius kicked back to watch the state's constitutional crisis unfold.

She was safe: Gov. Sebelius's failure to provide leadership was not part of the narrative in this story, and whatever was outside that

---

69 January 12, 2005.

narrative was just too complicated. After all, the legislature hadn't really been "given another opportunity to find a real solution for funding our schools," had it? It had been given an opportunity to accept judicial policy-making or face a state full of closed schools. Gov. Sebelius' version of "legislative responsibility" was to use the courts to increase the size of government and raise taxes, since the chances are nobody would ever vote for such a thing, especially without a good reason, but that particular narrative took a little explaining. The conservatives rose to the bait. To give the legislature "another opportunity to find a real solution for funding our schools" the governor called a special session of the legislature to respond to the court's demand. The special session awarded the funding and so the upward spiral of spending began. By 2017, Alan Rupe, the attorney who had first jumped on the passing money truck, was still representing the state's school districts. And in June 2018, after more than a half-billion additional dollars had been promised by the legislature, the state supreme court once again ruled, for the third time in two years that it still wasn't enough. The court said state now has until summer, 2019, to come up with even more money.[70]

---

70 For a highly detailed account of the 2005 special session, see my *Superior Nebraska* (Doubleday 2007), p200ff.

14

DESCENT OF THE STRAW MAN.

As I was working on this book, a friend of mine from New York called to ask me what in the world was going on in Midwestern classrooms. He'd just read that Kansas, or maybe Nebraska? Anyway, one of those states out there had passed a law saying science teachers had to tell kids the world had been created in six days and that they couldn't mention Darwin. "No Darwin? Are they crazy? Or just stupid?"

The answer is neither, of course—although I couldn't blame my friend, since the press' coverage of the suggested revisions in the Kansas state science standards had been less than scientific itself. Schools are often a battleground in the culture wars, covered with the smoke of hocus-pocus and superstition, like the belief that Kansas conservatives wanted the Bible to be used as a science text. That wasn't the case of course.

So what had happened? Well, not much. The state board of education had changed a passage in the state's science standards, from this:

"Science is the human activity of seeking natural explanations for what we observe in the world around us."

To this:

"Science is a systematic method of continuing investigation that uses observations, hypothesis testing, measurement, experimentation, logical argument and theory building to lead to more adequate explanations of natural phenomena."

The Board also suggested that students should be required to "understand the major concepts of the theory of biological evolution," and they also allowed that some teachers may want to inform their students that there is controversy surrounding evolution.

It seemed minor, but since a million words or so had been written damning Kansans for being religious primitives, I felt I should look into this sudden eruption of medievalism. So I went to the state's education department and asked somebody to explain to me exactly what effect this revision would have in classrooms. One woman, who asked not to be named, told me she had felt pressure "to say it would have a big effect. But really," she added conspiratorially, "it won't change a thing. There are 300 school districts in Kansas and each of them decides what will and won't be taught in their classrooms and nothing we say will affect that."

Maybe, but that message wasn't getting through to those who were concerned most—including many smart but worried parents. For example, Keith Roe, a longtime former state representative who went on to serve on his local education board, explained to me that while the state board of education "has almost no real power," like many Kansans, he was concerned that the board's influence could be significant. And his wife, Bethany, a teacher, was deeply worried that she might be asked to teach something scientifically indefensible in a science class.

To the board members, however, the science standards question was a non-issue. "We don't want religion taught in the schools," Kathy Martin — at the time, a conservative state board member from Clay Center — told me. "We don't want intelligent design taught in schools. We want science taught in schools." For Martin, and for the other members of the state board of education, that meant that when it came time to discuss the emergence of life on earth, the theory of evolution would do, controversy or not.

The claim that there could be anything controversial about evolution of course ratcheted up the already deafening level of the controversy considerably. Eventually, it evolved into full hysteria.

Whatever their intentions may have been, the Kansas state board of education produced a fabulously effective set-piece of political theater, complete with a special effect in which a dead but eminent British naturalist—that would be Charles Darwin—evolves first into a straw man and then into a baby seal, while earnest, middle-class board members morph into huge, club-swinging Canadians.

The history of this kind of controversy is as old as Scopes' monkey: In fact, the famous courtroom battle between Clarence Darrow and William Jennings Bryan was an event staged by the ACLU, eager to beat up on Biblical literalists. All they needed was a little casting and a good location. In 1925, they found a town willing to volunteer for pitiless self-parody in Dayton, Tennessee, and a willing "victim" in John Scopes, a part-time biology teacher. The rest is bad history.

Eighty years later, the revival was playing in Kansas. The board's mouse-sized alteration in a set of practically meaningless "standards" caused those who would wish to be seen as serious thinkers to grab their skirts and scream at the top of their lungs. Everybody wanted to be Clarence Darrow—especially as played by Spencer Tracy—even if only for 1000 words.

For Ted Koppel, the Kansas standards, this, not gross overfunding, "really could lead ultimately to the undermining of the public school system." The late Charles Krauthammer took to Fox News to accuse the Board of Ed of causing "a national embarrassment" and "forcing intelligent design into the statewide biology curriculum." George Will found the Board members were "the kind of conservatives who make conservatism repulsive to temperate people" and seemed to agree with a *New York Times* reporter who claimed the standards revision would "require that challenges to Darwin's theories be taught in the state's classrooms [and] change the definition of science itself." For pundits like Salman Rushdie, "In dumping Darwin, Kansas becomes a kind of Oz."

To find out how this had happened, I went to visit the state board of education's most controversial member, Connie Morris.

Morris is the wife of a plumbing and heating contractor and lives in the northwest corner of the state, near the quiet, dusty town of St. Francis—which was not named after the critter-loving monk from Assisi, but for the *wife* of a poor man named Captain A. L. Emerson in 1885. The town's on US 36, near where the Republican River crosses beneath the highway the first time, out by the Colorado border, but there aren't many good reasons for blue-staters to be on this stretch of 36, unless it's to write about how empty it is for *The New York Times*. I-70, not far to the south, siphons off most of the Denver-bound traffic through Goodland, where there's 32-by-24-foot reproduction of one of van Gogh's "Sunflower" paintings sitting on an 80-foot easel sold to the town by a Canadian artist for a mere $150,000. You can see it from the highway. It looks tiny.

Everything's super-sized out here, from the sky on down to the end of the road that connects Goodland to 36 and St. Francis. This end of Kansas is the wide, high, dry, flat part people from someplace else think about when they think about nothing in particular. It contrasts in obvious ways with the eastern side of the state, which, in comparison, is a lush, green paradise.

Even for folks in Holcomb, this is out there; you certainly can't help having the feeling that you're a long way from everyplace else—and you are. As the sign on the highway reminds you, St. Francis is "As Good as It Gets"—unless you're willing to turn around and drive all the way back to Goodland.

Courthouse, St. Francis, Kansas

Self-sufficiency is the civic subtext. St. Francis is prepared for the rest of the world to go away. The town even owns its own midway rides and parks them in the fairgrounds so there's no need to import those nasty carnies with their colorful tats and habits just for a once-a-year shindig. For fifty-one weeks, the Ferris wheel, the hammer, the tilt-a-whirl and the rest just sit there, way of context, until the first week in August, when they cut down all the weeds, plug everything in, turn the switch, rev up the cotton candy machine and everybody in St. Francis goes to the fair. (Oberlin, Kansas, a couple of counties to the east, does the same thing every year at about the same time.) The complete artifice of metropolitan life is evident everywhere in northwestern Kansas, where all the streets are extra-wide because *everything* is extra-wide.

Morris lives in a new home surrounded by miles and miles of emptiness. When I arrived, one of the first things she told me was where she wanted to locate her alligator farm—and she was serious. "Shoes, bags, that kind of thing," she said. Then she took me inside her temporary shelter—a mobile home parked in a barn while work on the new house nearby wrapped up—and told me about the two boys who had come out to make a video documentary about her to show at Sundance. I looked around, then rolled my eyes—but she caught me. "No, I trust them. I think they'll be fair." To the alligators, maybe.

Morris is young, pretty and fits the description I think is meant by the word "pert." She's got short brown hair and dresses tomboy-style, and is remarkably frank. Did she call Darwinism a "fairly tale"? Yes. Does she believe in evolution? No. Does she believe in good and evil? "Yes, I do. I believe in the traditional Judeo-Christian teachings." Does she think the book of Genesis should be used to teach science in Kansas? "Goodness no!" How about evolution? Even if you don't believe in it, should that be taught? "Of course. It's the dominant theory we have and it would be ridiculous not to teach it. I believe there are holes in the theory, and I don't know if it should be spoon-fed as *fact* when it's a theory, but I'm okay with that. I mean, it's science and it's what we have and I think we should teach what we know." Was she prepared for what had happened to her in the press? "No, I've been around—I've been hurt, abused, molested and raped twice. I've been around, but I wasn't prepared for *this*."

"This" is a relentless barrage by the press not only in Kansas, but across the country. It's been intensely personal, going far beyond the usual "conservatives are mean" and "conservatives are stupid" pieces that are staples of the press. When a Kansas City tabloid ran a hatchet job[71] under the headline: "The strange redemption of Connie Morris, high school slut turned Kansas State Board of Education anti-evolutionist," a journalist sent an emailed message around to his colleagues touting the piece as a good read. It certainly got around. If you Google "Connie Morris" and "slut" you get nearly 2000 citations.

When I asked her about the media in general, and that piece specifically, she was visibly upset. For the first time, her voiced cracked as she accused the writer of having just regurgitated the "ugliest" parts of a tell-all memoir[72] she had written earlier. It was true that the piece contained nothing that hadn't already seen ink elsewhere. "But he [the *Pitch* writer] hit a new low. He called my parents, who are nearly 80, and my father..." her voice broke off for a moment. "Well, that hurt me. I hate to admit it, but it did. It's something we had settled in our family years ago. To see them smear your name—for what? A political issue? One they don't even understand?"

The board of education in Kansas is divided into two permanently warring camps, with control going back and forth. Liberals on the board are especially angry, perhaps because the last time around conservatives were voted in to replace them—a reversal of the liberal *putsch* that had taken place the election before. Conservatives are less cohesive; they recently split on some sex-ed policies, for example. But in the back-and-forth of things, Morris had become a favored target of other liberal members of the board, no doubt because of her no-nonsense style. Everything she did was examined once, then again. When a travel item was audited, for example, and her opponents complained about her hotel bill, headlines flared and

---

71 *The Kansas City Pitch*, August 17, 2005.
72 *From the Darkness: One woman's rise to nobility*, 2002. "I hate that sub-title," she said. "The publisher chose it, but it's embarrassing!" I agreed.

she had to reimburse the board for expenses she incurred attending a conference when—or, in one case, for a $50 lunch that, according to Morris, "never even happened."

When it comes to explaining the revised standards she and other conservatives had put in place, Morris had been consistent in her explanations of what the standards do and don't do. "Intelligent design doesn't have anything to do with what we're debating," she told CNN. "I know that lots of people want to make it true that we're trying to insert intelligent design or, heaven forbid, creationism in the standards, but that's not what we're doing. Nowhere near that. We're not trying to insert religion whatsoever."

At one board of education meeting, she finally challenged one of the board's liberals, Sue Gamble, to shine a little light on the debate. "I asked if somebody, anybody would show me where [in the standards] there is religion or 'creationism' in any form, because I'd like to take it out. She hemmed and hawed and finally said, 'I don't have to.' She's a very unhappy woman."

Morris thought the whole issue was being blown out of proportion for reasons she doesn't quite understand, but suspects may be an effort to make a liberal-friendly issue where there isn't one in order to beat up on conservatives. "Even the president fell for it!" When a reporter had asked Bush if kids should be exposed to intelligent design, he had said he thought kids should be exposed to all kinds of different views. "That really infuriated me," Morris said. "The headlines said, 'Kansas seeks to insert religion into science' and somebody took it into the president and he comes out in favor of intelligent design! It was infuriating! We weren't trying to put intelligent design into the schools at all." Morris thinks they were hurt by allowing the intelligent-design people to help organize the discussions about science, since that meant that pro-evolution scientists would refuse to attend—although Morris pointed out that there were plenty of people at the board of education hearing that disagreed with intelligent design. "John Calvert [a leader in the intelligent design movement] organized the hearings, and maybe that was a mistake, but really, it was not an ID event. You can read it for yourself in the transcript,"[73] she said. "But nobody bothered to do that."

Morris told me she believes "the government is taking over" family life in America and "they're doing it in our public schools. We are doing some dreadful things to our children in public schools. I'm trying to hold that back some. If the people who elected me don't want that, they'll vote me out and that will be fine." Morris has been the target of recall efforts and there was a crowded field of candidates ready to run against her in 2006. She lost. If she hadn't, it would have been one of those miracles scientists hate. "I may not last long [in public office]," she told me before that became truth, "but you know what? That's a plus for me."

Justified or not, parents no longer trust schools to teach the sort of stuff that reinforces what they hope their children will believe about the world and how to behave in it. The frustration of mothers and fathers is often brought to a boil when schools force a set of secularized assumptions on children, forbidding mentions of Christmas or trying to impose Easter on a drunken spring break. Nobody in Kansas or Nebraska this side of a tongue-talking snake-juggler wants schools that teach religion instead of science. But many do object to fostering a kneejerk disrespect for religion and suggesting to children that religious belief is the refuge of morons offends the people who pay for the schools.

---

73 At http://www.ksde.org/

Yet when parents protest these violations of common sense in the name of political correctness, they are slapped down by educators and judges. Attempting to influence curriculum through the governing bodies that rule schools is really about all that most parents feel they can do—and so that is exactly what they have done in Kansas and in many other states and localities around the nation.

Of course, as political debates go, the skirmish over evolution seems like it was made in heaven for atheists and agnostics on the political left. It casts their advocates as thoughtful and open-minded thinkers and conservatives as zealots or simpletons or sluts. It doesn't matter that according to a USA Today/CNN/Gallup Poll 88 percent of Americans of all political persuasions believe that God had at least some hand in the creation of life, or how many times you remind worried people, as writer Jonah Goldberg once memorably did, "Your Darwin fish are safe," the élite on both sides of the political spectrum will still seize on the caricatures of that debate to pillory dissent, drowning out the rest of the conversation with a shrieking that approaches hysteria.

The issue of course is not science. Most of the pundits, journalists and politicians who were arguing for or against evolution or "intelligent design" or creationism are as clueless as all those guys in college in the '60s and '70s who took "rocks for jocks" as their science elective. Those who do actually have a claim to know about science have been hopelessly polarized by this crazy debate: most fall on the Darwinian side of the argument, but that argument is mostly about biological sciences. The further you get from that bailiwick of botanists and biologists, the more difficult it seems it is to claim evolution as a way of looking at "creation." Try explaining to yourself the "evolution" of light or gravity or of a glass of water. In fact, the closer you get the proto-nugget of creation, the goofier *everyone's* theories become: Some scientists, eager to cling to the god of random chance and desperate to avoid the implication obvious to most people that somebody up and out there must know something more than all of us put together, posit theoretical, parallel universes, an infinity of them. We just got the lucky one. There is less proof for this theory than there is for my daughter Maggie's brilliant panentheistic theory of creation, first advanced by her at age three: "We're just God's idea." For most of us, that works.

I'm certainly no partisan of Biblical creationism; I don't seem to be alone in thinking that interpreting the book of Genesis literally diminishes God and insults man. Dogmatic Darwinists and Biblical literalists both share an ambition to reduce God, whatever God is, to something more reasonable, something about the size of a man—or at least something the size of a man's ability to comprehend.

But I have to say, I don't know what difference it makes what people believe, even in a science class. An 8th-grader who doesn't properly understand how to read and write is probably going to have *The Origin of Species: By Means of Natural Selection or the Preservation of Favoured Races* [!] *in the Struggle for Life* wasted on him, including the fact that there's nothing in the book, other than the seeds of racism, that would suggest to most thoughtful readers a Godless creation.

Besides, there are plenty of college graduates out there who believe all kinds of really stupid things: Millions of bourgeois environmentalists believe DDT is the devil's brew and they're willing to consign millions of the poorest, weakest people on earth to death by malaria to prove their point. Leftwing politicians believe George W. Bush can make hurricanes. Dick Durbin, the senior US senator from Illinois, believes that US soldiers guarding terrorist prisoners have a lot in common with Nazi storm-troopers. My wife believes

I'm good-looking and my children think I'm smart. Believing God had something to do with creation isn't all that crazy in comparison.

Yet there is virtually no public person who has not yet pronounced critics of evolution—or even those who think evolution doesn't explain everything—dangerous lunatics out to wreck America's excellent education system, a system that now performs at such a miserable level of incompetence that most high school graduates can only read at a basic level, if that.[74] The chances that offering a critique of Darwin in a 10th-grade science class is going to make an iota of difference to the evolution and development of scientific thought is much, *much* more far-fetched than claiming, as Genesis does, that you and I are descendents of a handful of dust— which, if you add water and stir, is pretty much what Darwin said too. The posturing is impressive because the mantle of scientific reason looks great and is irresistible no matter who's posing in it: Charles Krauthammer, George Will and other putative intellectuals on the right and almost every commentator on the left has called the critics of evolution names and played loose with the facts in order to justify their calumnies. Bret Stephens, an otherwise reliably buttoned-down op-ed writer at *The New York Times* looked into a Fox News camera on February 18, 2006, nearly a *decade* after the latest round of the evolution debate started and said, "I think the losers in this debate would tell you that all they want to do is teach the controversy but, in fact, it was just an effort to introduce intelligence design discussions through the back door....it should not be taught in science classrooms. And I think it's time somebody said that." What he meant was, "It's time I had my chance to say that on TV," since literally thousands of other writers, policy-makers and com-

---

74 According to the National Institute for Literacy, the mean prose literacy scores of U.S. high school grads ranked 18th out of 19 countries. If the kids had 2-3 years of college, they went all the way up to 15.

mentators, including people like Connie Morris, had already said *exactly* that, some of them many, many times and at great volume.

Of course, it would be cynical to suggest that the "controversy" in play here may exist solely to introduce "intelligence design discussions" into Fox News' talk-shows. New York conservatives are as happy as New York liberals to take a cheap shot at those red-state hicks in Kansas.

In fact, virtually the entire establishment intelligentsia, left and right, has thrown their support in this "controversy" behind the people who run the country's public schools into trillions of debt. For the left, this debate works to their obvious advantage: It's hard to argue the virtues of a complex issue such as school choice, for example, while all the shouting is about what a lousy science book the Bible makes. For those on the right, it provides a golden opportunity to distance themselves from those they find slightly unwashed, intellectually speaking.

Nonetheless, the synthetic furor gave a genuine boost to Kansas' "moderate" Republicans and Democrats on a wide range of issues, none of which have any more to do with creationism than the Kansas state science standards. The Left believes no other issue has the potential to turn this red state blue, which is why it will rage on. It's allowed the secularists to demean the religiously inclined with impunity and brought to the surface irreligious nuts—just more proof that the evolution debate makes anyone who touches it look terrible.

To find out how terrible, just go to Lawrence, home of the University of Kansas, one of the two areas in the state to vote for Kerry over Bush[75] in 2004. Wading into the evolution controversy,

---

75 The other area was my old neighborhood in Kansas City.

the university announced "courses" — really, '60s-style teach-ins — designed not to teach but to ridicule the religious Right, each taught by a prof with an agenda.

Personally, I think it's a good thing that universities are finally being used for satire rather than self-parody, and on this point I appear to agree with the former chairman of KU's religious-studies department, Paul Mirecki, and the campus group he mentors, the 120-member "Society of Open-minded Atheists and Agnostics", or SOMA.

In the fall of 2005, Mirecki had announced plans to teach "the fundies" — as he referred to his spiritual demons — a lesson by offering a course called "Intelligent Design, Creationism and other Religious Mythologies." The course announcement was instantly picked up by AP, CNN, and a bunch of daily papers and TV stations across the country.

"The KU faculty has had enough," Mirecki told reporters with gusto.

Conservatives were irritated, of course, but universities — well, what can you do? The class would have passed into the archive of goofy courses all colleges offer for whatever reason. However, Mirecki had made the strategic error of using SOMA's Yahoo usergroup— open to any who cared to click and join it—to post to the list his admission that the purpose of the course was not education at all. It was agitprop.

"To my fellow damned," he wrote, "Its [sic] true, the fundies have been wanting to get I.D. and creationism into the Kansas public schools, so I thought 'why don't I do it?' I will teach the class with several other lefty KU professors...The fundies want it all taught in a science class, but this will be a nice slap in their big fat face [sic]...I expect it will draw much media attention. The university public relations office will have a press release on it in a few weeks. I also have contacts at several regional newspapers." No doubt.

The forum post was forwarded to an ad-hoc group of conservative Kansas bloggers and writers led by John Altevogt, a former *Kansas City Star* columnist, a political activist—and perhaps the only man in Kansas as angry as Mirecki. Altevogt blew the whistle and the embarrassing post caused KU chancellor Bob Hemenway — a fervent backer of the course — to blink. Calling many Christian Protestant voters "fundies" wasn't helpful to a public university.

After nearly a week of backpedaling, Mirecki apologized for the statement: "I have always practiced my belief that there is no place for impertinence and name calling in a serious academic class," he wrote. "My words in the email do not represent my teaching philosophy or the style I use in class." The word "Mythologies" was dropped from the description. The chancellor said he would conducting a "review" of Mirecki's e-mail. The university insisted the show would go on.

But the cat was out of the bag. As Hemenway was telling reporters the course was "serious," Mirecki was telling readers of his SOMA list, "This thing will be a hoot." At the same time, conservatives had set about conducting a review of their own, sorting through and circulating the rest of Mirecki's SOMA posts on the Internet. They came away more concerned than ever.

"These aren't just lighthearted messages," said Altevogt.

In looking through the posts he had written, it became clear Mirecki seemed to enjoy adolescent outrageousness as much as his students. In one note, for example, a SOMA member suggests creating anti-Gideon pamphlets: "While the Gideons are distributing their propaganda, we would distribute a single folded page of the same height and width of a Gideon bible. The cover would contain wording on the order of 'For complete assurance that your soul will be safe from the Fires of Hell...' The inside would continue 'quit believing that F---ING God and Jesus BULLS--T. — Join us, the Society of Open Minded Atheist and Agnostics. Our Bible is a quicker read.'"

Mirecki's response: "I think the language is a bit strong in what you suggest, but I still like the general idea..." and went on to offer his own version. In another, Mirecki explained to students that German Christians saw "Nazism as compatible (the fulfillment of?) Christianity [sic], with Hitler as final messiah."

Mirecki offered an explanation of his point of view in a post he published to the list in May 2005: "I had my first Catholic 'holy communion' when I was a kid in Chicago and when I took the bread-wafer the first time, it stuck to the roof of my mouth, and as I was secretly trying to pry it off with my tongue as I was walking back to my pew with white clothes and with my hands folded, all I could think was that it was Jesus' skin, and I started to puke, but I sucked it in and drank my own puke. That's a big part of the Catholic experience. I don't think most Catholics really know what they are supposed to believe, they just go home and use condoms and some of them beat their wives and husbands." Mirecki went on to explain that he was going to meet with Monsignor Vince Krische, then at the university's Catholic Center.

What did Msgr. Krische remember about the meeting? Not much, he told me. Although Mirecki claimed in his posts that the two were "very good friends," Msgr. Krische tells me had met Mirecki only twice, once at the Catholic Center and once at dinner. The priest could offer no explanation for the comments. "I just don't know why he would say such a thing. I think this is a very offensive and irresponsible thing for him to say. What is it based on? Why would he say this?" Mirecki did not return a call from me—or from most other journalists—asking for comment and clarification.

That left room for many others to make comments of their own, and to Altevogt and many other conservatives, the controversy was no laughing matter. "Our concerns," Altevogt told me, "are simple and not related to one particular course, but to more general issues. First, we're worried about the academic decline of the university under [Chancellor] Hemenway: KU has slipped seven places during his tenure and things like this may be one reason why. Second, we are concerned when an entire category of people — including the very students he is most likely to run into in his current assignment as an instructor teaching classes about religion — is maligned by the faculty sponsor of a university-sanctioned organization." Third, Altevogt said, is the concern many Kansans' have for the religious studies department itself. It had, he told me become "a hotbed of religious bigotry and intolerance."

For Mirecki, the reaction must have seemed like a kind of religious epiphany, since it so closely resembled the wrath of God. State Sen. Karin Brownlee told me she felt Mirecki's SOMA comments were "consistent with the tone and attitude of his other remarks" concerning the course he wants to teach. "I think students look up to a professor, whether he's an adviser or in a classroom...but as the head of a religion department he clearly has a disdain for those who have a Christian belief." Brownlee's complaint was echoed by many others as the story passed online from blog to blog.

Eventually, Mirecki had to forget the class and resign his chairmanship.[76] Another prof—this one a fervent devotee of Burning

---

76 The AP, invested in the narrative that held that Mirecki was the victim of religious "fundies" reported this news this way: "A University of Kansas professor who drew criticism for e-mails he wrote deriding Christian fundamentalists resigned Wednesday as chairman of the Department of Religious Studies."
This abbreviation of the facts so offended the University of Kansas that a spokeswom-

Man ceremonies—said he would stand in the gap and take a bash at those goofy Christians.

Of course Mirecki is very much in the mainstream of academics whose views on religion—no matter how bizarre—are accepted with an enthusiasm that can cause thoughtful parents to wince. There seems to be a Midwestern strain of nutty irreligiousity. For example, just north of Lawrence, at Omaha's Creighton University, the religious studies department published a document called "Cross-National Correlations of Quantifiable Societal Health with Popular Religiosity and Secularism in the Prosperous Democracies: A First Look," by a man named Gregory Paul in its "peer-reviewed" *Journal of Religion and Society*. The article was picked up by the London *Times* "religion correspondent" Ruth Gledhill, who reported it this way:

> Religious belief can cause damage to a society, contributing towards high murder rates, abortion, sexual promiscuity and suicide according tot research published today.
>
> According to the study, belief in and worship of God are not only unnecessary for a healthy society but may actually contribute to social problems.

---

an told me she had called the AP to protest and explain that it was Mirecki's views about Christians in general and Catholics in particular that had caused him grief. "If it had just been one group [ie, the "fundies"], this would not be as much of an issue," she told me.

The AP flatly refused her request to correct the story, and the newspapers of Kansas and around the world carried the tale that "Christian fundamentalists" had driven Mirecki from his chairmanship. A few weeks later, Mirecki claimed he had been followed through morning darkness by thugs in a pick-up truck and when he pulled over, he said, they gave him a black eye while angrily denouncing his proposed class. The local police were unable to shed any light on the alleged incident, but it too was carried by the AP and accepted as fact by Darwinians everywhere.

The study counters the view of believers that religion is necessary to provide the moral and ethical foundations of a healthy society.

It compares the social peformance of relatively secular countries, such as Britain, with the US, where the majority believes in a creator rather than the theory of evolution. Many conservative evangelicals in the US consider Darwinism to be a social evil, believing that it inspires atheism and amorality.

Many liberal Christians and believers of other faiths hold that religious belief is socially beneficial, believing that it helps to lower rates of violent crime, murder, suicide, sexual promiscuity and abortion....But the study claims that the devotion of many in the US may actually contribute to its ills.

The paper, published in the *Journal of Religion and Society*, a US academic journal, reports:

- Many Americans agree that their churchgoing nation is an exceptional, God-blessed, shining city on the hill that stands as an impressive example for an increasingly sceptical world.

- In general, higher rates of belief in and worship of a creator correlate with higher rates of homicide, juvenile and early adult mortality, STD infection rates, teen pregnancy and abortion in the prosperous democracies.

- The United States is almost always the most dysfunctional of the developing democracies, sometimes spectacularly so."

Gregory Paul, the author of the study and a social scientist, used data from the International Social Survey Programme, Gallup and other research bodies to reach his conclusions. [77]

The story traveled around the world in a heartbeat, thanks to gullible editors who would believe this stuff long before they'd believe there's any controversy over theories of creation. Apparently, neither Redhill's editor nor anyone else bothered to look at the credentials of Gregory Paul, social scientist, before giving the article credibility. If they had, they'd have seen nothing that would suggest he's a "social scientist" in the academic sense at all. Instead, he's a "freelance paleontologist" best known for painting pictures of dinosaurs; it appeared he had no professional credentials in either social science or religion and that his obsession about religion before this caused him to link it causally to Nazism.[78] His best-known published work, other than the paper the *Times's* reporter celebrates, is a so-called "transhumanist" book he co-authored called

77 September 27, 2005. There should be a warning label slapped on British journalists who cover religion. The BBC's "religious affairs" correspondence once was caught rattling away on the radio about the "American Epicopalian" church and its "same-sex bishops."

78 "The Great Scandal: Christianity's Role in the Rise of the Nazis," *Free Inquiry*, Vol 3, No. 24. Free Inquiry is published by the Council for Secular Humanism, an organization dedicated to advancing "the secular humanist eupraxophy as an alternative naturalistic life-stance." A man named Paul Kurtz is the L. Ron Hubbard of secular humanism—and the inventor of "eupraxophy," as it happens. The center is a resource for those who need experts to speak about the evils of intelligent design. Paul is one such "expert": "His book, Beyond Humanity, discusses the impact of intelligent cybertechnology on religion, further equipping him to speak on the role of religion in society. Because of his scientific background, Paul is also able to speak on broad debate issues, such as evolution v. creationism and the like."

Beyond Humanity: Cyberevolution and Future Minds. If I understand it properly, the book asserts that evolution won't be complete until humans and computers get it together sufficiently to cross-breed. Even George Gallup objected to the use of his stats by Paul, who is familiar to education lawyers as an avid anti-creationist, appearing as a witness whenever an "expert" is needed to testify on behalf of Darwin, et al., against a school district's outlandish wish to suggest that there may be something controversial about theories of creation.

If Paul's piece had been about how atheists and evolutionary true-believers had been responsible for 80-100 million deaths in the 20th century—as communism was—nobody would have noticed because it would never have been published. When I called the editor of the *Journal* to ask what he was thinking when he ran the article, he nervously repeated over and over than the journal was "peer-reviewed"—which of course was precisely the problem.

Faced with people like Paul and Mirecki, who are given serious consideration despite what seems to be a pathological hatred of people who order their lives around convictions of faith, it's not surprising that people are worried about the schools in their communities and want, however slightly, some dignity allowed for the values they hold. Surely, against men like these, having a teacher devote less than a minute to simply stating the obvious—that there is some controversy about the scientific theories of creation—before going on to study Darwinism isn't the end of reason in the 21st century.

Altevogt and others, including some members of the legislature — the source of the university's funding, after all — are concerned that even in red-state Kansas the educational establishment, and especially the state's university, is so disconnected from the people who pay for it that somebody so apparently "lacking in respect [for religion]," as Karin Brownlee put it, was given charge of KU's department of religious studies. As Altevogt notes, asking a man who apparently believes that Catholics "beat their wives" to run the religious-studies department has the feel of asking David Duke to oversee the African-American studies department.

In interviews and in their email lists, religious conservatives said they hoped both Mirecki and Hemenway would retreat to doing what they were hired to do and leave political theater to the drama department. But the religious-studies department may not be the healthiest environment for any kind of retreat: "The majority of my colleagues here in the dept[ment] are agnostics or atheists, or they just don't care," Mirecki wrote in explaining, correctly, that it wasn't the job of the department to make converts. "If any of [the other professors] are theists, it hasn't been obvious to me in the 15 years I've been here."

For most people out here, religion isn't actually a very contentious issue. While Wichita has its huge megachurches, there are thousands of country churches scattered across the Midwestern prairie, many of them the last living remnant of what must have been at one time a bustling little village. Some, like the church in St Joseph, are huge buildings; that particular Catholic parish is practically all that's left of St. Joseph, Kansas. Completed in 1908, it used to serve two masses every Sunday for 800 people. Now the vast building is used only for occasional weddings and funerals and the last parish priest left years ago. Further west is the "Cathedral of the Plains," St. Fidelis Baslica (completed in 1911), whose twin limestone steeples soar 141 feet over tiny Victoria, Kansas. The sanctuary, still used for regular masses, is 220 feet long and seats 1,100—about the population of the town itself. The dramatic size of the building, its elegant architectural exclamation, more than doubles the population of the town every month by drawing gawkers to look and see.

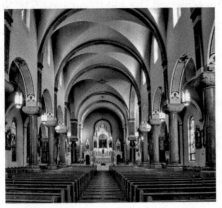

St. Fidelis basilica

But most churches are like the tiny church most of my family members have attended at one time or another, Olive Hill Church. It's not near anything, really—just a crossroads out in the country, its quiet presence indicated only by a sign pointing down a dirt road off highway 14 south of Superior on the Kansas side of the river.

It's a non-denominational church, and when I was little, a very hot one. I remember coloring in pictures of Jesus while the perspiration dropped off my nose and the sweat bees swarmed. For as long as I can remember, my uncles—Neal, Gerald and Delmar—sang in the church, as had my father, while my grandmother played the piano and my grandfather sat and smiled. My uncle Gerald is a great guitar-player and singer—in the tenor tradition of Ralph Stanley, you might say—and his renditions of great white gospel hymns, especially in duets with his piano-playing daughter, Gloria, are some of the greatest musical memories of my life. If you're in the vicinity on a Sunday morning, stop in, see Gloria, and Bill and Rita Blauvelt, too, and a bunch of others. They're all there, singing "How Great Thou Art."

The Olive Hill Church, like the little church in Ada, the one in Norway, and a pile of other towns you'd have to look up to find, had a way of extending its message far beyond the dirt crossroads where it was located. Once, I had to call an editor at Harper Collins to tell her I would be away during a closing of a manuscript. When I got through to her office, it turned out the company was going through one of the many shuffles that characterized the 1980s on East 53rd St. I finally reached a temp, some poor guy who'd been parked in front of a phone to tell everybody who called that nobody was home. I asked if I could leave a message saying I'd be away.

"Where you going?" the guy asked.

"Someplace you've never heard of," I said, with what I thought was Midwestern smugness.

"Try me."

"Okay. Burr Oak, Kansas."

"Doesn't Lester Snider give the *best sermons you've ever heard?*" Amazing. Tom Zoellner had just arrived in Manhattan from his trip across country, one that had involved taking his first newspapering job in Superior as a way of unwinding after a stint as a straight shepherd in Montana, then worked his way across US 36 until he eventually walked into Bill's office at the *Express*, got a job and a ride out with Bill and Rita to the Olive Hill Church.

The preacher in those days was the remarkable Lester Snider, a lean, silver-haired, hawk-faced man in cowboy boots. He resembled John Brown in those statehouse murals—all forward-leaning intensity. He had a past in the Society of Friends and the oratorical style of a country preacher, with cadences that sung, punctuated by long, dramatic silences; Lester had so many pregnant pauses that you thought he could give birth to a full year once a week. Plus, he had mastered the art—well, not of the rhetorical question, exactly, but of the rhetorical grill: *"Do you like fun?"* he would say, leaning forward and frightening the children behind their funeral home fans. *"I* like fun." A relief. Then the trap: *"Heaven's fun—but if you want to have fun in heaven you better be good here on Earth!"*

When my grandmother finally died aged nearly 99, leaving the Olive Hill Church behind at last, the whole neighborhood turned out to say goodbye. For most of her life, she had been the most intimidating woman I had ever known. I'd spend summer after summer with her and my grandfather, spending the days swatting sweat bees in a grain truck and the evening reading *True Detective* and closely examining the lingerie inventory in the Sears catalog.

When a circulatory problem finally took her leg, I was tempted to send her a peg, an eye-patch and a clip-on parrot. But amazingly the amputation also removed her fierceness, and for the last few decades of her long, exemplary life, she was the sweetest, kindest soul I ever knew.

Delivering a eulogy for my grandmother in that church was the hardest thing, and the most mortifying thing I've ever done, and that's going some. All I could think about was how often she'd prayed in there for all of us, even including me, and I did my usual terrible, choked-up job, so at least I was inaudible. (Cousin Gloria's was better.) And old Lester presided over the funeral, smiling mirthlessly, leaning forward hawkishly, telling stories about Granny and her life in the nursing home. He didn't know about her other life, burying a five-year-old son named Evan, dead of pneumonia during the Dust Bowl years; or her brave trip to New York City in 1918 and her tearful dismay at losing her best hat out the window; or her endless nights when three of her surviving four sons were all off fighting World War II at the same time. She spent a lifetime of Sundays in that old church praying for all of us, even me. Lester just got there at the end of the run.

"She lost her leg, yes," he told us. "But that couldn't keep her down! I can see her now, up there in heaven now, having *fun*—running around on all her legs."

Me, too, Lester.

I don't know what politics the congregation at Olive Hill has, but I suspect there's not a lot of room for meanness and intolerance in it. Religion is important to most Americans, no matter what their political point of view might be. The tradition of civic respect for religious belief used to be a hallmark of red-state politics. It still is, even if it's been pushed into the margins of public life by the media, academics, cynics and politicians. The red states of America don't own traditional morality, but the secular tide of the last decade or so that's flooding the nation with hatred for faith and ridicule of those who try to navigate life using ethics based on religious precepts—including simple rules of respect—that tide threatens to drown everyone. Conservatives in Kansas and Nebraska destroy the virtue of their point of view by dismissing those whose views on the right to life differ as "pro-aborts" and those who disagree with them on strict immigration policies as "embracing barbarism". Indeed, conservatives themselves don't agree on these issues, but even their fraternal quarrels are repellent to those who prefer respect and good faith as prerequisites for debate.

Concordia's most prominent native son is Frank Carlson—a six-term representative, a two-term governor, a three-term US senator and one of the most popular politicians in Kansas history. Ross Doyen—another Kansas political leader from Concordia—told me Carlson was a brilliant at knowing "how to do the right thing at the right time, so people thought a lot of him. But for us, the best thing about him was he never forgot where he came from."

How could he? Just to get to Concordia, you have to take the Frank N. Carlson Memorial Highway into town. Walk into the Frank N. Carlson library and go to the Frank N. Carlson room and there you'll find a cluttered and colorful record of Frank N. Carlson's many achievements. He was a politician in the old-fashioned Kansas

Republican mold, so the artifacts in the Carlson room are modest and homey. He was a moderate who didn't use the word to deceive, but to fairly describe his attention to the broad, middle way, and he was an avid, early supporter of Ike's.

The room is filled with presidential signing pens, copies of highway bills, notes about civil rights legislation from back in the days when Republicans were about the only hope African-Americans had of gaining political equality with whites. Carlson quietly lived his faith and made it the basis for his views of the world—without also seeking to force those views on others. The most ostentatious thing in the room is a tasteful display of the talk Carlson gave to a Senate breakfast group on June 19, 1968. Here's a taste of the kind of thing that is rarely heard in Washington any more. But even after forty years these Concordian values still echo loudly even all the way out here:

> Never before have so many hated on such flimsy cause. Never have so many denounced so many with such little knowledge. Never has the dollar been as important as it is today. Never has wild pleasure or physical abandonment been considered fitting human behavior as it is today.

> Never before have public officials been so brazen and open in seeking the vote of the people through promises of things that are morally and spiritually wrong. Never have ministers of the Gospels turned their pulpits and their pastoral duties toward the direction of the social order to the near exclusion of the salvational order as abounds in our time…

[The] daily press – notoriously indifferent to religious news – reports a few lines on the inner and back pages that tells us clearly how growing numbers of Americans treat holy things with irreverence and contempt.

Not only have vast numbers of Americans lost all sense of the sacred, the moral, and the ethical, but the spiritual leaders from both the laity and the priesthood are often found in the forefront of this irreligious pursuit of comfort rather than conviction – of accommodation rather than truth – of the pleasant life rather than the meaningful life....

You cannot pick up a paper, magazine or book that is not in and of itself critical of something or somebody, even including among its victims almighty God Himself. In truth, the criticisms of God rank well above almost all other criticisms of the hour. More people – in more ways and on more occasions – cast doubt, hurl darts, and throw charges against God such as this country has never seen in all of its history.

To accept the doctrine of universal criticism leaves up with almost nothing that is sacred – almost nothing that is absolute – and nothing that is eternal.[79]

Nothing, that is, except wheat, weather and common sense.

---

79 The full text is reprinted in an appendix to this book as it appeared in US News and World Report, July 1, 1968.

APPENDICES.

1. FRANK CARLSON. SENATE BREAKFAST SPEECH, 1968.

This speech was given by Frank Carlson to the Senate Breakfast Group, on June 19, 1968, as the Poor Peoples's March took place in Washington. The text that follows is as appeared in US News and World Report, *July 1, 1968 edition.*

The subject of the text I am using is "Wanted a Man – a Man Who Will Stand." We have had men in both ancient and modern society who have had the courage to take a stand and stand firm...

In Ezekiel 22:30, the Prophet says:

"And I sought for a man among them who would build up the wall and stand in the breach before me for the land that I should not destroy it."

God is searching for men who are unique, thoroughly saved, and filled to running over with His spirit. God and the world need men who will stand in the gap...

Modern Americans have accepted and are tolerating conditions never before permitted by any generation of our ancestors.

Never before have so many hated on such flimsy cause. Never have so many denounced so many with such little knowledge. Never has the dollar been as important as it is today. Never has wild pleasure or physical abandonment been considered fitting human behavior as it is today.

Never before have public officials been so brazen and open in seeking the vote of the people through promises of things that are morally and spiritually wrong. Never have ministers of the Gospels turned their pulpits and their pastoral duties toward the direction of the social order to the near exclusion of the salvational order as abounds in our time.

In that same 22nd chapter of Ezekiel, the Prophet speaks of Israel's leaders in these words:

"Her priests have done violence to my law and have profaned holy things; they have made no distinction between the holy and the common, neither have they taught the difference between the unclean and the clean, and they have disregarded my Sabbaths so that I am profaned among them."

Israel's religious leaders of that earlier time would be appalled to observe what is transpiring in the churches of God today. Even the daily press – notoriously indifferent to religious news – reports a few lines on the inner and back pages that tells us clearly how growing numbers of Americans treat holy things with irreverence and contempt.

Not only have vast numbers of Americans lost all sense of the sacred, the moral, and the ethical, but the spiritual leaders from both the laiety and the priesthood are often found in the forefront of this irreligious pursuit of of comfort rather than conviction – of accommodation rather than truth – of the pleasant life rather than the meaningful life.

If God is to have men who will stand in the gap and hold back the flood of destructive emotional and spiritual forces, we must first understand the nature of the problem, and why things are the way they are.

There are three major forces that have brought about this chaos, frustration and anti-Christian era in which we live. They touch both the philosophical and religious bases, were first voiced by the few in number whose intensity deceived millions, and have been permitted to flourish by both the unwary and the fearful.

First, we live in this age of uncertainty because we have either accepted or endured a doctrine of universal conformity.

The forces that reduce the power of an influence of God and Christ in the lives of our people are seeking to become levelers of men. It is their conviction that only through lowering mankind to a dependence upon the ideas, ideals, and material judgments of superior people can we live together in harmony and peace.

Evidence is rampant that this kind of meddling and interference with God's natural law brings fearful conflict, death, destruction, riots, crime and disregard of decency and principle among our people.

Today, there is widespread devotion to the idea that nothing, absolutely nothing, can remain the same. All things must change, and there is practically no consideration given as to whether change is good or bad – right or wrong – easy or difficult – necessary or unnecessary.

The doctrine of change stands on just the precise idea that change is inevitable. That is absolutely true. But irresponsible, erratic, violent change only for the sake of making things different is as illogical and as unreasonable as it is misguided.

No intelligent person argues against the necessity of question marks after many of our inherited notions and preconceived ideas. But when the question mark is turned into a totem pole or a marble altar on which the people are supposed to lay sacrificial offerings, such people have escaped the general limit of common sense and sound judgment and have launched off into material idolatry and a rushing toward a degree of spiritual insanity.

If human reason has so totally lost its respectability and no one is allowed to go from a major and a minor premise to some sort of orderly conclusion, then the welfare of our people is entrusted to the care of strange and weird people.

Great changes had to take place during these recent years, and even greater changes will have to take place in the future. But no safe and proper change is seen in recent times – and certainly none of the irrational changes that outnumber the sane ones – can justify the wholesale abandonment of the safe and sure principles of God and this country which have brought us safely this far. In the face of great changes, we Christians have to remember that we have a firm point of view and that we operate from certain unchanging foundations.

We believe in a God who does not change – in human nature which does not change except for its accommodation and acceptance of God – in standards of right and wrong that do not change – in death and judgment which are inescapable – and we believe in a truth that is absolute, not relative, and which is forever settled in heaven and can never pass away.

The Christian today – even in the midst of the erratic and erotic commitments of its irreligious leaders – does not follow the failing steps of the priests of Israel. Christians make a clear distinction between the holy and the common. They teach the difference between the clean and unclean. They observe and keep the Sabbath and they do not profane either the name, the spirit, or the power of God.

The third cause of our uncertainties in this time is the doctrine of universal criticism. Today, man is taught not to accept anything until he has first put it under strong and critical examination. Trust nobody – believe nobody – have faith in nothing – and accept no truth until it has been proved to you with mathematical exactness and material demonstration. That is the agony of hour when the doctrine of criticism has taken over our people.

You cannot pick up a paper, magazine or book that is not in and of itself critical of something or somebody, even including among its victims almighty God Himself. In truth, the criticisms of God rank well above almost all other criticisms of the hour. More people – in more ways and on more occasions – cast doubt, hurl darts, and throw charges against God such as this country has never seen in all of its history.

To accept the doctrine of universal criticism leaves up with almost nothing that is sacred – almost nothing that is absolute – and nothing that is eternal. So real has our acceptance of the doctrine of criticism become that even the word "indoctrination" has been turned into and evil word that must be shunned like "discipline," "disciple" or "patriotism."

These three doctrines – universal conformity, universal change, and universal criticism – have left our nation without moorings or anchors. We are being tossed in the sea of doubt and uncertainty that is about to sink the ship of God before our very eyes.

The world today is looking for:
Men who are not for sale;

Men who are honest, sound from center to circumference, true to the heart's core;

Men with consciences as steady as the needle to the pole;

Men who will stand for the right if the heavens totter and the earth reels;

Men who can tell the truth and look the world right in the eye;

Men who neither brag nor run;

Men who neither flag nor flinch;

Men who can have courage without shouting it;

Men in whom the courage of everlasting life runs still, deep, and strong;

Men who know their message and tell it;

Men who know their place and fill it;

Men who know their business and attend to it;

Men who will not lie, shirk or dodge;

Men who are not too lazy to work, nor too proud to be poor;

Men who are willing to eat what they have earned and wear what they have paid for;

Men who are not ashamed to say "No" with emphasis and not ashamed to say "I can't afford it."

God is looking for men. He wants those who can unite together around a common faith – who can join hands in a common task – and who have come to the kingdom for such a time as this. God give us men.

2. WILLIAM ALLEN WHITE. WHAT'S THE MATTER WITH KANSAS?

Editorial, *The Emporia Gazette*, August 16, 1896.

Today the Kansas Department of Agriculture sent out a statement which indicates that Kansas has gained less than two thousand people in the past year. There are about two hundred and twenty-five thousand families in the state, and there were about ten thousand babies born in Kansas, and yet so many people have left the state that the natural increase is cut down to less than two thousand net.

This has been going on for eight years.

If there had been a high brick wall around the state eight years ago, and not a soul had been admitted or permitted to leave, Kansas would be a half million souls better off than she is today. And yet the nation has increased in population. In five years ten million people have been added to the national population, yet instead of gaining a share of this-say, half a million-Kansas has apparently been a plague spot and, in the very garden of the world, has lost population by ten-thousands every year.

Not only has she lost population, but she has lost money. Every moneyed man in the state who could get out without loss has gone. Every month in every community sees someone who has a little money pack up and leave the state. This has been going on for eight years. Money has been drained out all the time. In towns where ten years ago there were three or four or half a dozen money-lending concerns, stimulating industry by furnishing capital, there is now none, or one or two that are looking after the interests and principal already outstanding.

No one brings any money into Kansas any more. Which community knows over one or two men who have moved in with more than $5,000 in the past three years? And what community cannot count half a score of men in that time who have left, taking all the money they could scrape together?

Yet the nation has grown rich; other states have increased in population and wealthier neighboring states. Missouri has gained over two million, while Kansas has been losing half a million. Nebraska has gained in wealth and population while Kansas has gone downhill. Colorado has gained every way, while Kansas has lost every way since 1888.

What's the matter with Kansas?

There is no substantial city in the state. Every big town save one has lost in population. Yet Kansas City, Omaha, Lincoln, St. Louis, Denver, Colorado Springs, Sedalia, the cities of the Dakotas, St. Paul and Minneapolis and Des Moines-all cities and towns in the West-have steadily grown.

Take up the Government Blue Book and you will see that Kansas is virtually off the map. Two or three little scrubby consular places in yellow-fever-stricken communities that do not aggregate ten thousand dollars a year is all the recognition that Kansas has. Nebraska draws about one hundred thousand dollars; little old North Dakota draws about fifty thousand dollars; Oklahoma doubles Kansas; Missouri leaves her a thousand miles behind; Colorado is almost seven times greater than Kansas-the whole west is ahead of Kansas.

Take it by any standard you please, Kansas is not in it.

Go east and you hear them laugh at Kansas; go west and they sneer at her; go south and they "cuss" her; go north and they have forgotten her. Go into any crowd of intelligent people gathered anywhere on the globe, and you will find the Kansas man on the defensive. The newspaper columns and magazines once devoted to praise of her, to boastful facts and startling figures concerning her resources, are now filled with cartoons, jibes and Pefferian speeches. Kansas just naturally isn't in it. She has traded places with Arkansas and Timbuctoo.

What's the matter with Kansas?

We all know; yet here we are at it again. We have an old mossback Jacksonian who snorts and howls because there is a bathtub in the state house; we are running that old jay for Governor. We have another shabby, wild-eyed, rattle-brained fanatic who has said openly in a dozen speeches that "the rights of tee user are paramount to the rights of the owner"; we are running him for Chief Justice, so that capital will come tumbling over itself to get into the state. We have raked the old ash heap of failure in the state and found an old human hoop-skirt who has failed as a businessman, who has failed as an editor, who has failed as a preacher, and we are going to run him for Congressman-at-Large. He will help the looks of the Kansas delegation at Washington. Then we have discovered a kid without a law practice and have decided to run him for Attorney General. Then, for fear some hint that the state had become respectable might percolate through the civilized portions of the nation, we have decided to send three or four harpies out lecturing, telling the people that Kansas is raising hell and letting the corn go to weeds.

Oh, this is a state to be proud of! We are a people who can hold up our heads! What we need is not more money, but less capital, fewer white shirts and brains, fewer men with business judgment, and more of those fellows who boast that they are "just ordinary clodhoppers, but they know more in a minute about finance than John Sherman"; we need more men who are "posted," who can bellow about the crime of `73, who hate prosperity, and who think, because a man believes in national honor, he is a tool of Wall Street. We have had a few of them- some hundred fifty thousand-but we need more.

We need several thousand gibbering idiots to scream about the "Great Red Dragon" of Lombard Street. We don't need population, we don't need wealth, we don't need well-dressed men on the streets, we don't need standing in the nation, we don't need cities on the fertile prairies; you bet we don't! What we are after is the money power. Because we have become poorer and ornerier and meaner than a spavined, distempered mule, we, the people of Kansas, propose to kick; we don't care to build up, we wish to tear down.

"There are two ideas of government," said our noble Bryan at Chicago.

"There are those who believe that if you just legislate to make the well-to-do prosperous, this prosperity will leak through on those below. The Democratic idea has been that if you legislate to make the masses prosperous their prosperity will find its way up and through every class which rests upon them."

That's the stuff! Give the prosperous man the dickens! Legislate the thriftless man into ease, whack the stuffings out of the creditors and tell debtors who borrowed the money five years ago when money "per capita" was greater than it is now, that the contraction of currency gives him a right to repudiate.

Whoop it up for the ragged trousers; put the lazy, greasy fizzle, who can't pay his debts, on an altar, and bow down and worship him. Let the state ideal be high. What we need is not the respect of our fellow men, but the chance to get something for nothing.

Oh, yes, Kansas is a great state. Here are people fleeing from it by the score every day, capital going out of the state by the hundreds of dollars; and every industry but farming paralysed, and that crippled, because its products have to go across the ocean before they can find a laboring man at work who can afford to buy them. Let's don't stop this year. Let's drive all the decent, self-respecting men out of the state. Let's keep the old clodhoppers who know it all. Let's encourage the man who is "posted." He can talk, and what we need is not mill hands to eat our meat, nor factory hands to eat our wheat, nor cities to oppress the farmer by consuming his butter and eggs and chickens and produce. What Kansas needs is men who can talk, who have large leisure to argue the currency question while their wives wait at home for that nickel's worth of bluing.

What's the matter with Kansas?

Nothing under the shining sun. She is losing wealth, population and standing. She has got her statesmen, and the money power is afraid of her. Kansas is all right. She has started in to raise hell, as Mrs. Lease advised, and she seems to have an over-production. But that doesn't matter. Kansas never did believe in diversified crops. Kansas is all right. There is absolutely nothing wrong with Kansas.

"Every prospect pleases and only man is vile."

ABOUT THE AUTHOR

Denis Boyles is co-editor of *The Fortnightly Review*. He lives in France, where he teaches literature in the Chavagnes Studium and journalism ethics at l'Institut catholique d'études supérieures in La Roche-sur-Yon.

denisboyles.com